Spelling Connections

J. Richard Gentry, Ph.D.

ZB **Zaner-Bloser**

Author

J. Richard Gentry, Ph. D.

Reviewers

Paula Boales, Killeen ISD, Killeen, TX
Sherry Durham, Ed. D., Lufkin ISD, Lufkin, TX
Karyn L. Huskisson, Klein Instructional Center, Spring, TX
Carmen Ramos, San Benito CISD, San Benito, TX
Susan Shogan, Round Rock ISD, Round Rock, TX
Linda Stout, Crawford ISD, Crawford, TX

ELL and Spanish Consultants

Ellen Riojas Clark, Ph.D., Professor, College of Education
 and Human Development, Division of Bicultural-Bilingual
 Studies, The University of Texas at San Antonio, TX
Bertha Pérez, Ed.D., Professor Emeritus of Literacy,
 College of Education and Human Development,
 The University of Texas at San Antonio, TX
Rocio Reyes-Moore, Spanish Language Productions,
 Alexandria, OH

ISBN 978-0-7367-6869-6

Copyright © 2012 Zaner-Bloser, Inc.

Zaner-Bloser, Inc., P.O. Box 16764, Columbus, Ohio 43216-6764
1-800-421-3018
www.zaner-bloser.com
Printed in the United States of America   11 12 13 14 15 997 6 5 4 3 2

SUSTAINABLE FORESTRY INITIATIVE

Certified Chain of Custody
Promoting Sustainable
Forest Management
www.sfiprogram.org

This SFI label applies to the text paper.

Table of Contents

Writer's Handbook

Spelling Dictionary

Writing Thesaurus

Index

Word Sorting

A word sort helps you become a Word Detective. When you sort, you look for patterns in your spelling words. You see how words are the same and how they are different. Word sorting can help you remember how to spell words.

Buddy Sort using the word sort cards

Word sort on an interactive whiteboard

There are different kinds of word sorts you can use with your spelling words.

- **Individual Sort**—Use word sorting to practice your spelling words.
- **Buddy Sort**—Do a word sort with a partner.
- **Speed Sorts on Your Own**—Time yourself as you sort your spelling words. Then do it again and try to improve on the number of seconds it takes to complete the word sort.
- **Speed Sorts With a Team**—See which team can complete the sort in the shortest time and with the greatest accuracy.

Spell Check

Most computers have a spell checker. Spell check is a tool that can find many spelling mistakes, but it can't find them all!

Sometimes a writer types the wrong word. For example, if you type **there** instead of **their**, the spell checker will not catch your mistake because the word you typed is spelled correctly. The spell checker does not know you meant to write a different word.

Spell check can help you find and correct mistakes in your writing. But you still must proofread everything you write!

Spelling Study Strategy

Look, Say

1
Look at the word.

2
Say the letters in the word. Think about how each sound is spelled.

Cover, See

3
Cover the word with your hand or close your eyes.

4
See the word in your mind. Spell the word to yourself.

Write, Check

5
Write the word.

6
Check your spelling against the spelling in the book.

Taking a Test

1. **Get** ready for the test. Make sure your paper and pencil are ready.

2. **Listen** carefully as your teacher says each word and uses it in a sentence. Don't write before you hear the word **and** the sentence.

3. **Write** the word carefully. Make sure your handwriting is easy to read. If you want to print your words, ask your teacher.

4. **Use** a pen to correct your test. Look at the word as your teacher says it.

5. **Say** the word aloud. Listen carefully as your teacher spells the word. Say each letter aloud. Check the word one letter at a time.

6. **Circle** any misspelled parts of the word.

7. **Look** at the correctly written word. Spell the word again. Say each letter out loud.

8. **Write** any misspelled words correctly.

Connections to THINKING

Read the spelling words and sentences.

1. crust	*crust*	Lucas cut the **crust** off his bread.
2. pass	*pass*	I **pass** that computer store every day.
3. else	*else*	Who **else** is coming to this party?
4. skill	*skill*	Writing poetry is a **skill** I admire.
5. brag	*brag*	It is rude to **brag** about your deeds.
6. zipper	*zipper*	Maria sewed a **zipper** into her skirt.
7. began	*began*	He was so happy he **began** to sing.
8. collar	*collar*	Mom has a lace **collar** on her dress.
9. drag	*drag*	We **drag** our boats into the water.
10. smell	*smell*	Did you stop to **smell** the roses?
11. brick	*brick*	Follow the yellow **brick** road.
12. felt	*felt*	In the sun the sand **felt** hot.
13. spill	*spill*	You must not **spill** your milk.
14. button	*button*	Kwan lost a **button** from his shirt.
15. held	*held*	I **held** the injured bird in my hand.
16. trust	*trust*	Can I **trust** you to keep a secret?
17. kept	*kept*	This show has **kept** me in suspense.
18. trick	*trick*	The magician tried to **trick** us.
19. shell	*shell*	The turtle's head was in its **shell**.
20. begin	*begin*	Let me **begin** to tell you a story.

Think & Sort the spelling words.

1–4. Write the words that have the **short a** sound spelled **a**.

5–10. Write the words that have the **short e** sound spelled **e**.

11–16. Write the words that have the **short i** sound spelled **i**.

17. Write the word that has the **short o** sound spelled **o**.

18–20. Write the words that have the **short u** sound spelled **u**.

Remember

Many short vowel sounds are spelled with a single letter: **a** as in **pass**, **e** as in **held**, **i** as in **skill**, **o** as in **collar**, and **u** as in **trust**.

 TEKS 4.22D Use spelling patterns and rules and print and electronic resources to determine and check correct spellings.

Connections to VOCABULARY

Word Analysis

Write the spelling word that does not belong in each group.

1. start, begin, felt
2. dump, brag, spill
3. collar, drag, sleeve
4. kept, trick, fool
5. boast, held, brag
6. began, faith, trust

Double Consonants

Write the words with double consonants in the middle of the word. Draw a line between the syllables.

7. _____   8. _____   9. _____

Plurals

A. Write the spelling words that are singular forms of the plurals that are formed by adding **-s**.

   10. shells   12. crusts   14. tricks
   11. skills   13. bricks

B. Write the spelling word that is the singular form of the plural that is formed by adding **-es**.

   15. passes

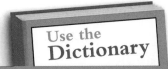

Use the **Dictionary**

16–20. Words in a dictionary are in alphabetical order. Write these words in alphabetical order.

      held   else   trust   kept   begin

Dictionary Check Be sure to check the alphabetical order of the words in your **Spelling Dictionary**.

 TEKS 4.22Ai Spell words with more advanced orthographic patterns and rules: plural rules. **4.22Aiii** Spell words with more advanced orthographic patterns and rules: double consonants in middle of words. **4.22D** Use spelling patterns and rules and print and electronic resources to determine and check correct spellings.

15

crust	pass	else	skill	brag
zipper	began	collar	drag	smell
brick	felt	spill	button	held
trust	kept	trick	shell	begin

Complete the Analogies

Write a spelling word to complete each analogy.

1. **Skin** is to **apple** as _____ is to **bread**.
2. **Stroller** is to **push** as **sled** is to _____.
3. **See** is to **eye** as _____ is to **nose**.
4. **Sleep** is to **slept** as **keep** is to _____.
5. **Say** is to **said** as **hold** is to _____.

Make Inferences

Write a spelling word to solve each riddle.

6. I am round and have eyes.
7. I rhyme with **glass** and mean "to go by."
8. I am the "yesterday" word of "today's" word **feel**.
9. One of the three little pigs used me to build a house.
10. I am a two-syllable word that means "started."

Use Context Clues

Write a spelling word to complete each sentence.

11. A tortoise goes into its _____ when it is frightened.
12. If you fill your glass too full, you may _____ your drink.
13. It takes great _____ to play professional sports.
14. The magician taught us a new _____.
15. I hope I can _____ you to keep this secret.
16. I like to _____ about my brother's paintings.
17. Because I was hot, the _____ of my shirt got wrinkled.
18. A _____ in a jacket makes it easy to open and close.
19. Did anyone _____ get the right answer to that question?
20. We will _____ each sentence with a capital letter.

 TEKS 4.22D Use spelling patterns and rules and print and electronic resources to determine and check correct spellings.

Connections to WRITING

Proofread a Realistic Story

Proofreading means reviewing your paper for errors in spelling, grammar, capitalization, and punctuation. To show where changes are needed, use **proofreading marks**. The symbol ≡ means **make a capital letter**. The symbol / means **make a small letter**.

Proofread the story below for ten misspelled words. Then rewrite the story. Write the spelling words correctly and make the corrections shown by the proofreading marks.

A Gift From the Beach

I cannot beginn to explain how happy the beach makes Me. There is no place els i like better. I found a shall there I could not passe by. It had a pink edge that looked like a colar. when I hild it in my hand, it felled smooth. I could smel the sea on it. I keppt the shell and brought it home. I trusst it will always remind me of that happy Day.

Proofreading Marks

≡	Capital Letter
/	Small Letter
∧	Add
ℯ	Delete
⊙	Add a Period
⌗	Indent

NARRATIVE Writing Prompt
Write a Realistic Story

Write or type a short story about an interesting place that you have visited. Use as many spelling words as you can.

- Use the writing process: prewrite, draft, revise, edit, and publish.
- Include details about the characters you met and the setting.
- Build your story to a climax that explains the most interesting thing you saw and how you felt about it.
- Use descriptive words to help the reader visualize the place that your story is about.
- Use complete sentences with correct capitalization, punctuation, grammar, and spelling.
- Read your writing. Circle three words that may be misspelled. Use a print dictionary to check the spelling.

Transfer
Think of three more words with a short vowel sound.

Write the words in your Spelling Journal. Circle the letters that stand for the short vowel sound.

 TEKS 4.22D Use spelling patterns and rules and print and electronic resources to determine and check correct spellings.

17

Extend & Transfer

Word Study

crop	began	begin	brick	public
dinner	collar	crust	spill	swift
land	felt	else	trick	perhaps
lunch	button	skill	shell	catfish
test	held	brag	camera	ticket
pass	trust	drag	contest	begun
zipper	kept	smell	discuss	vinegar

Pattern Power

Use words from the spelling list to answer these questions.

1–2. Which pair of rhyming words has the **short e** pattern as in **bed**?

3–6. Which two pairs of rhyming words have the **short i** pattern as in **pin**?

7–8. Which pair of rhyming words has the **short u** pattern as in **fun**?

9–10. Which pair of rhyming words has the **short a** pattern as in **cat**?

Meaning Patterns

11–13. Write the spelling words that represent different tenses of the same verb.

Double Consonants

Write the spelling words that share the same double consonant pattern and rhyme with the words below.

14. chipper   **15.** dollar   **16.** glutton

Add Endings

17–20. When a syllable ends in a vowel and a consonant, double the consonant when adding the ending **-ed** or **-ing**. Write the four spelling words that follow this rule, and then add **-ing** to each word. Draw a line between the syllables.

TEKS 4.22Aiii Spell words with more advanced orthographic patterns and rules: double consonants in middle of words. **4.22B** Spell base words and roots with affixes. **4.22D** Use spelling patterns and rules and print and electronic resources to determine and check correct spellings.

Science
Word Hunt

Read the paragraphs below. Look for words with the short vowel patterns you have studied in this unit.

Did you ever see a kangaroo baby? Was it held in its mother's pouch? Kangaroos are *marsupials*. That means they are land animals that have pouches. Today, most marsupials live in Australia, but scientists think that many once lived in the Americas.

The Virginia opossum is the only marsupial left in North America. It probably began to migrate from South America thousands of years ago. The opossum has survived for more than 50 million years. It is called a living fossil.

The opossum looks like a large rat. It is the size of a house cat. It has short legs, a long nose, and silvery hair. It has no hair on its ears and tail. Opossums are not swift. They don't see very well, but they have a great sense of smell. They also have good hearing.

Opossums live in forests and in cities. They make homes in hollow logs, under buildings, and in sheds. They cram into burrows dug by other animals. Their skill in adapting is key to their survival.

The opossum is known for a trick. It plays dead, lying completely still for hours. This fools the opossums' enemies. Perhaps that's how they kept from being eaten by dinosaurs!

WORD SORT

1–2. Write the words that contain the **short a** sound spelled **consonant-consonant-short vowel a-consonant**.

3–8. Write the words that contain short vowels with the **consonant-consonant-short vowel a, e, i,** or **u-consonant-consonant** pattern.

19

 TEKS 4.22D Use spelling patterns and rules and print and electronic resources to determine and check correct spellings.

Unit 2

Vowel-Consonant-e

Connections to THINKING

Read the spelling words and sentences.

1. wise	*wise*	Owls are described as **wise** birds.
2. huge	*huge*	An elephant is a **huge** animal.
3. case	*case*	We bought a **case** of spring water.
4. alone	*alone*	Are you **alone** or with friends?
5. rise	*rise*	Soap bubbles **rise** in the air.
6. cube	*cube*	A **cube** has six sides.
7. fame	*fame*	Movie stars earn **fame** and money.
8. beside	*beside*	Lisa sits **beside** me in school.
9. blame	*blame*	He did not **blame** us for the mistakes.
10. chose	*chose*	They **chose** sides for the game.
11. tire	*tire*	My bicycle **tire** is flat.
12. became	*became*	The hiker **became** lost in the woods.
13. awhile	*awhile*	Rest **awhile** if you are tired.
14. spoke	*spoke*	Joy **spoke** her lines well.
15. wife	*wife*	I met Uncle Theo's new **wife**.
16. drove	*drove*	Mother **drove** the truck to work.
17. surprise	*surprise*	Aunt Belle paid us a **surprise** visit.
18. scale	*scale*	Use the **scale** to check the cat's weight.
19. alive	*alive*	Grandfather is **alive** and well.
20. invite	*invite*	I will **invite** you to the party.

Think & Sort the spelling words.

1–5. Write the words that spell the long vowel sound **a-consonant-e**.

6–14. Write the words that spell the long vowel sound **i-consonant-e**.

15–18. Write the words that spell the long vowel sound **o-consonant-e**.

19–20. Write the words that spell the long vowel sound **u-consonant-e**.

Remember

The long vowel sounds you hear in **case, rise, chose,** and **cube** are spelled with the **vowel-consonant-e** pattern.

20

 TEKS 4.22D Use spelling patterns and rules and print and electronic resources to determine and check correct spellings.

Connections to VOCABULARY

Use Synonyms

Words that have the same or almost the same meaning, such as **simple** and **easy,** are called **synonyms**. Write a spelling word that is a synonym for each of these words.

1. carton
2. gigantic
3. recognition
4. accuse
5. smart

Word Structure

6–12. Write the spelling words that have two syllables. Draw a line between the syllables. Use the **Spelling Dictionary** to check the syllables.

13. Write the spelling word whose plural is formed by changing **f** to **v** and adding **-s**.

Adding Suffixes

Write the spelling words that are related in meaning to the words below. Circle the words in which the silent **e** was dropped when the suffix was added.

14. tiring
15. spoken
16. scaling
17. cubic
18. chosen

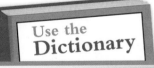

Use the Dictionary

Each word that appears in a dictionary is called an **entry word**. Entry words appear in dark print. Find the words **rise** and **drove** in your **Spelling Dictionary**. Write the word that answers each question.

19. Which word is in the past tense?

20. Which word can mean to "move upward or ascend"?

4.22Ai Spell words with more advanced orthographic patterns and rules: plural rules. **4.22Av** Spell words with more advanced orthographic patterns and rules: silent letters. **4.22B** Spell base words and roots with affixes. **4.22D** Use spelling patterns and rules and print and electronic resources to determine and check correct spellings.

21

Connections to READING

wise	huge	case	alone	rise
cube	fame	beside	blame	chose
tire	became	awhile	spoke	wife
drove	surprise	scale	alive	invite

Complete the Analogies

Write a spelling word to complete each analogy.

1. **Small** is to **tiny** as _____ is to **big**.
2. **Down** is to **up** as **descend** is to _____.
3. **Skate** is to **foot** as _____ is to **car**.
4. **Ruler** is to **measure** as _____ is to **weigh**.
5. **Ignorance** is to **wisdom** as **ignorant** is to _____.
6. **Came** is to **come** as _____ is to **become**.
7. **Four** is to **six** as **square** is to _____.

Word Substitution

Write one spelling word for each of these phrases.

8. ask to come
9. a box for carrying something
10. went by car
11. for a short time
12. at the side of
13. the quality of being well known

Use Context Clues

Write the spelling words from the box that complete the paragraph.

The detective __14.__ to the __15.__ of the missing man. "It will come as no __16.__ to learn that your husband is __17.__ and well. You __18.__ knew where he was hiding, and you __19.__ to keep it a secret. You and he must take the __20.__ for this deceit."

surprise
alone
chose
alive
blame
spoke
wife

 TEKS 4.22D Use spelling patterns and rules and print and electronic resources to determine and check correct spellings.

Connections to WRITING

Proofread a Friendly Letter

The symbol ∧ means **add**. The symbol ℓ means **take out,** or **delete**. Proofread the letter below for ten misspelled words. Then rewrite the letter. Write the spelling words correctly and make the corrections shown by the proofreading marks.

17 Oak Drive

Willowdale, Ohio 43011

September 17, 2012

Dear Joe,

    I paid ∧ᵃ surpris visit to Mr. Jackson and his wize wive. Mom drov me to see them. They live alon on a huje farm. Their house was built besid a beautiful ~~lake~~ lake. They want me to stay with them awile. they spoak with Mom and M̶e about when to come. Maybe they'll invyte you to stay, too.

Love,

ricky

Proofreading Marks

≡	Capital Letter
/	Small Letter
∧	Add
ℓ	Delete
⊙	Add a Period
⊬	Indent

NARRATIVE Writing Prompt
Write a Friendly Letter

Write a letter to a friend about a movie that you liked or a fun day that you spent with a family member. Use as many spelling words as you can.

- Use the writing process: prewrite, draft, revise, edit, and publish.
- Include the parts of a friendly letter: the heading, the greeting, the body of the letter, the closing, and your signature.
- Use complete sentences with correct capitalization, punctuation, grammar, and spelling.
- Read your writing. Circle three words that may be misspelled. Use a print dictionary to check the spelling.

Transfer
Find three words in your letter that have a long vowel sound spelled with the **vowel-consonant-e** pattern. Circle the letter that stands for the vowel sound. Underline the **silent e**.

 TEKS 4.22D Use spelling patterns and rules and print and electronic resources to determine and check correct spellings.

close	alone	invite	tire	locate
face	beside	wise	spoke	underline
size	became	rise	scale	fuse
write	awhile	cube	alive	female
wrote	wife	fame	complete	trapeze
huge	drove	blame	froze	antelope
case	surprise	chose	include	otherwise

Pattern Power
Use words from the spelling list to answer these questions.

1–3. Which three rhyming words have the **long i-consonant-e** pattern?

4–6. Which three rhyming words have the **long a-consonant-e** pattern?

Base Words
Write the spelling word that is a base word for one of these words.

7. cubic   8. invitation   9. casement

Verb Tenses
Write the spelling word that is the past tense of each of these words.

10. speak   12. drive   14. write

11. choose   13. freeze   15. become

Meaning Mastery
Write the spelling word that has the same meaning as each word or phrase.

16. living   19. get sleepy

17. a short time   20. used for weighing

18. a married woman

 TEKS 4.22B Spell base words and roots with affixes. **4.22D** Use spelling patterns and rules and print and electronic resources to determine and check correct spellings.

Social Studies

Word Hunt

Read the paragraphs below. Look for words with the **vowel-consonant-e** pattern.

Good citizens try to improve their communities. A Navajo woman named Annie Dodge Wauneka was such a citizen.

Annie was born in Arizona in 1910. Her father was a wise Navajo leader. Annie worked beside him. The Navajo had some huge problems to face. Annie wanted to help them solve these problems.

Annie was the first female on the Navajo council. She chose to work on medical care for her people. She wanted to stop the spread of tuberculosis, or TB. Many of her people died of this lung disease. It broke Annie's heart to see her people suffer.

The Navajo used only natural medicines to cure disease. Annie thought they should use modern medicine. She spoke about this on the radio. Soon her people began to combine both modern and natural medicines to wipe out TB.

Annie continued to strive for better health conditions. She worked to complete college. Then she worked in the field of public health. Annie became the first Native American to receive the Medal of Freedom. She was not interested in fame. But she took pride in the work that she did for her people.

WORD SORT

1–5. Write the two-syllable words that contain **long a, i,** or **e** spelled **long vowel-consonant-e.** Circle the **vowel-consonant-e** pattern.

6–10. Write the words that contain **long o** or **u** spelled **long vowel-consonant-e.** Circle the **vowel-consonant-e** pattern.

 TEKS 4.22D Use spelling patterns and rules and print and electronic resources to determine and check correct spellings.

Connections to THINKING

Read the spelling words and sentences.

1.	aim	*aim*	Her **aim** is to become a doctor.
2.	holiday	*holiday*	Which **holiday** falls on January 1?
3.	paper	*paper*	Todd forgot to sign his **paper**.
4.	station	*station*	The radio **station** went off the air.
5.	able	*able*	Humans are **able** to travel in space.
6.	crayon	*crayon*	Blue **crayon** is good for coloring sky.
7.	flavor	*flavor*	I use toothpaste with mint **flavor**.
8.	lazy	*lazy*	Successful people are usually not **lazy**.
9.	brain	*brain*	Our **brain** controls our emotions.
10.	anyway	*anyway*	You may not win, but try **anyway**.
11.	remain	*remain*	Sleep and eat well to **remain** healthy.
12.	favor	*favor*	Do a **favor** for your friends.
13.	rail	*rail*	The **rail** for the train was made of steel.
14.	grayest	*grayest*	This was the **grayest** day of the month.
15.	trailer	*trailer*	I got a **trailer** to pull my boat.
16.	lady	*lady*	A **lady** is known for her good manners.
17.	nation	*nation*	Our **nation** is a vast land.
18.	relay	*relay*	I will **relay** the good news to all.
19.	fail	*fail*	Try again if at first you **fail**.
20.	radio	*radio*	Karl is host of a **radio** talk show.

Think & Sort the spelling words.

1–9. Write the words that have the **long a** sound spelled **a**.

10–15. Write the words that have the **long a** sound spelled **ai**.

16–20. Write the words that have the **long a** sound spelled **ay**.

Remember

The **long a** sound can be spelled **a** as in **lady**, **ai** as in **aim**, and **ay** as in **relay**.

 TEKS 4.22D Use spelling patterns and rules and print and electronic resources to determine and check correct spellings.

Connections to VOCABULARY

Word Structure

1–2. Write the spelling words that have two syllables and have the **long a** sound in the second syllable. Draw a line between the syllables. Refer to your **Spelling Dictionary** if you need help.

3–13. Write the spelling words that have two syllables and have the **long a** sound in the first syllable. Draw a line between the syllables. Refer to your **Spelling Dictionary** if you need help.

Word Clues

Write a spelling word for each clue.

14. Thanksgiving is an example.

15. It is the opposite of **pass**.

16. It is located in your skull.

Use the **Dictionary**

Write each pair of words in alphabetical order.

   17–18. anyway, aim   **19–20.** radio, rail

Dictionary Check Be sure to check the alphabetical order of the words in your **Spelling Dictionary**.

TEKS 4.22D Use spelling patterns and rules and print and electronic resources to determine and check correct spellings.

27

aim	holiday	paper	station	able
crayon	flavor	lazy	brain	anyway
remain	favor	rail	grayest	trailer
lady	nation	relay	fail	radio

Complete the Analogies

Write a spelling word to complete each analogy.

1. **Paint** is to **canvas** as **pencil** is to _____.
2. **Gentleman** is to **man** as _____ is to **woman**.
3. **Heart** is to **chest** as _____ is to **head**.
4. **Country** is to _____ as **car** is to **automobile**.
5. **Slim** is to **thin** as **idle** is to _____.
6. **Black** is to **blackest** as **gray** is to _____.

Use Context Clues

Write a spelling word to complete each sentence.

7. I used pencil and _____ to draw and color that picture.
8. I never _____ to enjoy a good book.
9. You must be strong if you are _____ to carry that heavy load.
10. If your _____ is poor, you will not hit the target.
11. Please _____ in your seat until your name is called.
12. Jimmy and I went to the bus _____ to meet my aunt.
13. Goods are often sent by _____ or by sea.
14. The car pulled a _____ full of furniture.
15. Dad told Jim not to open the present, but he did _____.
16. We heard a traffic report on our car's _____.
17. Do me the _____ of returning a book to the library.
18. Chocolate is my favorite ice cream _____.
19. The player will _____ the coach's message to the team.
20. Columbus Day is a _____ that is observed on October 12.

TEKS 4.22D Use spelling patterns and rules and print and electronic resources to determine and check correct spellings.

Connections to WRITING

Proofread a Diary Entry

The symbol ⊙ means **add a period**. The symbol ⊬ means **indent**. Proofread the diary entry below for ten misspelled words. Then rewrite the entry. Write the spelling words correctly and make the corrections shown by the proofreading marks.

⊬ Each weekend is a hollidaiy at our house. we remane

at home and listen to music on our favorite raydio station,

read the daily payper, and are laisy without feeling guilty.

I give my brane a rest from school, and we All relax. It is

good we are ayble to do this most weekends. I miss it

when we faill to spend a weekend at home. We make it

our aime to spend time with each other. i did have to do

some chores, but it was a great weekend enyway⊙

Proofreading Marks

≡	Capital Letter
/	Small Letter
∧	Add
℘	Delete
⊙	Add a Period
⊬	Indent

NARRATIVE Writing Prompt
Write a Diary Entry

Write a diary entry to help you remember a special day that you spent with a friend. Use as many spelling words as you can.

- Use the writing process: prewrite, draft, revise, edit, and publish.
- Use descriptive words about your day so that when you look at your diary months—or even years—from now, you will be able to picture the day as though it were only yesterday.
- Use complete sentences with correct capitalization, punctuation, grammar, and spelling.
- Use the **Spelling Dictionary** in this book or an online dictionary to check spelling if you are not sure.

Transfer

Think of three words that have a **long a** sound spelled **a, ay,** or **ai**. Write the words in your Spelling Journal. Circle the letter(s) that stand for the **long a** sound.

TEKS 4.22D Use spelling patterns and rules and print and electronic resources to determine and check correct spellings.

29

Word Study

away	station	radio	remain	prepaid
laid	able	aim	rail	reclaim
mail	favor	crayon	grayest	contain
maybe	trailer	flavor	fail	stadium
paint	lady	lazy	explain	replay
holiday	nation	brain	refrain	regain
paper	relay	anyway	midday	trainer

Pattern Power

1–3. Write three one-syllable rhyming words that have the **long a** sound spelled **ai**.

4–5. Write two rhyming words that differ by only one letter and have **long a** in the first syllable.

6–8. Write the spelling words whose first syllable ends with **long a** spelled **ay**.

9. Write the spelling word whose plural is formed by dropping **y** and adding **-ies**.

Adding Suffixes

The suffix **-ion** means "condition of." Write the spelling words that are the base words for these words. Circle the letters in each word that spell /**sh**/.

10. nationality
11. explanation
12. reclamation
13. stationary

The suffix **-er** can mean "one that performs a specified action." Add **-er** to each of these words.

14. trail
15. train

The ending **-er** can also mean "more."

16. Write the spelling word in which the final **y** is changed to **i** before adding this ending.

TEKS 4.22Ai Spell words with more advanced orthographic patterns and rules: plural rules. **4.22Aiv** Spell words with more advanced orthographic patterns and rules: other ways to spell sh. **4.22B** Spell base words and roots with affixes.

Art
Word Hunt

Read the paragraphs below and look for words with the **long a** sound spelled **a, ai,** or **ay**.

Some very famous artists paint very simple pictures. Anna Mary Robertson is one. This lady is better known as Grandma Moses. Maybe you've heard of her.

Anna grew up on a farm in upstate New York. She did needlework for many years. When she got older, holding a needle became too painful for her aching fingers. Anna's sister said, "Try painting." Anna was 75.

That's how one of this nation's most beloved artists got started. Anna had no art training, but folks liked her work. A local store put her paintings on display in their window.

One day, a New York art collector named Louis Caldor saw the paintings. He bought them all. Caldor was able to show the paintings in a famous art museum. The art world met Grandma Moses. Her paintings received wide acclaim.

Art critics have tried to explain the appeal of her art. Grandma Moses captured the flavor of the world around her. Her paintings were a taste of a simpler life and time.

When she was 100 years old, Grandma Moses completed her final painting, called *Rainbow*. What is simpler or more beautiful than a rainbow?

WORD SORT

1–2. Write the two-syllable words that contain the **long a** sound spelled **ay**.

3–8. Write the two-syllable words that contain the **long a** sound spelled **a**.

9–10. Write the two-syllable words that contain the **long a** sound spelled **ai** only in the second syllable.

 TEKS 4.22D Use spelling patterns and rules and print and electronic resources to determine and check correct spellings.

Connections to THINKING

Read the spelling words and sentences.

1. field	*field*	The cows are grazing in the **field**.
2. lead	*lead*	If you **lead**, I will follow.
3. speed	*speed*	Do bikers **speed** on this path?
4. believe	*believe*	I **believe** you are telling the truth.
5. deal	*deal*	That **deal** was too good to be true.
6. piece	*piece*	We lost a **piece** of the puzzle.
7. reach	*reach*	Ava cannot **reach** the top shelf.
8. breeze	*breeze*	The **breeze** helped cool us today.
9. speak	*speak*	We are learning to **speak** Italian.
10. agree	*agree*	Yes, I **agree** with your plan.
11. least	*least*	It has rained for at **least** six days.
12. season	*season*	Summer is the **season** I like best.
13. between	*between*	This secret is **between** you and me.
14. chief	*chief*	A **chief** is head of a group.
15. steam	*steam*	You can **steam** these vegetables.
16. degree	*degree*	The temperature rose one **degree** today.
17. reason	*reason*	What is your **reason** for being so early?
18. brief	*brief*	A **brief** tale is a short story.
19. repeat	*repeat*	Do not **repeat** everything you hear.
20. peach	*peach*	The skin of a **peach** is fuzzy.

Think & Sort the spelling words.

1–10. Write the words that have the **long e** sound spelled **ea**.

11–15. Write the words that have the **long e** sound spelled **ee**.

16–20. Write the words that have the **long e** sound spelled **ie**.

Remember

The **long e** sound can be spelled in different ways: **ea** as in **deal**, **ee** as in **speed**, and **ie** as in **field**.

 TEKS 4.22D Use spelling patterns and rules and print and electronic resources to determine and check correct spellings.

Connections to VOCABULARY

Word Meanings

Write a spelling word for each definition.

1. a fuzzy, sweet fruit
2. a leader; head of a group
3. to handle in a certain way; cope
4. gas made from water
5. to talk
6. to march at the head of the line
7. smallest in size or amount
8. to extend

Word Categorization

Write a spelling word to complete each category.

9. area, meadow, _____
10. current, wind, _____
11. swiftness, rapidity, _____
12. short, concise, _____

Syllables

13–19. Write the spelling words that have two syllables. Draw a line between the syllables.

Use the Dictionary

20. Words that have exactly the same pronunciation but different meanings and different spellings are called **homophones**. Write the spelling word that is a homophone for **peace**.

Dictionary Check Be sure to check your answer in your **Spelling Dictionary**.

 TEKS 4.22C Spell commonly used homophones. **4.22D** Use spelling patterns and rules and print and electronic resources to determine and check correct spellings.

33

field	lead	speed	believe	deal
piece	reach	breeze	speak	agree
least	season	between	chief	steam
degree	reason	brief	repeat	peach

Complete the Analogies

Write a spelling word to complete each analogy.

1. **Carrot** is to **vegetable** as _____ is to **fruit**.
2. **Rain** is to **mist** as **wind** is to _____.
3. **Monarch** is to **ruler** as **talk** is to _____.
4. **Happy** is to **sad** as **follow** is to _____.
5. **Country** is to **state** as **whole** is to _____.
6. **Seek** is to **search** as _____ is to **short**.
7. **Heat** is to _____ as **cold** is to **ice**.
8. **Question** is to **ask** as _____ is to **think**.

Make Inferences

Write a spelling word to complete each sentence. The spelling word rhymes with the underlined word.

9. The farmer's _____ will surely <u>yield</u> a crop.
10. You must never _____ that dangerous <u>feat</u>.
11. I swim at a <u>beach</u> that is not out of _____.
12. When biking, you <u>need</u> to be aware of your _____.
13. We dined at a <u>feast</u> with five courses at _____.
14. To appoint him a _____ is beyond my <u>belief</u>.
15. A five-dollar <u>meal</u> is a very good _____.

Use Context Clues

Write spelling words to complete the paragraph.

My friends and I have different ideas about which **16.** is best. I **17.** summer is perfect, but Marcie does not **18.** She prefers winter, while Paul is torn **19.** spring and fall. He needs a high **20.** of cool, brisk weather.

believe
agree
degree
between
season

 TEKS 4.22D Use spelling patterns and rules and print and electronic resources to determine and check correct spellings.

Connections to WRITING

Proofread a Newspaper Ad

Proofread the newspaper ad below for ten misspelled words. Then rewrite the ad. Write the spelling words correctly and make the corrections shown by the proofreading marks.

For Rent

¶ Why pay high Hotel rates? Rent for the summer
sieson. a peech of a house on a lovely piese of
land beetween a grassy feild and a clear blue
lake. You will not beelieve how nice the place
is. Enjoy the summer brieze and catch a load of
fish. $175 per week. I will not be able to
repeet this offer. this price is good for only
a breef time. Call 555-1111 to speke to me.

Proofreading Marks

≡ Capital Letter

/ Small Letter

∧ Add

℘ Delete

⊙ Add a Period

¶ Indent

PERSUASIVE Writing Prompt
Write a Newspaper Ad

Write or type a newspaper ad to sell something you own. Write your ad to appeal to the type of person who would be interested in your item. Use as many spelling words as you can.

- Use the writing process: prewrite, draft, revise, edit, and publish.
- Include a description of the item's condition and the price. Include at least three details that would make someone want to buy the item.
- Use complete sentences with correct capitalization, punctuation, grammar, and spelling.
- Read your writing. Circle three words that may be misspelled. Use an electronic resource to check your spelling.

Transfer

Think of three words that have the **long e** sound. One word should have the sound spelled **ea,** one should have the sound spelled **ee,** and one should have the sound spelled **ie**. Write the words in your Spelling Journal. Circle the letter(s) that stand for the **long e** sound.

 TEKS 4.22D Use spelling patterns and rules and print and electronic resources to determine and check correct spellings.

35

Word Study

cheese	believe	reason	degree	freedom
leave	piece	speed	brief	make-believe
mean	reach	deal	repeat	wreath
peace	speak	breeze	peach	treason
speech	agree	least	beliefs	keenly
field	between	season	beneath	breed
lead	chief	steam	decrease	belief

Pattern Power

1. Write the spelling word that has the same second syllable as **agree**.
2–4. Write the three rhyming words that have **long e** spelled **ie**.
5–7. Write the three rhyming words that end with the digraph /**ch**/.
8–9. Write the two words that rhyme with **fleas**.

Adding Prefixes

The prefixes **dis-** and **mis-** mean "not" or "wrong." Write the spelling word that is a base word for one of the words below.

10. mislead	12. disagree	14. disbelieve
11. misspeak	13. misdeal	

Adding Suffixes

The suffix **-er** means "one who." Write the spelling word that is a base word for one of the words below.

15. speeder	17. leader	19. repeater
16. steamer	18. speaker	

Figurative Language: Idioms

20. If something is last but not _____, it is at the end but not last in importance.

 TEKS 4.22B Spell base words and roots with affixes. **4.22D** Use spelling patterns and rules and print and electronic resources to determine and check correct spellings.

Math

Word Hunt

Read the paragraphs below and look for words that have the **long e** sound spelled **ea, ee,** or **ie**.

Every baseball season, fans cheer their favorite teams. Some fans use math to calculate statistics on every player and every team.

Statistics are called "stats" for short. Baseball fans keep stats for each player on the field. To do this, fans need to divide with decimals and understand percentages.

Fans keep a player's batting averages to tell how many hits the batter gets each time he or she comes to bat. A baseball is not easy to hit. A batting average of .300 is great! That means a batter got a hit once every three times at bat. Fans also keep stats on how many times a runner gets on base. A runner needs a lot of speed to reach base after a hit.

Baseball records have been kept for a long time. They are a piece of sports history, and they mean a lot to baseball fans. Maybe one day a fan will teach you how to figure out averages. That's a good reason to learn math, but it will be worth it. At least that's what real baseball fans believe.

WORD SORT

1–2. Write the two-syllable rhyming words that contain the **long e** sound spelled **ea** in the first syllable.

3. Write the two-syllable word that begins with the **long e** sound. Circle the letters that make that sound.

4–5. Write the one-syllable words that contain the **long e** sound spelled **ie**.

6–9. Write the five-letter words that contain the **long e** sound spelled **ee**.

TEKS 4.22D Use spelling patterns and rules and print and electronic resources to determine and check correct spellings.

Connections to THINKING

Read the spelling words and sentences.

1.	eyes	*eyes*	Sunglasses protect our **eyes**.
2.	icicle	*icicle*	An **icicle** is a hanging stick of ice.
3.	tight	*tight*	My shoes are too **tight** for comfort.
4.	climb	*climb*	Some bears can **climb** trees.
5.	umpire	*umpire*	The **umpire** called the pitch a strike.
6.	highway	*highway*	A **highway** is wider than a street.
7.	idea	*idea*	Whose **idea** was it to hold this meeting?
8.	flight	*flight*	In **flight,** bats scoop up insects.
9.	cycle	*cycle*	The water **cycle** supports life.
10.	fright	*fright*	The haunted house gave us a **fright**.
11.	iron	*iron*	Steel and **iron** are strong materials.
12.	slight	*slight*	A **slight** rip can be sewn easily.
13.	tiny	*tiny*	A dot is a **tiny** mark.
14.	higher	*higher*	Go to **higher** ground during floods.
15.	shy	*shy*	A **shy** person tries to avoid notice.
16.	hire	*hire*	Will the city **hire** more workers?
17.	buy	*buy*	I **buy** my shoes at that store.
18.	might	*might*	She was afraid they **might** be late.
19.	reply	*reply*	I must **reply** to the invitation.
20.	title	*title*	What is the **title** of your story?

Think & Sort the spelling words.

1–6 Write the words that have **long i** spelled **i**.

7–8. Write the words that have **long i** spelled **i-consonant-e**.

9–11. Write the words that have the **long i** sound spelled **y**.

12–18. Write the words that have the **long i** sound spelled **igh**.

19. Write the word that has the **long i** sound spelled **ey**.

20. Write the word that has the **long i** sound spelled **uy**.

Remember

The **long i** sound is spelled **i** as in **climb**, **i-consonant-e** as in **hire**, **y** as in **cycle**, **igh** as in **might**, **ey** as in **eyes**, and **uy** as in **buy**.

 TEKS 4.22D Use spelling patterns and rules and print and electronic resources to determine and check correct spellings.

Word Meanings

Replace each underlined word or group of words with a spelling word.

1. Last summer, we took a <u>plane ride</u> from Denver to Seattle.
2. Because we were on a <u>close</u> schedule, we had to hurry through the airport.
3. After a <u>brief</u> delay, the plane took off.
4. I <u>could</u> have relaxed, but then I realized I had forgotten my suitcase.
5. That gave me quite a <u>scare</u>.

Word Structure

6–15. Write the spelling words that have more than one syllable. Draw a line between the syllables.

16. Write the one-syllable spelling word that ends with a consonant that is not sounded.

17. Write the one-syllable spelling word that ends with a **silent e** and is a homophone for **higher**.

18. Write the one-syllable spelling word that starts with the sound you hear at the beginning of **ship** and ends with the sound you hear at the end of **try**.

Use the Dictionary

Look at these dictionary respellings. Say each word. Write the spelling word for each dictionary respelling. Circle the word that is a homophone for **by** and **bye**.

19. /bī/   20. /īz/

Dictionary Check Be sure to check your answers in your **Spelling Dictionary**.

 TEKS 4.22Av Spell words with more advanced orthographic patterns and rules: silent letters. **4.22C** Spell commonly used homophones. **4.22D** Use spelling patterns and rules and print and electronic resources to determine and check correct spellings.

39

Connections to READING

eyes	icicle	tight	climb	umpire
highway	idea	flight	cycle	fright
iron	slight	tiny	higher	shy
hire	buy	might	reply	title

Make Inferences

Write a spelling word to solve each riddle.

1. I am little; I rhyme with **fight**. What am I?
2. As a verb, I press; as a metal, I am heavy. What am I?
3. I am wide and black; cars ride on my back. What am I?
4. I am best in the cold but drip in the heat. What am I?

Complete the Analogies

Write a spelling word to complete each analogy.

5. **Big** is to **huge** as **small** is to _____.
6. **Up** is to **down** as **loose** is to _____.
7. **Gallop** is to **horse** as _____ is to **bird**.
8. **Canoe** is to **paddle** as **bike** is to _____.
9. **Leave** is to **go** as **scare** is to _____.
10. **Ask** is to **question** as _____ is to **answer**.
11. **Peace** is to **piece** as **higher** is to _____.

Use Context Clues

Write a spelling word to complete each sentence.

12. Volunteering to help the needy is a good _____.
13. Even _____ people can learn to speak in public.
14. You're a sight for sore _____.
15. Many people have tried to _____ Mount Everest.
16. The _____ called the player out at third base.
17. What is the _____ of the book you are reading?
18. Hang the picture _____ so I can see it better.
19. I want to _____ my mother a birthday present.
20. Powerful people think "_____ makes right."

40

TEKS 4.22D Use spelling patterns and rules and print and electronic resources to determine and check correct spellings.

Connections to WRITING

Proofread a Poster

Proofread the poster below for ten misspelled words. Then rewrite the poster. Write the spelling words correctly and make the corrections shown by the proofreading marks.

The Man in the Iren mask

by by that famous theater group

The Season Cicle Players!

Where?   Main street Theater, Hiway 66

When?   June 17–20

Your eys will pop out of your Head. Your heart will pound. You mite even scream. Chills, joy, and frite. All for the slite price of $4.50. Don't be shi. Call 555-2633 now to buye your tickets. You will pay a hyer price at the door

SEE YOU THERE!

Proofreading Marks

≡	Capital Letter
/	Small Letter
∧	Add
ℓ	Delete
⊙	Add a Period
¶	Indent

PERSUASIVE Writing Prompt
Write a Poster

Write a poster to persuade people to come to an event. Use as many spelling words as you can.

- Use the writing process: prewrite, draft, revise, edit, and publish.
- Use persuasive language to tell people why they should come. Be sure to include the name of the event, the location, the date, the time, and the price of tickets.
- Use complete sentences with correct capitalization, punctuation, grammar, and spelling.
- Read your writing. Circle three words that may be misspelled. Use an electronic dictionary to check the spelling.

Transfer
Think of six words that have a **long i** sound spelled **i, i-consonant-e, y, igh, ey,** or **uy**.
Write the words in your Spelling Journal. Circle the letter(s) that stand for the **long i** sound.

 TEKS 4.22D Use spelling patterns and rules and print and electronic resources to determine and check correct spellings.

Extend & Transfer
Word Study

fight	idea	might	higher	style
find	flight	icicle	hire	supply
price	cycle	tight	reply	dial
right	iron	umpire	title	rely
wild	tiny	highway	arrive	hydrant
eyes	shy	fright	delight	lightly
climb	buy	slight	silent	blight

Pattern Power
1–3. Write three words that end in **light**.

Parts of Speech
Write a spelling word by changing the part of speech of each of these words by dropping the prefix, suffix, or ending.

4. from adjective **entitled** to noun _____

5. from verb **idealize** to noun _____

6. from noun **climber** to verb _____

7. from noun **replication** to verb _____

8. from noun **tininess** to adjective _____

Meaning Mastery
9. Write the spelling word, which means a baseball official, that is sometimes confused with the word **empire,** meaning a territory ruled by a monarch or emperor.

10. Write the spelling word that is a homophone for **higher**.

11. Write the spelling word that can mean "frozen ice piece" or "an aloof, cold person."

12. Write the spelling word that has a silent **gh** in the final syllable and means "great pleasure."

TEKS 4.22Av Spell words with more advanced orthographic patterns and rules: silent letters. **4.22B** Spell base words and roots with affixes. **4.22C** Spell commonly used homophones. **4.22D** Use spelling patterns and rules and print trand electronic resources to determine and check correct spellings.

Technology
Word Hunt

Read the paragraphs below and look for words that have the **long i** sound spelled **i, i-consonant-e, y, igh, ey,** or **uy**.

The Internet is sometimes called the information super-highway. Perhaps it should be called the information super-railway. Can you guess why?

It's because search engines ride the Internet. A search engine is a tool devised to help people find information. It searches the Internet to find websites that can answer questions based on the words you type. For example, do you want to know the name of the first female professional baseball umpire? Just type the words *first female professional baseball umpire* into a search engine. You'll find out that her name is Bernice Gera. She umpired in the minor leagues.

You might need to find a flight to Grimes County, Texas. Just type *Grimes County flights* into a search engine. There's more than a slight chance you'll arrive at an answer. Do you want to know the title of a book about Sam Houston? Ask a search engine. You could get more than eight hundred answers.

Want to try a search engine? Just remember one thing. You can't absolutely rely on every answer you get. Sometimes, the best search engine is the one right inside your own head.

 WORD SORT

1–4. Write the one-syllable words that contain the **long i** sound spelled **igh**.

5–10. Write the two-syllable words that contain the **long i** sound spelled **i-consonant-e**.

 TEKS 4.22D Use spelling patterns and rules and print and electronic resources to determine and check correct spellings.

Unit 6

Assess for Transfer

Assessment

Each word in the box fits one of the spelling patterns and rules you have studied over the past five weeks. Read the unit descriptions. Then write each assessment word under the unit number it fits.

Unit 1

1–4. Many short vowel sounds are spelled with a single letter: **a** as in **pass, e** as in **held, i** as in **skill, o** as in **collar,** and **u** as in **trust**.

Unit 2

5–10. The long vowel sounds you hear in **case, rise, chose,** and **cube** are spelled with the **vowel-consonant-e** pattern.

Unit 3

11–14. The **long a** sound can be spelled **a** as in **lady, ai** as in **aim,** and **ay** as in **relay**.

Unit 4

15–18. The **long e** sound can be spelled in different ways: **ea** in **deal, ee** in **speed,** and **ie** in **field**.

Unit 5

19–20. The **long i** sound is spelled **i** in **climb, i-consonant-e** in **hire, y** in **cycle, igh** in **might, ey** in **eyes,** and **uy** in **buy**.

Words for Assessment

skull

stroke

betray

series

magic

fired

icy

beast

slope

rainy

crime

raft

claim

gift

male

screen

basin

type

seep

sty

Review

Unit 1: Short Vowel Sounds

begin	kept	trust	zipper	pass
collar	held	button	began	felt

Write the spelling word that rhymes with each of these words.

1. slept   3. melt   5. flipper

2. mass   4. yelled   6. just

Write a spelling word to complete each sentence.

7. The dog wore a red _____.

8. I lost one shiny gold _____ from my new coat.

9. What time does the school day _____?

10. Last year, school _____ one hour earlier.

Unit 2: Vowel-Consonant-e

awhile	became	beside	invite	case
drove	huge	wife	surprise	alone

Write the missing spelling word. Use the underlined word as a clue.

11. They are <u>husband</u> and _____.

12. These horses ran <u>together</u> while one stood _____.

13. One package was <u>big</u>, but the other was _____!

14. There are seats <u>behind</u> and also _____ me.

Find the misspelled word in each sentence. Write the word correctly.

15. My party was a real suprise.

16. Don't wait for me; I will be along in awile.

17. Anna will inveit the whole class to her party.

18. Mary bicame ill from eating too much ice cream.

19. Can the lawyer win this kase?

20. We were lost and drov three blocks out of our way.

Review

Unit 3: Long a: a, ai, ay

favor	holiday	relay	trailer	able
paper	nation	radio	station	lady

Write the spelling word that is related to each word below.
Circle the word in which the vowel sound changed from
short a to **long a**.

1. ladies
2. favorite
3. national
4. stationary
5. holidays

6. papery
7. trail
8. ability
9. relayed
10. radioed

Unit 4: Long e: ea, ee, ie

agree	believe	field	reason	between
reach	speak	lead	chief	piece

Write the spelling word that completes each sentence.

11. What is your _____ for saying that?
12. You will need a stool to _____ that upper shelf.
13. I _____ that is the right answer.
14. The house stands _____ two huge old trees.
15. Tall corn grew in the farmer's _____.
16. Would you like a _____ of chocolate cake?
17. If we follow Rover, he will _____ us to the right place.
18. The _____ reason I can't go is that I have homework to do.
19. Please _____ a little more softly.
20. Do you _____ that the party was a big success?

Unit 5: Long i: i, i-C-e, y, igh, ey, uy

buy	climb	might	cycle	flight
eyes	tiny	idea	iron	shy

Write the spelling words for these clues.

1–2. These words rhyme with **right**.

3. This word has three syllables.

Write the spelling word that completes each sentence.

4. Rain is part of the water _____.

5. It is fun to _____ that big old tree in our yard.

6. I have just enough money to _____ that book.

7. Most animals have two _____.

8. A very small insect is a _____ ant.

9. A tool we use to press clothes is called an _____.

10. Speak up. Don't be _____.

Spelling Study Strategy

Spelling Tic-Tac-Toe

Here's a fun way to practice spelling words.

1. Write your spelling words in a list. Ask your friend to do the same with his or her spelling words. Trade spelling lists.

2. Draw a tic-tac-toe board on a piece of scrap paper. Decide who will use **X** and who will use **O**.

3. Ask your partner to call the first word on your spelling list to you. Spell it out loud. If you spell it correctly, make an **X** or an **O** (whichever you are using) on the tic-tac-toe board. If you misspell the word, ask your partner to spell it out loud for you. You miss your turn.

4. Now you call a word from your partner's spelling list.

5. Keep playing until one of you makes "tic-tac-toe."

Directions: Read the introduction and the passage that follows. Then read each question and fill in the correct answer on your answer sheet.

Kate and Alison are best friends. They do lots of things together. Their favorite thing is to have sleepovers. Alison wrote this paper about something scary and funny that happened at a sleepover at her house. Here is the draft of Alison's paper. As you read the paper, think about the corrections and improvements Alison should make when she revises.

A Scary Night for Kate and Alison

(1) Kate and I have sleepovers a lot. (2) The last time she slept at my house we got a gigantic scare and a hug surprise for a very funny reason.

(3) Kate and I saw a monster movie on TV before I turned off the station, got in betwien the covers, and turned off the lights. (4) I was able to fall asleep right away, but not Kate. (5) Too many monsters kept her awake. (6) Suddenly, I felt Kate reach over and pull my colar. (7) "Do you hear that?" she asked in terror. (8) I did hear something, so I turned on the lights. (9) I did not believe my eyes; a payper bag was skittering across the floor.

(10) I had no ideer where that bag came from or why it was running around my bedroom. (11) Kate thought there mite be a tiny monster in the bag, but I did not agree. (12) I saw two eyez peeking out, and came to find the surprise was Chipper, my sister's new kitten. (13) She became stuck inside and could not get out! (14) I had to drag Chipper out before I could climb back into bed. (15) Chipper begayne to cry and drove me nuts. (16) So I got out of bed again and let her sleep with Kate and me. (17) We went to sleep in peace, and Chipper slept on my head all night!

1 What change, if any, should be made in sentence 2?

   A Change *hug* to **huge**

   B Change *surprise* to **surpris**

   C Change *reason* to **reeson**

   D Make no change

2 What change, if any, should be made in sentence 3?

   F Change *station* to **stashun**

   G Change *betwien* to **between**

   H Change *lights* to **lites**

   J Make no change

3 What change, if any, should be made in sentence 4?

   A Change *able* to **ayble**

   B Change *asleep* to **a sleep**

   C Change *right* to **ryte**

   D Make no change

4 What change, if any, should be made in sentence 6?

   F Change *felt* to **filt**

   G Change *reach* to **reech**

   H Change *colar* to **collar**

   J Make no change

5 What change, if any, should be made in sentence 9?

   A Change *believe* to **beleeve**

   B Change *eyes* to **ise**

   C Change *payper* to **paper**

   D Make no change

6 What change, if any, should be made to sentence 10?

   F Change *ideer* to **idea**

   G Change *bag* to **bug**

   H Change *why* to **whi**

   J Make no change

7 What change, if any, should be made to sentence 11?

   A Change *mite* to **might**

   B Change *tiny* to **tighny**

   C Change *agree* to **agrea**

   D Make no change

8 What change, if any, should be made in sentence 12?

   F Change *find* to **fined**

   G Change *surprise* to **surprize**

   H Change *eyez* to **eyes**

   J Make no change

9 What change, if any, should be made to sentence 15?

   A Change *begayne* to **began**

   B Change *cry* to **crie**

   C Change *begayne* to **begun**

   D Make no change

10 What change, if any, should be made in sentence 17?

   F Change *peace* to **piece**

   G Change *Chipper* to **chipper**

   H Change *night* to **nite**

   J Make no change

STOP

Grammar, Usage, and Mechanics
Possessive Nouns

A **possessive noun** shows ownership.
Some possessive nouns are singular. Only one
person or animal is the owner.

- **Jess's** bike is old, but **Jill's** is new.

- Do not remove the **dog's** collar.

Other possessive nouns are plural. More than
one person or animal is the owner.

- All the **boys'** teams are here but not the **men's** teams.

- The **horses'** hooves could be heard in the canyon as
  they galloped over the hill.

Practice Activity

A. Write the correct possessive form in each sentence.
   1. My (mothers'/mother's) birthday is tomorrow.
   2. One (teams'/team's) coach is late.
   3. A (pigs'/pig's) tail is curly.
   4. I knit both of my (uncles'/uncle's) hats.
   5. It was (Jakes'/Jake's) turn to feed the rabbits.

B. Change each underlined phrase to make one possessive
   noun.
   6. I will borrow the sweater of Carlos.
   7. The shoes of everyone need to be polished.
   8. The kennel where the dogs stay is very clean.
   9. Kim found the lost key that belongs to your cousins!
   10. The books of the student were piled high.

The Writing Process: Narrative
Writing a Realistic Story

PREWRITING
Some stories sound like they really happened, but they didn't. The writer might include names of real people, but the events are invented. Think about your town or community. How do you think it was started? Look in books at the library to help you get ideas. Ask your teacher to help you find information about where you live on the Internet, too.

DRAFTING
Review the information you have gathered. Develop a plot outline that includes a beginning, a climax, and an ending. Support your plot with details about setting and characters. Stop and gather more information if you need to make your story more accurate. If possible, use a word processor to type your draft. A word processor allows you to revise and edit your work easily.

REVISING
When you have finished your first draft, read your story from beginning to end. Check to see if you have included all of the points in your outline. Does each sentence support the topic? Now write your final draft.

EDITING
Use the **Editing Checklist** to proofread your story. Be sure to use proofreading marks when you make corrections. As you proofread, find three words you are not sure how to spell. Use the spell-check feature of the word processor to check the spelling.

PUBLISHING
Make a copy of your realistic story and share it with your readers.

EDITING CHECKLIST

Spelling
- ✓ Circle words that contain the spelling patterns and rules learned in Units 1–5.
- ✓ Check the circled words in your **Spelling Dictionary**.
- ✓ Check for other spelling errors.

Capital Letters
- ✓ Capitalize important words in the title.
- ✓ Capitalize the first word in each sentence.
- ✓ Capitalize proper nouns.

Punctuation
- ✓ End each sentence with the correct punctuation.
- ✓ Use commas, apostrophes, and quotation marks correctly.

Grammar, Usage, and Mechanics
- ✓ Use singular and plural possessive nouns correctly.

TEKS 4.22D Use spelling patterns and rules and print and electronic resources to determine and check correct spellings.

Connections to THINKING

Read the spelling words and sentences.

1.	poet	*poet*	Which **poet** wrote those lines?
2.	coast	*coast*	Along the **coast** lie sunken ships.
3.	pillow	*pillow*	A soft **pillow** cradled her head.
4.	hotel	*hotel*	The **hotel** was ten stories high.
5.	also	*also*	I can sing and **also** dance.
6.	clothes	*clothes*	My **clothes** hang in a closet.
7.	pony	*pony*	The **pony** trotted around the ring.
8.	bold	*bold*	Catching the snake was a **bold** move.
9.	moment	*moment*	In a **moment** the sun will set.
10.	obey	*obey*	Dogs can learn to **obey** commands.
11.	grown	*grown*	She has **grown** an inch this year.
12.	hello	*hello*	I say **hello** to everyone I know.
13.	motel	*motel*	A **motel** is a motor hotel.
14.	boast	*boast*	Do not **boast** of our success yet.
15.	glow	*glow*	I followed the **glow** of the lamp.
16.	goal	*goal*	The ball bounced over the **goal** line.
17.	poem	*poem*	That **poem** contains rhyming words.
18.	shown	*shown*	We were **shown** to our room.
19.	hero	*hero*	A **hero** does brave deeds.
20.	fold	*fold*	Do not **fold** or wrinkle your paper.

Think & Sort the spelling words.

1–12. Write the words that have the **long o** sound spelled **o**.

13–15. Write the words that have the **long o** sound spelled **oa**.

16–19. Write the words that have the **long o** sound spelled **ow**.

20. Write the word that has the **long o** sound spelled **o-consonant digraph-e**.

Remember

The **long o** sound can be spelled in different ways: **o** as in **pony**, **oa** as in **goal**, **ow** as in **glow**, and **o-consonant digraph-e** as in **clothes**.

 TEKS 4.22D Use spelling patterns and rules and print and electronic resources to determine and check correct spellings.

Connections to VOCABULARY

Word Meanings

Write a spelling word for each definition. Use your **Spelling Dictionary** to check the meaning and the spelling of each word. Find the words that have a double consonant in the middle and draw a line between the syllables.

1. a greeting
2. land along the ocean
3. a place offering guest rooms, meals, and other services
4. a form of **show**
5. something usually found on a bed

Use Syllables

Say a word to yourself and listen to the beats to determine how many syllables it has. You can also tell how many syllables a word has by the number of vowel sounds it contains. Check a dictionary to be sure.

6–9. Write the four-letter spelling words that have one syllable.

10–15. Write the four-letter spelling words that have two syllables.

Use the
Dictionary

16–20. The dictionary lists the part of speech for an entry word after the respelling. Write these spelling words in alphabetical order. Then look in the **Spelling Dictionary** to find the abbreviation for the word's part of speech. Write the abbreviation next to each word.

motel   grown   clothes   moment   boast

TEKS 4.22Aiii Spell words with more advanced orthographic patterns and rules: double consonants in middle of words. **4.22D** Use spelling patterns and rules and print and electronic resources to determine and check correct spellings.

poet	coast	pillow	hotel	also
clothes	pony	bold	moment	obey
grown	hello	motel	boast	glow
goal	poem	shown	hero	fold

Solve the Riddles

Write a spelling word for each riddle.

1. I am a brief period of time. Who am I?
2. Everyone loves me because I am brave. Who am I?
3. I am something everyone wants to reach. Who am I?
4. Sometimes I rhyme, and sometimes I do not. Who am I?
5. I am something you do with paper and with clothes. Who am I?

Make Inferences

Write a spelling word to complete each sentence.

6. While driving to Chicago, we stopped for the night to stay at a _____ near the highway.
7. A soft _____ was at the head of the bed.
8. Mother has _____ both flowers and vegetables.
9. Many beachgoers swam and picnicked along the sandy _____.
10. Say _____ to your brother for me.
11. We play ball and _____ fly kites in the park.
12. Peter was _____ a map of the city when he was lost.
13. She is a _____, a writer, and a musician.
14. He greets visitors at a fancy _____ in New York City.
15. The _____ of fireflies lights up the night sky.

Use Context Clues

Write spelling words from the box to fill in the blanks in the story.

Children, dressed in their best __16.__, were taking turns riding a __17.__. They were having their pictures taken and felt quite __18.__ when they could make the pony __19.__. I heard one boy __20.__ that he was the best rider and was going to be a cowboy.

pony
bold
obey
boast
clothes

 4.22D Use spelling patterns and rules and print and electronic resources to determine and check correct spellings.

Proofread a Poem

Proofread the poem below for ten misspelled words. Then rewrite the poem. Write the spelling words correctly, and make the corrections shown by the proofreading marks.

A Pom by Grover, the Dog

I obay you when you call me or order me to sit.

And when i chew your close up, you never throw a fit.

We allso watch TV together, and when you laugh, I bark.

You give me an extra mowment to sniff when we go to the park.

You've shone me how to fetch fetch a ball and bring it back to you.

You're my teacher and my herro, and I'm stuck to you like glue.

We've groan up together and Have always been best friends.

My greatest gole is to make sure that our friendship never ends

We've been together through oh, so much, through happiness and tears,

And I'm bolde enough to hope you'll live to be a hundred in doggy years!

NARRATIVE Writing Prompt
Write a Poem

Write or type a poem that a pet, such as a cat, dog, fish, or bird, might write to you. Use as many spelling words as you can.

- Use the writing process: prewrite, draft, revise, edit, and publish.
- To create rhythm in your poem, try to have the same number of syllables in each pair of lines.
- Use sensory language to make your poem paint a picture of the funny things that pets do and that you do for them.
- Use correct capitalization, punctuation, grammar, and spelling.
- Read your poem. Circle each pair of rhyming words. Use an online rhyming dictionary to check the spelling and make sure the words truly rhyme.

Transfer
Think of three words that have a **long o** sound spelled **o, oa,** or **ow**. Write the words and their definitions in your Spelling Journal. Circle the letter(s) that stand for the **long o** sound.

 TEKS 4.22D Use spelling patterns and rules and print and electronic resources to determine and check correct spellings.

55

Extend & Transfer
Word Study

below	also	shown	glow	loaves
nobody	clothes	poet	goal	narrow
over	moment	hotel	hero	bonus
rainbow	obey	pony	fold	banjo
soap	grown	bold	bowl	poach
coast	hello	motel	groceries	stroll
pillow	poem	boast	growth	following

Use words from the spelling list to answer these questions.

Rhyming Words

1–2. Which one-syllable rhyming words have the **long o** sound spelled **oa**?

3–4. Which two-syllable rhyming words have the **long o** sound spelled **o**?

5. Which one-syllable word with **long o** spelled **ow** rhymes with **flow** and can be both a noun and a verb?

Plurals

A. Write the word that is the plural form of each of these words.

    6. grocery   7. loaf

B. Write the word that is the singular form of each of these words.

    8. ponies   11. poets   14. moments

    9 pillows   12. heroes   15. rainbows

   10. hellos   13. folds   16. bonuses

Homophones

Write the word that is a homophone for each word below.

17. shone   19. groan

18. close   20. bowled

 TEKS 4.22Ai Spell words with more advanced orthographic patterns and rules: plural rules. **4.22C** Spell commonly used homophones. **4.22D** Use spelling patterns and rules and print and electronic resources to determine and check correct spellings.

Language Arts
Word Hunt

Read the paragraphs below. Look for words with the **long o** sound spelled **o, oa,** and **ow**.

I like poems called limericks. They are often so senseless that they make people groan. Below is an example of a ridiculous limerick:

> There once was a Man of the Coast,
> Who meekly sat down on a post;
> But when it was cold,
> He let go of his hold,
> And demanded some hot buttered toast.

Edward Lear is the poet who wrote that limerick more than 200 years ago. Some of his language sounds old, so I revised it a little. Lear's limericks are very well known, and he is a special hero of mine. Lear was also an artist. His drawings are shown in *A Book of Nonsense*. This was the first book ever published with illustrations by the author.

The goal of a limerick is not just to be silly; it has to follow very narrow rules. A limerick must be five lines in length. The first two lines must rhyme with the last line. That's called a *triplet.* The third and fourth lines must rhyme with each other. That's called a *couplet.* Do you think you could write a limerick? Why not give it a try?

WORD SORT

1–3. Write the two-syllable words that contain the **long o** sound spelled **ow** in the last syllable.

4–6. Write the two-syllable words that contain the **long o** sound spelled **o** in the last syllable.

7–10. Write the one-syllable words that contain the **long o** sound spelled **oa.**

 TEKS 4.22D Use spelling patterns and rules and print and electronic resources to determine and check correct spellings.

Read the spelling words and sentences.

1. flute	*flute*	A **flute** is a musical instrument.
2. view	*view*	We had a clear **view** of the sea.
3. student	*student*	The **student** studied for her test.
4. whose	*whose*	I wonder **whose** shoes these are.
5. clue	*clue*	That **clue** helped solve the mystery.
6. human	*human*	We all belong to the **human** race.
7. juice	*juice*	Orange **juice** is a healthful drink.
8. few	*few*	She has **few** faults and many friends.
9. true	*true*	Is that story **true** or false?
10. tube	*tube*	That thin **tube** is a drinking straw.
11. truth	*truth*	The **truth** serves better than a lie.
12. glue	*glue*	We can **glue** the pieces together.
13. dew	*dew*	The grass sparkled with morning **dew**.
14. lose	*lose*	Win or **lose,** be a good sport.
15. tulip	*tulip*	The **tulip** is a flower of spring.
16. used	*used*	My bike, though **used,** is new to me.
17. due	*due*	Yesterday's homework is **due** today.
18. fruit	*fruit*	Those **fruit** trees bear sweet pears.
19. music	*music*	I listen to **music** to relax.
20. rule	*rule*	No school **rule** should be broken.

Think & Sort the spelling words.

1–15. Write the words with the /o͞o/ vowel sound.

16–20. Write the words with the /yo͞o/ vowel sound.

Remember

The vowel sound you hear in **true** and the vowel sound you hear in **few** can be spelled in many different ways. When /o͞o/ is spelled **ew** or **oo,** it is sometimes called an abstract vowel.

 TEKS 4.22D Use spelling patterns and rules and print and electronic resources to determine and check correct spellings.

Word Meanings

Write a spelling word for each definition. Circle the two words that are **homophones,** words that sound alike but have different spellings and meanings.

1. a scene; a range or field of sight
2. water droplets that form on cool surfaces
3. expected or scheduled
4. information that helps solve a problem
5. a sticky liquid that holds things together
6. a musical instrument

Use Phonics

Follow the directions to write spelling words.
Check the spellings in your **Spelling Dictionary**.

7. toy – oy + ube = _____
8. rail – ail + ule = _____
9. useful – ful + d = _____
10. train – ain + ue = _____
11. fool – ool + ew = _____
12. jug – g + ice = _____
13. whole – le + se = _____
14. frost – ost + uit = _____
15. troop – oop + uth = _____
16. low – w + se = _____

Use the
Dictionary

Find each word in your **Spelling Dictionary**. Write the word and draw a line between the syllables.

17. tulip
18. student

19. music
20. human

TEKS 4.22C Spell commonly used homophones. **4.22D** Use spelling patterns and rules and print and electronic resources to determine and check correct spellings.

flute	view	student	whose	clue
human	juice	few	true	tube
truth	glue	dew	lose	tulip
used	due	fruit	music	rule

Complete the Analogies

Write a spelling word to complete each analogy. Check your answers in a dictionary or thesaurus.

1. **Make-believe** is to **real** as **false** is to _____.
2. **Suggest** is to **hint** as **sign** is to _____.
3. **Locate** is to **misplace** as **find** is to _____.
4. **Teacher** is to **pupil** as **instructor** is to _____.
5. **More** is to **less** as **many** is to _____.
6. **Tree** is to **maple** as **flower** is to _____.
7. **Cereal** is to **box** as **toothpaste** is to _____.
8. **They** is to **theirs** as **who** is to _____.
9. **Brass** is to **trumpet** as **woodwind** is to _____.
10. **String** is to **tie** as **paper** is to _____.

Use Context Clues

Write the spelling word that completes each idiom or saying.

11. *A bird's eye* ____ is being able to look at something clearly from above.
12. If something is _____ *to your ears,* it's exactly what you wanted to hear.
13. You can disagree with someone politely by saying *with all* ____ *respect.*
14. If something is *fresh as the morning* ____, it is really fresh.
15. If you ____ *the roost,* then you are the boss.
16. *They don't make them like they* ____ *to.*
17. If there is a *grain of* ____ to what you say, it is partly true.
18. *To err is* ____ *but to forgive is divine* means a person should be forgiven because everyone makes mistakes.
19. To *pick low-hanging* _____ means to do something that is easy.
20. If you ____ *something up,* you turn on the electricity.

TEKS 4.22D Use spelling patterns and rules and print and electronic resources to determine and check correct spellings.

Connections to WRITING

Proofread a Descriptive Essay

Proofread the descriptive essay below for ten misspelled words. Then rewrite the essay. Write the spelling words correctly. Then make the corrections shown by the proofreading marks.

¶ it was a frigid day but as fine as any humen could want. As a

rool, I would shun the cold, but I am a tru football fan. Therefore,

I appeared when I was doo at the Stadium. The vue was

breathtaking. The band, sparkling with bright colors, was playing

spirited musik. I hoped to someday play the floote in the band.

Soon the teams, in splendid uniforms, trotted onto the turf.

I did not have a clew whether my team would win or loze.

The trooth is, either way i'd enjoy the game.

Proofreading Marks

=	Capital Letter
/	Small Letter
∧	Add
ℯ	Delete
⊙	Add a Period
¶	Indent

DESCRIPTIVE Writing Prompt

Write a Descriptive Essay

Write or type an essay describing a person or place you remember fondly. Think about the things you like about the person or place. Use as many spelling words as you can.

- Use the writing process: prewrite, draft, revise, edit, and publish.
- Begin your essay with a topic sentence. Use supporting details and facts to help the reader "see" the person or place. Follow the form used in the proofreading sample to write a concluding sentence.
- Use complete sentences with correct capitalization, punctuation, grammar, and spelling.
- Read your writing. Circle three words that may be misspelled. Type your essay into a word processor and use the spell-check feature to check the spelling.

Transfer

Circle the words in your essay that have the /$\overline{oo}$/ sound and the words that have the /y$\overline{oo}$/ sound. Then circle the letter(s) that stand for the /$\overline{oo}$/ or /y$\overline{oo}$/ sound in each word.

TEKS 4.22D Use spelling patterns and rules and print and electronic resources to determine and check correct spellings.

balloon	few	rule	glue	movies
drew	true	flute	dew	suitcase
news	tube	view	tulip	menu
pool	lose	student	due	fuel
threw	used	clue	amuse	nephew
whose	fruit	juice	beauty	duties
human	music	truth	continue	blueberry

Plurals

1–2. Write the words that are plural forms of these words.

movie   duty

3–6. Write the words that are singular forms of these words.

tulips   juices   fruits   tubes

7. Write the word whose singular form is **dew drop**.

8–9. Write the words whose plurals are formed by dropping **y** and adding **-ies**.

Prefixes and Suffixes

A. The prefix **un-** means "not." Write the spelling words that are base words for these words.

10. unruly   **12.** untruth   **14.** unglue

11. untrue   **13.** unused

B. The suffix **-y** in **unruly** means "somewhat like." Write the words that are base words for these words.

15. fruity   **16.** juicy

Use Antonyms

Change the meaning of each sentence by replacing the underlined words with an antonym from the spelling list.

17–18. How did you <u>find</u> the <u>new</u> flute?

19–20. <u>Many</u> statements were <u>false</u>.

 TEKS 4.22Ai Spell words with more advanced orthographic patterns and rules: plural rules. **4.22B** Spell base words and roots with affixes. **4.22D** Use spelling patterns and rules and print and electronic resources to determine and check correct spellings.

Connections to VOCABULARY

Word Meanings

Write the spelling word that most closely matches each definition.
Circle the letters that are not sounded in the vowel spelling. Use the
Spelling Dictionary to check your answers.

1. past tense of **buy**
2. a harbor town where ships dock
3. and not; or not; not either
4. forward; into full sight
5. past tense of **bring**
6. a game, often a competition
7. an account

Identify Synonyms

Write the spelling word that is a synonym for each word.
Circle the letters that are not sounded in the vowel spelling.

8. carry
9. should
10. battled
11. arrange
12. idea
13. captured
14. instructed

Use the
Dictionary

The dictionary identifies stressed syllables with an accent mark
(') and boldface type. Find these spelling words in your **Spelling
Dictionary**. Write each word and underline the syllable that
receives the greater stress.

15. forgot
16. because
17. forest
18. daughter
19. report
20. forty

TEKS 4.22Av Spell words with more advanced orthographic patterns and rules: silent letters. **4.22D** Use
spelling patterns and rules and print and electronic resources to determine and check correct spellings.

71

forgot	bought	nor	haul	ought
forest	sport	thought	daughter	port
sort	record	taught	brought	forth
because	fought	report	forty	caught

Replace the Words

For each sentence, write the spelling word that is the past tense form of the underlined verb.

1. Mrs. King <u>teaches</u> us how to paint with watercolors.
2. I almost <u>forget</u> that today is your birthday.
3. Carlos <u>brings</u> his stamp collection to school.
4. Show me what you <u>buy</u> at the store.
5. Before they became friends, the two boys <u>fight</u> a lot.
6. I <u>think</u> the answer was simple.
7. Maria <u>catches</u> the ball for the third out.

Word Clues

Write a spelling word for each clue. Check your answers in your **Spelling Dictionary**.

8. a good place for ships
9. a parent's female child
10. to put in groups
11. one more than thirty-nine

Use Context Clues

Write a spelling word to fill each blank in the story.

My favorite __12.__ is horseback riding. Sometimes I ride through the __13.__ . When I return, I like to __14.__ my experiences to my friends and __15.__ my thoughts in my diary. A horseback rider __16.__ to carry as little as possible. That is __17.__ the more you __18.__ , the harder it is for your horse. A rider should go __19.__ with a respect for nature. He or she should disturb neither animals __20.__ plants, so they will still be there for all to enjoy.

forth
ought
sport
record
forest
because
report
nor
haul

 TEKS 4.22D Use spelling patterns and rules and print and electronic resources to determine and check correct spellings.

Connections to WRITING

Proofread a Story

Proofread the story below for ten misspelled words. Then rewrite the story. Write the spelling words correctly and make the corrections shown by the proofreading marks.

Some Fun!

Sylvia went camping in the forist, a trip which oght to have been fun. She cawt three fish and ate them for dinner. then she had a good night's sleep⊙

¶Her trip home, however, was neither pleasant noar fun bicause she fergot her compass and lost her way. Then she remembered what her mother had taugt her: Moss grows on the north side of trees. Home is south of here, she thot, so I should go in the opposite direction from the Moss. Sylvia smiled as she thought of how proud Mom would be of her dawter⊙

Sylvia went south and it braught her home. Sylvia had had learned an important lesson: Before going camping, check to see that you have all your supplies.

Proofreading Marks

≡	Capital Letter
/	Small Letter
∧	Add
℮	Delete
⊙	Add a Period
¶	Indent

NARRATIVE Writing Prompt

Write a Story

Write a story from your imagination. Be sure to include details about the characters and the setting of the story. Use as many spelling words as you can.

- Use the writing process: prewrite, draft, revise, edit, and publish.
- Be sure to build the plot to a climax. Follow the form used in the proofreading sample to conclude your story.
- Use complete sentences with correct capitalization, punctuation, grammar, and spelling.
- Read your story. Circle three words that may be misspelled. Use an electronic dictionary to check the spelling.

Transfer

Think of two words that have the /ôr/ sound and two that have the /ô/ sound. Write the words in your Spelling Journal and circle the letters that make the /ôr/ or /ô/ sound.

TEKS 4.22D Use spelling patterns and rules and print and electronic resources to determine and check correct spellings.

73

Extend & Transfer

Word Study

before	forest	caught	taught	important
form	thought	forgot	forth	launch
morning	sort	haul	fought	audio
north	record	ought	forty	naughty
story	brought	sport	audience	oriole
bought	because	daughter	author	toward
nor	report	port	enormous	dinosaur

Pattern Power

Use words from the spelling list above to answer these questions.

1–3. Which one-syllable rhyming words contain the /ôr/ sound spelled **or**?

4–5. Which rhyming words contain the /ô/ sound spelled **augh**?

6–10. Which rhyming words contain the /ô/ sound spelled **ough**?

11–13. Which words contain the /ô/ sound spelled **au** in the first syllable?

Latin Roots

14–16. The root **port** means "to carry." Write the spelling words that have this root.

Homophones and Homographs

17. Write the homograph that can mean "to take notes" or "a vinyl disk that contains music."

18. Write the homophone for **mourning**.

19. Write the homophone for **hall**.

20. Write the homophone for **fourth**.

74

TEKS 4.22B Spell base words and roots with affixes. **4.22C** Spell commonly used homophones. **4.22D** Use spelling patterns and rules and print and electronic resources to determine and check correct spellings.

Science

Read the paragraphs below. Look for words with the /ôr/ or /ô/ sound.

About one third of the United States is covered with forest. The thought of our forests disappearing is scary. Yet, that is what's happening to the rainforest. That ought to worry us all. Most rainforests are in South and Central America. We live in North America. So why should it matter to us? It matters because the rainforest is valuable to our lives and our planet.

The rainforest is a sort of drugstore. Many of its plants are used to make medicines.

Do you like bananas? Have you ever bought a jar of peanuts? These foods and many others were first grown in the rainforest.

The rainforest breathes for us. Its plants take in carbon dioxide and send forth oxygen. Rainforests are the lungs of our planet. Yet, report after report states that acres of rainforest are destroyed every day. Some scientists think that the rainforests will vanish in less than forty years!

What is causing this to happen? People are clearing the land to plant crops. Wood is needed to build houses, so trees are cut down. People need the land, but a balance must be found. We must work to save the rainforest— the lungs of the planet!

1–3. Write the words with the /ô/ sound spelled **ough**.
4–5. Write the words with the /ô/ sound spelled **au**.
6–9. Write four two-syllable words with the /ôr/ sound.
10. Write the three-syllable word with the /ôr/ sound.

TEKS 4.22D Use spelling patterns and rules and print and electronic resources to determine and check correct spellings.

75

Connections to THINKING

Read the spelling words and sentences.

1.	near	*near*	I was **near** enough to touch the president.
2.	steer	*steer*	He is learning to **steer** his unicycle.
3.	certain	*certain*	Are you **certain** of the answer?
4.	return	*return*	My **return** address is on the card.
5.	tear	*tear*	The child wiped a **tear** from his eye.
6.	thirst	*thirst*	The heat of the day increased our **thirst**.
7.	perfect	*perfect*	He threw a nearly **perfect** pitch.
8.	fear	*fear*	Those who **fear** failure should try anyway.
9.	term	*term*	The first school **term** is over.
10.	cheer	*cheer*	They came to **cheer** for our team.
11.	turkey	*turkey*	We will eat **turkey** on Thanksgiving.
12.	firm	*firm*	Once on **firm** ground, I was safe.
13.	ear	*ear*	I held the seashell up to my **ear**.
14.	burst	*burst*	The soap bubble **burst** in the air.
15.	rear	*rear*	We marched at the **rear** of the parade.
16.	serve	*serve*	The waiter came to **serve** our party.
17.	year	*year*	A **year** is twelve months long.
18.	person	*person*	The price was $5 per **person**.
19.	clear	*clear*	We expect **clear** and sunny weather.
20.	herd	*herd*	In the field was a **herd** of cows.

Think & Sort the spelling words.

1–7. Write the words with the /îr/ sound spelled **ear**.

8-9. Write the words with the /îr/ sound spelled **eer**.

10–11. Write the words with the /ûr/ sound spelled **ir**.

12–17. Write the words with the /ûr/ sound spelled **er**.

18–20. Write the words with the /ûr/ sound spelled **ur**.

Remember

The **r-controlled vowel** sound you hear in **near** (/îr/) can be spelled **ear** as in **near** and **eer** as in **cheer**. The **r-controlled vowel** sound you hear in **firm** (/ûr/) can be spelled **ir** as in **firm, er** as in **herd,** or **ur** as in **burst**.

 TEKS 4.22D Use spelling patterns and rules and print and electronic resources to determine and check correct spellings.

Connections to VOCABULARY

Word Meanings

A. Write the spelling word that most closely matches each definition.

1. come back
2. a need for liquid
3. sure; without doubt
4. close by
5. offer food
6. a group of animals

B. Write the word that has both meanings.

7. corn on the cob or a sensory organ for sound
8. steady or a business unit
9. the back part or to raise a child
10. cloudless or to get approval

Add Suffixes

The suffix **-ion** means "being" or "the result of." Write the spelling word that is a base word for each word.

11. perfection
12. termination
13. impersonation

Plurals

Write the singular form of each plural noun below.

14. tears
15. fears
16. years
17. bursts
18. turkeys

Find these multiple-meaning words in your **Spelling Dictionary**. Beside each word write the number of the definition and the letter that tells what part of speech it is.

19. steer
20. cheer

TEKS 4.22Ai Spell words with more advanced orthographic patterns and rules: plural rules. **4.22B** Spell base words and roots with affixes. **4.22D** Use spelling patterns and rules and print and electronic resources to determine and check correct spellings.

Connections to READING

near	steer	certain	return	tear
thirst	perfect	fear	term	cheer
turkey	firm	ear	burst	rear
serve	year	person	clear	herd

Word Categorization

Write the spelling word that goes with each group.

1. sparrow, crow, chicken, _____
2. shout, yell, _____
3. day, week, month, _____
4. solid, stiff, hard, _____
5. alarm, fright, horror, _____
6. drive, guide, operate, _____
7. sure, positive, definite, _____
8. correct, excellent, _____
9. liquid, droplet, _____

Complete the Analogies

Write the spelling word that completes each analogy.
Check the spelling of your answers in a dictionary or thesaurus.

10. **Food** is to **hunger** as **water** is to _____.
11. **Glass** is to **break** as **balloon** is to _____.
12. **Cloudy** is to **overcast** as **sunny** is to _____.
13. **Face** is to **front** as **back** is to _____.
14. **Birds** is to **flock** as **cattle** is to _____.

Use Context Clues

Write two spelling words to complete each sentence.

15–16. Whitney would like to _____ one _____ as the class president.
17–18. Please wait _____ this bench until I _____.
19–20. That _____ has a voice that is pleasing to the _____.

TEKS 4.22D Use spelling patterns and rules and print and electronic resources to determine and check correct spellings.

Review

Unit 7: Long o: o, oa, ow

clothes	hello	moment	pillow	coast
grown	also	poem	obey	shown

Write the spelling word that completes each sentence.

1. Hang your _____ in the closet.
2. Here is another _____ for your bed.
3. I'll be right there in a _____.
4. Say _____ to your aunt for me.
5. The lighthouse is on the _____.
6. I cannot teach that dog to _____ commands.
7. When Joan is fully _____, she will be very tall.
8. Joe will be very tall, _____.
9. A spring day makes me want to write a _____.
10. He has to be _____ how to do that problem.

Unit 8: Vowel Sounds: /yo͞o/, /o͞o/

few	lose	used	whose	music
true	fruit	human	tube	rule

Write the spelling word that fits each blank.

11–12. Is it _____ that there are just a _____ seats left?
13. Apples, bananas, and oranges are _____.
14. Who left the top off the _____ of toothpaste?
15. It's a club_____ that no food is allowed inside.
16. Do you know _____ books were left outside?
17. I'll be in trouble if I _____ my homework.
18. You can get a good price on a _____ bike.
19. All people are _____ beings.
20. We sang three songs in _____ class.

Review

Unit 9: Diphthongs: /oi/, /ou/

amount	choice	flower	moist	however
joy	mouth	power	vowel	crowd

Write the spelling word that fits each meaning.

1. slightly damp
2. many people
3. not a consonant
4. strength or force
5. quantity or sum
6. where your teeth are
7. the opposite of sorrow
8. a selection
9. a bloom or blossom
10. anyway

Unit 10: Vowel Sounds: /ôr/, /ô/

because	brought	caught	thought	sort
forest	record	bought	report	nor

Find each misspelled word. Write the word correctly.

11. Neither my sister nur I will be able to go to the play.
12. The weather repoort promises a fine day.
13. I brawght the book with me.
14. Mom caut five trout.
15. Please sourt the clean socks.
16. I'll be late becauze our car has a flat tire.
17. I really thout that was the right answer.
18. The teacher will recored our test grades.
19. There are tall pines in that fourist.
20. We bawte new tires for our car.

Unit 11: r-Controlled Vowels: /îr/, /ûr/

| certain | return | tear | year | cheer |
| person | firm | near | fear | clear |

Write the spelling word that has the opposite meaning.

1. go

2. uncertain

3. far

4. soft

5. foggy

6. sadness

Write the spelling word for each meaning.

7. to be afraid

8. water in the eye

9. a human being

10. twelve months

Spelling Study Strategy

Sorting by Spelling Pattern

One good way to practice spelling is to place words into groups according to a spelling pattern. Here is a way to practice some of the words you studied in the past few weeks.

Write each of the spelling patterns for Units 7 through 11 at the top of its own long strip of paper. For example, for Unit 7 you will need four strips of paper: **long o spelled o; long o spelled oa; long o spelled ow;** and **long o spelled o-consonant digraph-e.**

Then sort your spelling words and write each one in the column for that spelling pattern. Try to add other words that fit the pattern, too.

Directions: Read the introduction and the passage that follows. Then read each question and fill in the correct answer on your answer sheet.

Keisha's favorite stuffed animal is an old, worn-out Teddy Bear that she's had since she was a little girl. Now she wants to find out how the bear got its name. Keisha wrote a school report to tell what she found out. Here is the draft of Keisha's report. As you read the report, think about the corrections and improvements Keisha should make when she revises it.

How Teddy Bear Got His Name

(1) Teddy Bear sits on my pillo with a glow in his button eyes. (2) I didn't have a clue, hoyever, about the reason his name is Teddy. (3) I thot I'd do a school report about who chose that name and why.

(4) I learned that Teddy was named after President Teddy Roosevelt. (5) Here's why.

(6) One day President Roosevelt went hunting for bear. (7) A croud of newspeople also went with him to report about the hunt.

(8) A bear did not show up. (9) After a while, the president got tired of being kept waiting in the fourest. (10) He went to his tent for a nap. (11) A short while later, another purson caught a bear. (12) He tied it up to a tree for the president to shoot.

(13) The president thought it was a bad idea and not good sport to shoot a tied-up bare. (14) So he freed it.

(15) A certin cartoonist had the idea to draw a picture for the nation to see. (16) But he showed the president freeing a tiny bear cub, not a huge groan one.

(17) A shopkeeper saw the cartoon and asked his wife to make a tiny stuffed bear to sell in their store. (18) They put the bear in the window with a pitcher of the cartoon and called the bear "Teddy." (19) So that's how Teddy Bear got his name. (20) The clever shopkeeper got very rich.

GO ON

1 What change, if any, should be made in sentence 1?

   A Change *pillo* to **pillow**

   B Change *glow* to **glo**

   C Change *button* to **butten**

   D Make no change

2 What change should be made in sentence 2?

   F Change *clue* to **clew**

   G Change *hoyever* to **however**

   H Change *reason* to **reeson**

   J Change *about* to **abowt**

3 What change, if any, should be made in sentence 3?

   A Change *thot* to **thought**

   B Change *report* to **repourt**

   C Change *chose* to **chos**

   D Make no change

4 What change, if any, should be made in sentence 7?

   F Change *also* to **alsow**

   G Change *croud* to **crowd**

   H Change *report* to **repourt**

   J Make no change

5 What change should be made in sentence 9?

   A Change *a while* to **awhyl**

   B Change *waiting* to **wayting**

   C Change *kept* to **kipt**

   D Change *fourest* to **forest**

6 What change, if any, should be made in sentence 11?

   F Change *short* to **shourt**

   G Change *purson* to **person**

   H Change *caught* to **caut**

   J Make no change

7 What change should be made in sentence 13?

   A Change *thought* to **thot**

   B Change *idea* to **ideea**

   C Change *sport* to **spourt**

   D Change *bare* to **bear**

8 What change, if any, should be made in sentence 15?

   F Change *certin* to **certain**

   G Change *idea* to **idee**

   H Change *nation* to **nasion**

   J Make no change

9 What change, if any, should be made in sentence 16?

   A Change *tiny* to **tighny**

   B Change *huge* to **huje**

   C Change *groan* to **grown**

   D Make no change

10 What change should be made in sentence 18?

   F Change *bear* to **bare**

   G Change *window* to **wyndow**

   H Change *pitcher* to **picture**

   J Change *cartoon* to **cartune**

STOP

Grammar, Usage, and Mechanics
Common and Proper Nouns

A **common noun** names any person, place, or thing.

- That **student** goes to my **school**.

- The **building** is in a **city**.

A **proper noun** names a particular person, place, or thing. A proper noun begins with a capital letter.

- **Carl Hansen** goes to **Roosevelt School**.

- **Reunion Tower** is a landmark in **Dallas, Texas**.

Practice Activity

A. What kind of noun is underlined in each sentence? Write **common** or **proper**.

   1. My friend <u>Alice</u> will bring oranges.
   2. Is one <u>horse</u> Black Beauty?
   3. My family moved here from <u>Florida</u>.
   4. The store is somewhere on <u>State Street</u>.
   5. Our <u>principal</u> is Ms. Everson.

B. Write a proper noun that could replace each underlined common noun in these sentences. Be sure to begin your proper noun with a capital letter.

   6. <u>She</u> lives across the street.
   7. I always enjoy visiting <u>the city</u>.
   8. We saw the <u>memorial</u> on our visit to Washington, D.C.
   9. There is no school on <u>a holiday</u>.
   10. We bought a recording of <u>my favorite singing group</u>.

The Writing Process: Descriptive
Writing a Descriptive Essay

PREWRITING

There are four seasons in a year: spring, summer, fall, and winter. Depending on where you live, each season is different. During the winter, some people can build a snowman while others can go swimming in the ocean! What is your favorite season? Think about the things you see, hear, smell, taste, and feel during that season. Write an outline that includes a topic sentence, your supporting details, and a concluding statement.

DRAFTING

Use your outline to write a descriptive essay. Try to use vivid words that really describe the season for your reader. Use as many spelling words as possible. If you don't know how to spell a word, make your best guess. You will be able to revise your essay later.

REVISING

When you have finished your first draft, read your essay from beginning to end. Check to see if you have included all of the points in your outline. Did you achieve your purpose for writing? Does each sentence support the topic? Now use a word processor to type your final draft.

EDITING

Use the **Editing Checklist** to proofread your essay. Be sure to use proofreading marks when you make corrections. Read your essay again. Find three words you are not sure how to spell. Use the spell-check feature of the word processor to check the spelling.

PUBLISHING

Make a copy of your descriptive essay. Include a drawing of the season and share it with your readers.

EDITING CHECKLIST

Spelling

✓ Circle words that contain the spelling patterns and rules learned in Units 7–11.

✓ Check the circled words in your **Spelling Dictionary.**

✓ Check for other spelling errors.

Capital Letters

✓ Capitalize important words in the title.

✓ Capitalize the first word in each sentence.

✓ Capitalize proper nouns.

Punctuation

✓ End each sentence with the correct punctuation.

✓ Use commas, apostrophes, and quotation marks correctly.

Grammar, Usage, and Mechanics

✓ Use common nouns to name any people, places, or things.

✓ Use proper nouns to name particular people, places, or things.

TEKS 4.22D Use spelling patterns and rules and print and electronic resources to determine and check correct spellings.

Read the spelling words and sentences.

1. share — *share* — I will do my **share** of the work.
2. cart — *cart* — The horse pulled a heavy **cart**.
3. beware — *beware* — We must **beware** of poison ivy.
4. march — *march* — Drummers will **march** in the parade.
5. rare — *rare* — A cold day in July is **rare**.
6. army — *army* — The **army** set up camp near here.
7. charge — *charge* — Put the **charge** on my bill.
8. stare — *stare* — We tried not to **stare** at the movie stars.
9. market — *market* — We bought food at the **market**.
10. compare — *compare* — Do not **compare** apples and oranges.
11. mark — *mark* — Please **mark** that date on your calendar.
12. alarm — *alarm* — That noise will **alarm** the baby.
13. parent — *parent* — Take this note to your **parent**.
14. chart — *chart* — Did you **chart** your progress?
15. spare — *spare* — Can you **spare** a pencil for me?
16. smart — *smart* — You made a **smart** play today.
17. charm — *charm* — The dancers have grace and **charm**.
18. scare — *scare* — The dark does not **scare** me.
19. apart — *apart* — He took the alarm clock **apart**.
20. spark — *spark* — Strike a **spark** to start a fire.

Think & Sort the spelling words.

1–12. Write the words with the /är/ sound spelled **ar**.

13–20. Write the words with the /âr/ sound spelled **are**.

Remember

The **r-controlled vowel** sound you hear in **cart** (/är/) is spelled **ar**.
The **r-controlled vowel** sound you hear in **spare** (/âr/) is spelled **are**.

90

 TEKS 4.22D Use spelling patterns and rules and print and electronic resources to determine and check correct spellings.

Word Meanings

Write the spelling word that most closely matches each definition.
Use the **Spelling Dictionary** to check your answers.

1. to examine two things for similarities and differences
2. a father or mother
3. to be careful of; to guard against
4. extra; more than is needed
5. a tiny piece of fire
6. intelligent
7. to frighten or terrify

Word Clues

Write a spelling word for each clue.

8. a synonym of **uncommon**
9. a homophone of **stair**
10. an antonym of **hoard**
11. begins with a vowel and rhymes with **harm**
12. ends with a **long e** sound
13. found in the word **apartment**

Use the Dictionary

Write each group of spelling words in alphabetical order.

14–16. mark, march, market
17–20. cart, chart, charm, charge

Dictionary Check Be sure to check the alphabetical order of the words in your **Spelling Dictionary**.

 TEKS 4.22C Spell commonly used homophones. **4.22D** Use spelling patterns and rules and print and electronic resources to determine and check correct spellings.

share	cart	beware	march	rare
army	charge	stare	market	compare
mark	alarm	parent	chart	spare
smart	charm	scare	apart	spark

Complete the Facts

Statements that can be checked and proven are facts. Write the spelling word that completes each fact.

1. A _____ is used to record a patient's progress over time.
2. The navy, marines, coast guard, and _____ are branches of our armed services.
3. You can make a _____ by striking flint on steel.
4. A _____ may have two or four wheels.
5. We can buy many different items in a _____.
6. Bands often _____ onto football fields.
7. A smoke _____ in the house can warn us of fires.
8. Wolves are _____ in most of our states.

Complete the Opinions

Statements that cannot be proven are opinions. Write the spelling word that completes each opinion and includes the word in parentheses.

9. Every adult wants to be a _____. (rent)
10. It is simple to take _____ all machines. (art)
11. We should _____ of making too many friends. (war)
12. Playing video games is a _____ way to pass time. (mar)
13. I should be in _____ of this club. (char)
14. The most important quality a person can possess is _____. (arm)
15. It is easy to _____ brands of canned goods. (are)

Rhyming Words

Complete the pattern to write the spelling word that rhymes.

16. **care** rhymes with **st** _____
17. **park** rhymes with **m** _____
18. **dare** rhymes with **sh** _____
19. **bare** rhymes with **sc** _____
20. **ware** rhymes with **sp** _____

 TEKS 4.22D Use spelling patterns and rules and print and electronic resources to determine and check correct spellings.

Connections to VOCABULARY

Word Meanings

Write a spelling word that has the same meaning as each definition.

1. the first meal of the day
2. by this time; before
3. in place of
4. a knitted garment worn on the upper part of the body

Word Structure

Change one letter at the beginning of each word to write a spelling word.

5. dread   7. blood
6. guild   8. quilt

Add one letter at the end of each word to write a spelling word.

9. mean   10. read

Antonyms

Write the spelling word that is an antonym of each word.

11. cry   14. life
12. smooth   15. light
13. tender   16. gather

Use the
Thesaurus

Write a spelling word to complete each synonym set.

17. adequate, ample, sufficient, _____
18. feel, handle, stroke, _____
19. before, forward, _____
20. juvenile, youthful, _____

Thesaurus Check Be sure to check the synonyms in your **Writing Thesaurus**.

 TEKS 4.22Av Spell words with more advanced orthographic patterns and rules: silent letters. **4.22D** Use spelling patterns and rules and print and electronic resources to determine and check correct spellings.

97

meant	build	flood	laugh	breakfast
enough	sweater	rough	bread	touch
spread	tough	already	built	ready
death	young	instead	heavy	ahead

Replace the Synonyms

Replace the underlined adjective in each sentence with a spelling word.

1. Please help me lift this <u>weighty</u> box.
2. The tire went flat on the <u>bumpy</u> road.
3. That <u>youthful</u> student enjoys writing about animals.
4. Be <u>prepared</u> to leave for the zoo at noon.

Complete the Idioms

An **idiom** is a saying that doesn't mean exactly what the words in it say. Read the meaning of each idiom. Then write the spelling word that completes it.

5. A _____ nut to crack. (a difficult problem)
6. A good _____. (a funny joke)
7. A soft _____. (easy)
8. I've had this old red coat since before the _____. (very old)

Use Context Clues

Write the spelling word to complete each sentence.

9. To make toast, you start with a slice of _____.
10. Katrina doesn't have _____ orange paint to finish the job.
11. Mandy Lee can _____ a tree house in the backyard.
12. Every news station reported the _____ of the famous author.
13. We can _____ this tablecloth on the ground for our picnic.
14. Did you know what that word _____?
15. Our school was _____ more than fifty years ago.
16. Let's read a book _____ of watching television.
17. Alex has _____ finished his homework.
18. We will go on _____ if they are late.
19. We had scrambled eggs for _____.
20. This heavy _____ is so warm, you won't feel the cold.

 TEKS 4.22Av Spell words with more advanced orthographic patterns and rules: silent letters. **4.22D** Use spelling patterns and rules and print and electronic resources to determine and check correct spellings.

Connections to WRITING

Proofread a Book Review

Proofread the book review below for ten misspelled words. Then rewrite the review. Write the spelling words correctly and make the corrections shown by the proofreading marks.

Bobby Baseball

by Robert Kimmel Smith

Bobby Ellis is a yung boy who loves baseball⊙He knows alredy that he wants to be a pitcher, but his father, the coach, thinks he was ment to play second base insted. bobby has a tuff choice to make. Will he be reddy to go ahed with his plans? Will Bobby be able to laff off his /father's interference, or will it be the deth of his dream? Read to find out. The ⋀uthor adds enugh detail to hold any reader's interest.

EXPOSITORY Writing Prompt
Write a Book Review

Write a book review about a book you have read. Use as many spelling words as you can.

- Use the writing process: prewrite, draft, revise, edit, and publish.
- Include the title of the book and the name of the author. Tell what the story is about and what problem the main character has. Tell whether or not you would recommend the book to another reader. Be sure to use information from the book to support your recommendation.
- Use correct capitalization, punctuation, grammar, and spelling.
- Read your writing. Circle three words that may be misspelled. Use a print dictionary to check the spelling.

Transfer

Think of four words about baseball that use more letters than sounds to spell the **short a, short e, short i,** and **short u** sounds. Write the words in your Spelling Journal. Circle the letters that spell each sound, and write the name of the sound below each word.

 TEKS 4.22Av Spell words with more advanced orthographic patterns and rules: silent letters. **4.22D** Use spelling patterns and rules and print and electronic resources to determine and check correct spellings.

99

head	breakfast	instead	tough	subhead
said	enough	flood	death	sweatshirt
friend	touch	laugh	heavy	wealth
read	already	sweater	ahead	threat
dead	built	rough	plaid	pheasant
meant	ready	bread	pleasant	biscuit
build	young	spread	pleasure	

Pattern Power

A. Use words from the spelling list above to complete these exercises.

1–9. Write the rhyming words that contain the **short e** sound. Circle the letters that spell that sound.

10–12. Write the rhyming words that contain the **short u** sound. Circle the letters that spell that sound.

B. Write the spelling words you can make from these words. (Hint: Look for the **ea** spelling pattern in these spelling words.)

13. fat breaks   **14.** waters this   **15.** pasta hen

Base Words

Write the spelling word that is a base word for each of these words. Circle the word whose base word changed spelling when the ending was added.

16. retouched   **17.** heavier   **18.** flooded

Meaning Mastery

19. Write the word that is the past tense of **build**.

20. Write the word that means "a knit jacket."

100

TEKS 4.22Av Spell words with more advanced orthographic patterns and rules: silent letters. **4.22B** Spell base words and roots with affixes. **4.22D** Use spelling patterns and rules and print and electronic resources to determine and check correct spellings.

Math
Word Hunt

Read the paragraphs below and look for words that use two letters to spell the **short a, short e, short i,** or **short u** vowel sound.

Aunt Sofia taught me how to knit a scarf. I just knitted until I decided it was long enough, and then I stopped. Cousin Josie adored my scarf, so I decided to knit her a surprise birthday sweater.

I kept my idea a secret. I felt a little guilty about not telling Aunt Sofia, but I was afraid she'd let it slip and spoil my surprise.

I bought some nice pink wool, but I didn't buy a pattern. Instead, I decided to use my own plan. That's where I went wrong.

My plan turned out badly. When I sewed the sweater together, the front and back didn't match and neither did the sleeves.

I showed it to Aunt Sofia, who took a deep breath and said, "Maria, you didn't measure, did you?"

"We measure in math class," I said. "I wasn't doing math; I was knitting."

"Math and knitting go together," Aunt Sofia explained.

"Will Cousin Josie laugh at this sweater?" I asked, in tears.

"Cousin Josie will treasure it. It's the thought that counts," Aunt Sofia said.

WORD SORT

1. Write the two-syllable word that contains the **short i** sound spelled **ui**. Draw a line between the syllables.

2–3. Write the words that contain the **short a** sound spelled **au**.

4–8. Write the words that contain the **short e** sound spelled **ea**.

9–10. Write the two-syllable words that contain the **short u** sound spelled **ou**. Draw a line between the syllables.

 TEKS 4.22Av Spell words with more advanced orthographic patterns and rules: silent letters. **4.22D** Use spelling patterns and rules and print and electronic resources to determine and check correct spellings.

101

Connections to THINKING

Read the spelling words and sentences.

1. often	*often*	We **often** call our grandparents.
2. knot	*knot*	I have a **knot** in my shoelace.
3. wring	*wring*	We **wring** the water from our wet socks.
4. island	*island*	You can reach the **island** by ferry.
5. lamb	*lamb*	A **lamb** is a young sheep.
6. answer	*answer*	Please **answer** the question.
7. knee	*knee*	He hurt his **knee** climbing a cliff.
8. written	*written*	They have **written** many letters.
9. though	*though*	He could read, **though** he was not six.
10. knock	*knock*	You should **knock** before entering.
11. echo	*echo*	Call and you will hear an **echo**.
12. known	*known*	Her address is not **known**.
13. comb	*comb*	Wait until I **comb** my hair.
14. wrong	*wrong*	No question that you ask is **wrong**.
15. limb	*limb*	The bird sat on the **limb** of the tree.
16. knife	*knife*	On the table were a **knife** and fork.
17. listen	*listen*	You must **listen** to each question.
18. honest	*honest*	Please give me an **honest** answer.
19. doubt	*doubt*	I do not **doubt** your story.
20. calm	*calm*	The sea was **calm** after the storm.

Think & Sort the spelling words.

1–9. Write the words in which the first letter is a silent consonant.

10–13. Write the words in which the last letter is a silent consonant.

14–16. Write the words in which the next to last letter is a silent consonant.

17–20. Write the words in which the silent consonant is in the middle of the word.

Remember

Some words are spelled with silent consonants: **k** in **knot** and **s** in **island**. Patterns such as **wr** and **kn** are sometimes called **complex consonants**.

 TEKS 4.22Av Spell words with more advanced orthographic patterns and rules: silent letters. **4.22D** Use spelling patterns and rules and print and electronic resources to determine and check correct spellings.

Connections to VOCABULARY

Word Meanings

Write a spelling word for each definition.

1. frequently
2. quiet; peaceful
3. a young sheep
4. to be unsure
5. a reply to a question
6. a large branch of a tree
7. to send back a sound
8. a tool with teeth; used to arrange hair

Silent Consonants

Write the spelling words that have the same silent consonant patterns as the words below.

9. aisle
10. honor
11. hasten
12–16. know
17–19. write

A conjunction can join two sentences or two parts of one sentence. Look up the following words in your **Spelling Dictionary**. Write the word that can be used as a conjunction.

20. often, honest, though, echo

Dictionary Check Be sure to check your answer in your **Spelling Dictionary**.

 TEKS 4.22Av Spell words with more advanced orthographic patterns and rules: silent letters. **4.22D** Use spelling patterns and rules and print and electronic resources to determine and check correct spellings.

often	knot	wring	island	lamb
answer	knee	written	though	knock
echo	known	comb	wrong	limb
knife	listen	honest	doubt	calm

Make Inferences

Write a spelling word for each clue.

1. I can make your shoelaces hard to untie.
2. I am your voice sent back to you.
3. I can mean "to search carefully."
4. I rhyme with **low** and can be a conjunction.
5. I am surrounded by water.
6. I am an arm, a leg, a flipper, or a wing.
7. I am something you do on a door.
8. I am a form of the word **know**.
9. I am a form of the word **write**.

Complete the Analogies

Write the missing spelling word to complete each analogy.

10. **Cow** is to **calf** as **sheep** is to _____.
11. **Loaves** is to **loaf** as **knives** is to _____.
12. **Arm** is to **elbow** as **leg** is to _____.
13. **Not** is to **knot** as **ring** is to _____.
14. **See** is to **watch** as **hear** is to _____.

Use Antonyms

Write the spelling word that is an antonym for each underlined word or phrase.

15. Are you sure this answer is <u>correct</u>?
16. An <u>untruthful</u> person will have many friends.
17. I <u>am sure</u> that Katera will come with us.
18. Please write the <u>question</u> on the board.
19. The sea was <u>rough</u> after the storm.
20. We <u>rarely</u> go shopping in the city.

 TEKS 4.22Av Spell words with more advanced orthographic patterns and rules: silent letters. **4.22D** Use spelling patterns and rules and print and electronic resources to determine and check correct spellings.

Connections to WRITING

Proofread a Letter of Complaint

Proofread the letter of complaint below for ten misspelled words. Then rewrite the letter. Write the spelling words correctly and make the corrections shown by the proofreading marks.

September 10, 2012

Dear Sir or Madam:

¶ I was billed the rong amount for a pair of pants your good Reputation is well knoan, so I am sure this was an honist mistake. I do not dout that you will correct the error. I've ofen heard that you take time to lissen to those who shop at your store. The price of the pants was $23.42, tho I was charged $32.42. They were marked down because of a hole in the knea. I would appreciate a writen anser to this letter.

Sincerely,

Thomas r. Whitman

Proofreading Marks

≡	Capital Letter
/	Small Letter
∧	Add
℮	Delete
⊙	Add a Period
¶	Indent

EXPOSITORY Writing Prompt
Write a Letter

Use the writing process to write a letter of complaint about a real or imaginary problem you have had with a store or company. Use as many spelling words as you can.

- Use language that the person you are writing to will understand.
- Explain what the problem is and tell how you would like it solved.
- Include the date, a greeting, a closing, and your signature.
- Use correct capitalization, punctuation, and grammar.
- Read your writing. Circle three words that may be misspelled. Use an electronic resource to check the spelling.

Transfer

Think of two words that have a silent letter at the beginning and two words that have a silent letter at the end. Write the words in your Spelling Journal and circle the letters that are silent.

TEKS 4.22Av Spell words with more advanced orthographic patterns and rules: silent letters. **4.22D** Use spelling patterns and rules and print and electronic resources to determine and check correct spellings.

half	answer	calm	comb	knapsack
hourly	knee	knot	limb	thorough
knew	though	wring	knife	gnaw
knight	known	lamb	doubt	gnat
wrap	wrong	written	beret	wretched
often	listen	knock	design	prompt
island	honest	echo	frighten	knuckle

Pattern Power

Use words from the spelling list above to complete these exercises.

1–9. Write the words that contain silent **k**.
10–13. Write the words that contain silent **b**.
14. Write the word that contains silent **s**.
15–16. Write the words that contain silent **t**.

Base Words

Write the spelling word that is a base word for each of these words.

17. echoed   **18.** wringer   **19.** calmly

Word History

20. In Old English, **comb** ended with a /b/ sound, and **knitting** began with a /k/ sound. Over time, the **b** and the **k** became silent, but the spellings of these words remained the same. Write the spelling word that once was pronounced /**kuh-ny-cht**/.

TEKS 4.22Av Spell words with more advanced orthographic patterns and rules: silent letters. **4.22B** Spell base words and roots with affixes. **4.22D** Use spelling patterns and rules and print and electronic resources to determine and check correct spellings.

Science
Word Hunt

Read the paragraphs below and look for words that contain silent consonants.

Do you believe there's a monkey that's the size of your thumb? It's not a finger puppet. It's a real monkey. Its scientific name is Pygmy Marmoset, and it lives in the South American rainforest.

Most people call this monkey a *thumb monkey.* Truthfully, it's a little bigger than your thumb. Its whole body is about as long as a twelve-inch ruler. It weighs about as much as a cup of sand.

The thumb monkey has a knack for adapting to survive. A tree is its main protection and source of food. Trees provide it with a safe hiding place from enemies because this tiny monkey can climb to a high limb and hide on a palm leaf. For food, it can fasten itself to the side of the tree, gnaw holes in the bark, and suck out the softened sap.

These little monkeys are very social creatures. They live together in groups. A mother thumb monkey has twins about every five months. The daddy and the rest of the group care for the babies, who really are the size of your thumb. Maybe one day you'll see one of these babies, and you can give it the "Thumbs Up" sign!

1–3. Write the words that have a silent **b** at the end.

4–6. Write the words that have a silent consonant at the beginning. Then circle the silent consonant in each word.

7–10. Write the words that have a silent consonant in the middle. Then circle the silent consonant in each word.

 TEKS 4.22Av Spell words with more advanced orthographic patterns and rules: silent letters. **4.22D** Use spelling patterns and rules and print and electronic resources to determine and check correct spellings.

Unit 16

Complex Consonants: qu, squ

Read the spelling words and sentences.

1. quick	quick	She is **quick** to learn her lessons.
2. quarter	quarter	I ate dinner at **quarter** till seven.
3. squint	squint	We had to **squint** in the bright light.
4. quiz	quiz	There will be a math **quiz** tomorrow.
5. squeeze	squeeze	I **squeeze** oranges for juice.
6. quote	quote	We would like to **quote** what you said.
7. quit	quit	I **quit** the game when I got tired.
8. squash	squash	We grew **squash** in our garden.
9. queen	queen	The king and **queen** rode in a carriage.
10. squirm	squirm	A worm will **squirm** in your hand.
11. quilt	quilt	A heavy **quilt** covered the bed.
12. quart	quart	I will buy bread and a **quart** of milk.
13. squeal	squeal	Children at play **squeal** with joy.
14. quake	quake	My cats **quake** with fear during storms.
15. quill	quill	A porcupine's **quill** is sharp.
16. quarrel	quarrel	A **quarrel** among friends is not serious.
17. square	square	A **square** has four sides.
18. quite	quite	It is not **quite** seven o'clock.
19. question	question	That **question** is easy to answer.
20. quiet	quiet	Thank you for being **quiet** while I study.

Think & Sort the spelling words.

1–14. Write the words that begin with **qu**.

15–20. Write the words that begin with **squ**.

Remember

The /**kw**/ sound is spelled **qu**: **quiz**, **squint**.

TEKS 4.22D Use spelling patterns and rules and print and electronic resources to determine and check correct spellings.

Connections to VOCABULARY

Word Meanings

Write a spelling word that has the same meaning as each definition.
Circle the word with double consonants in the middle.

1. a sentence that asks something
2. an argument
3. to turn and twist the body
4. to look at with partly opened eyes
5. to compress; to press together hard
6. a heavy bed covering

Rhymes

Write a spelling word that rhymes with each of these words.

7. whiz
8. take
9. short
10. pill
11. green
12. tight

Multiple-Meaning Words

Write the multiple-meaning spelling word for each pair of meanings.
Use a dictionary to help you.

13. a vegetable; to crush
14. a coin worth twenty-five cents; one fourth of a whole
15. an open four-sided area; a rectangle with four equal sides
16. a high-pitched cry; slang for telling on someone

Use the
Thesaurus

Write the spelling word that is a synonym for each of these words.

17. swift
18. recite
19. stop
20. silent

Thesaurus Check Be sure to check the synonyms in your
Writing Thesaurus.

TEKS 4.22Aiii Spell words with more advanced orthographic patterns and rules: double consonants in middle of words.
4.22D Use spelling patterns and rules and print and electronic resources to determine and check correct spellings.

109

quick	quarter	squint	quiz	squeeze
quote	quit	squash	queen	squirm
quilt	quart	squeal	quake	quill
quarrel	square	quite	question	quiet

Make Inferences

Write the spelling word that answers each question. Use the definitions in your **Spelling Dictionary** to check your answers.

1. Which word means "to argue or fight"?
2. Which word means "a fourth of something"?
3. Which word refers to an open space surrounded by streets?
4. For what can quotation marks be a clue?
5. What do you answer?
6. What can keep you warm at night?
7. Which word means "to shake or vibrate"?
8. Which word names a vegetable?
9. Which is the wife of a king?
10. Which used to be part of a pen?

Use Context Clues

Write spelling words to complete the story.

Last night it was very __11.__ in my house. I was studying for a math __12.__ . I decided to take a __13.__ break for a glass of milk. As I removed the __14.__ of milk from the refrigerator, I heard a loud __15.__ outside. It was so dark, I had to __16.__ to see better. As my eyes focused, I saw our smallest piglet trying to __17.__ through a hole in the fence. He had gotten caught, so I rescued him. He surely did __18.__ around in my arms when I picked him up! He __19.__ struggling and ran when I put him down. After being stuck, he seemed __20.__ happy to be inside the fence again.

squeal
squint
squeeze
squirm
quite
quart
quick
quiz
quit
quiet

TEKS 4.22D Use spelling patterns and rules and print and electronic resources to determine and check correct spellings.

Connections to WRITING

Proofread an E-Mail

Proofread the e-mail below for ten misspelled words. Then rewrite the e-mail. Write the spelling words correctly and make the corrections shown by the proofreading marks.

| Send | Save as a Draft | Cancel | Attach Files |

To: info@communitygarden.org

Subject: Starting a Community Garden

I read your website on starting a community garden⊙We have a sqware block set aside for a garden. w̲e̲ plan to use a qwarter of it as a kids' garden. I questshun whether that is enough land. I also want to ask if iꬵ planting sqwash is okay. Your website says vegetables need 6 hours of sunlight a day. We get only 5 sunny hours. Can we squeez in a vegetable with that amount of sun? Thanks for reminding us to keep out of quarells with folks who live near the garden. We will be qwiet and plant only in the ⊬Afternoon. That should be qwite enough time for us. Thanks for letting me quis you. We'll send you a qwaurt of strawberries from our first crop.

Proofreading Marks

☰	Capital Letter
/	Small Letter
∧	Add
℘	Delete
⊙	Add a Period
⊬	Indent

EXPOSITORY Writing Prompt
Write an E-Mail

Write or type an e-mail to a famous chef about how to make something you'd like to eat. Use as many spelling words as you can.

- Use the writing process: prewrite, draft, revise, edit, and publish.
- Begin with the reason you are e-mailing. Use proper Netiquette, such as typing a clear subject line and including a detailed salutation (your full name and e-mail address).
- Use correct capitalization, punctuation, grammar, and spelling.
- Use the spell-check function in your e-mail program or an online dictionary to check your spelling.

Transfer

Think of three words about cooking that have the /**kw**/ sound spelled **qu**. Write the words in your Spelling Journal and circle the letters that spell the /**kw**/ sound.

TEKS 4.22D Use spelling patterns and rules and print and electronic resources to determine and check correct spellings.

equal	square	squash	aquarium	quiver
quick	quite	squirm	quotient	squid
quarter	question	quart	squirrel	squirt
squeeze	quiet	squeal	quail	
quit	squint	quake	unequal	
queen	quiz	quill	quartz	
quilt	quote	quarrel	quaint	

Pattern Power

1. Write the word with the /**sh**/ sound spelled **ti**.
2-3. Write the words with **long e** spelled **ee**.
4-5. Write the words with double consonants in the middle of the word. Draw a line between the syllables.
6. Write the word that ends in a double consonant.

Prefixes and Suffixes

7-8. The prefix **un-** means "not" or "opposite of." Write the spelling words that are related to **unequal** and **unquiet**.
9-10. The suffix **-ness** means "quality of." Write the spelling words that are related to **quickness** and **quaintness**.

Verb Tense Endings

The endings **-ed** and **-ing** are added to verbs to form tenses. Write the present tense spelling words for each of these past and past progressive tense verbs. Circle the verbs that change their spelling before adding the **-ed** or **-ing** ending.

11. squinted, was squinting
12. quit or quitted, was quitting
13. squealed, was squealing
14. quoted, was quoting
15. quilted, was quilting
16. squirmed, was squirming
17. quaked, was quaking
18. questioned, was questioning

TEKS 4.22Aiii Spell words with more advanced orthographic patterns and rules: double consonants in middle of words. **4.22Aiv** Spell words with more advanced orthographic patterns and rules: other ways to spell sh. **4.22B** Spell base words and roots with affixes. **4.22D** Use spelling patterns and rules and print and electronic resources to determine and check correct spellings.

Art
Word Hunt

Read the paragraphs below. Look for words with the /**kw**/ sound spelled **qu**.

Quilt making has a long history in America. Quilting was early recycling. Throwing out old clothing was considered squandering resources. Colonists used scraps from old clothes to make bed covers. Farmers used quilts to shelter crops from rain or dust storms.

A quilt can be the equivalent of a family album. It might have a square from a baby's blanket sewn beside a scrap of clothing worn by a loved one.

Quilts can tell many stories. Some quilts tell Bible stories, such as the one made by a former slave named Harriet Powers. It is so exquisite that it is displayed in the Smithsonian National Museum of American History.

Quilts made between 1930 and 2000 by African American women of Gee's Bend, Alabama, are treasured. They are praised for their abstract design and artistic quality. Museums show them. Collectors quickly snap them up.

Do you have a quilt on your bed? Does it have pictures of squeaking mice and quacking ducks? Or does it have a design of squares and squiggles? Pull it up under your chin. Shut your eyes. Good night and sweet dreams.

WORD SORT

1–5. Write the two-syllable words that contain the /**kw**/ sound. Draw a line between the syllables.

6–8. Write the three-syllable words that contain the /**kw**/ sound. Draw a line between the syllables.

9. Write the four-syllable word that contains the /**kw**/ sound. Draw a line between the syllables.

 TEKS 4.22D Use spelling patterns and rules and print and electronic resources to determine and check correct spellings.

Connections to THINKING

Read the spelling words and sentences.

1.	badge	*badge*	She pinned the **badge** on her uniform.
2.	gym	*gym*	In **gym** we climb ropes and play ball.
3.	rigid	*rigid*	My teacher avoids **rigid** rules.
4.	gem	*gem*	A diamond is a precious **gem**.
5.	baggage	*baggage*	He checked his **baggage** at the airport.
6.	range	*range*	Their ages **range** from six to ten.
7.	dodge	*dodge*	In this game you must **dodge** the ball.
8.	package	*package*	The **package** was delivered yesterday.
9.	engine	*engine*	Oil keeps an **engine** from overheating.
10.	cottage	*cottage*	He built a **cottage** in six months.
11.	gigantic	*gigantic*	A **gigantic** wave crashed ashore.
12.	edge	*edge*	The **edge** of a ruler is straight.
13.	gentle	*gentle*	A calf is **gentle** and friendly.
14.	strange	*strange*	That book had a **strange** plot.
15.	ridge	*ridge*	Trees grew along the rocky **ridge**.
16.	cabbage	*cabbage*	A **cabbage** has a solid, round head.
17.	bridge	*bridge*	The **bridge** spanned the stream.
18.	hedge	*hedge*	He trimmed the **hedge** to lower it.
19.	village	*village*	The band played on the village **green**.
20.	judge	*judge*	The **judge** instructed the jury.

Think & Sort the spelling words.

1–7. Write the words with the /j/ sound spelled **dge**.

8–16. Write the words with the /j/ sound spelled **g** followed by **e**.

17. Write the word with the /j/ sound spelled **g** followed by **y**.

18–20. Write the words with the /j/ sound spelled **g** followed by **i**.

Remember

The /j/ sound can be spelled **g** followed by **e** (**gem**), **g** followed by **y** (**gym**), and **g** followed by **i** (**gigantic**). The /j/ sound can also be spelled **dge** (**edge**). These patterns are sometimes called **complex consonants**.

 TEKS 4.22D Use spelling patterns and rules and print and electronic resources to determine and check correct spellings.

Connections to VOCABULARY

Word Meanings

Write a spelling word for each clue. Use the definitions in your
Spelling Dictionary to check your answers.

1. Take me on your trip.
2. I am very big.
3. Use me for sports.
4. I can be gift-wrapped.
5. I've got a green head.

Words and Letters

Follow the directions to write spelling words.

6. Drop one letter in **frigid**.
7. Drop one letter in **ledge**.
8. Change the first letter of **fudge**.
9. Change the first letter of **pottage**.
10. Change the last two letters of **villain**.
11. Change the last two letters of **ranch**.
12. Add a letter at the start of **edge**.
13. Change the second letter in **budge**.
14. Add one letter to **ride**.
15. Add one letter to **bride**.
16. Drop one letter from **strangle**.

Use the Dictionary

Write the spelling word that would be on the same dictionary page as these guide words.

17. decimeter • dye
18. egg • envelope
19. gender • govern
20. gaze • gene

 TEKS 4.22D Use spelling patterns and rules and print and electronic resources to determine and check correct spellings.

Connections to READING

badge	gym	rigid	gem	baggage
range	dodge	package	engine	cottage
gigantic	edge	gentle	strange	ridge
cabbage	bridge	hedge	village	judge

Use Synonyms

Write the spelling word that is a synonym for each word below.
Use your **Writing Thesaurus** to check your answers.

1. span   **3.** unbending   **5.** avoid

2. border   **4.** mild   **6.** immense

Replace the Words

Write the spelling word to replace each underlined word or phrase below.

7. A ruby is a <u>precious jewel</u>.

8. All of our <u>luggage</u> was put onto the plane.

9. Did anyone deliver a <u>parcel</u> to 18 Locust Drive?

10. They live in a <u>place smaller than a town</u> in Ohio.

11. He trimmed the <u>fence of bushes</u> with his clippers.

12. The car <u>machine that creates motion</u> made a funny noise.

13. Sue boiled a <u>vegetable with a leafy head</u> for dinner.

14. The <u>person who presides over a court</u> wore a black robe.

15. I use the treadmill at the <u>short word for a workout place</u>.

Use Context Clues

Write the spelling words to complete the story.

    Yesterday we came across a **16.** scene. We saw a deserted **17.** on a pine-covered mountain **18.**. No one knew who lived there. The sheriff pinned on his **19.** and asked me to go with him. We rode across the **20.** over the river and entered the house. There we found nothing but cobwebs—and a newspaper dated July 1, 1898.

> badge
> cottage
> strange
> ridge
> bridge

TEKS 4.22D Use spelling patterns and rules and print and electronic resources to determine and check correct spellings.

116

Connections to WRITING

Proofread a Letter

Proofread the letter below for ten misspelled words. Then rewrite the letter. Write the spelling words correctly and make the corrections shown by the proofreading marks.

November 18, 2012

Dear Ms. Roget:

please consider me for the job of clerk in your store. I am a hard worker who knows most of the People in our vilage. Sam King, owner of a jim at the edj of town where I worked before, is a good juje of my ability. I am sure he will will give me a good recommendation. I have a ranj of talents and can sell anything from cabbige to baggije, and I can wrap a gift pakage very well. I wouldn't dodj any duty, and I have no problem following ridgud rules. I will be glad to come in and talk with you about the job.

Sincerely

Ima pearl

Proofreading Marks

☰	Capital Letter
/	Small Letter
∧	Add
ℯ	Delete
⊙	Add a Period
⌿	Indent

PERSUASIVE Writing Prompt

Write a Letter

Use the writing process to write or type a letter to apply for a job. Use as many spelling words as you can.

- Use language that the person you are writing to will understand.
- Name the job that you are applying for, and give at least three reasons that you would be a good candidate.
- Include the date, a greeting, a closing, and your signature.
- Use correct capitalization, punctuation, and grammar.
- Read your writing. Circle three words that may be misspelled. Use a print or online dictionary to check your spelling.

Transfer

Write three words from your letter that spell the /j/ sound **dge** or **g**. Write the words in your Spelling Journal and circle the letters that spell the /j/ sound.

TEKS 4.22D Use spelling patterns and rules and print and electronic resources to determine and check correct spellings.

age	range	judge	gentle	imagine
change	dodge	badge	ridge	judgment
larger	engine	gym	cabbage	gadget
largest	edge	rigid	hedge	gelatin
page	strange	package	apology	engage
gem	bridge	cottage	average	beverage
baggage	village	gigantic	general	rummage

Use words from the spelling list above to complete these exercises. Check your answers in a print or online dictionary.

Pattern Power

1–3. Write the three rhyming words that contain the /**j**/ sound spelled **g** followed by **e**.

4–5. Write the two rhyming words that contain the /**j**/ sound spelled **dge**.

6–11. Write the other spelling words that contain the /**j**/ sound spelled **dge**.

12–13. Write the two spelling words that dropped the final **e** before adding **-er** and **-est**.

Base Words

Write the spelling words that are base words for these words.

14. engineer   **16.** apologize   **18.** gymnast

15. gently   **17.** villager   **19.** prepackage

Multiple Meanings

20. Write the spelling word that can mean "part of a book" and "to call out a person's name on a loudspeaker."

  TEKS 4.22B Spell base words and roots with affixes. **4.22D** Use spelling patterns and rules and print and electronic resources to determine and check correct spellings.

Technology
Word Hunt

Read the paragraphs below. Look for words with the /j/ sound spelled **g** or **dge**.

Did you know that music videos were around even before television? George Thomas generated what we could call the original music videos. He filmed a song called "The Little Lost Child" more than 100 years ago.

How did George manage it? Here's how. He took pictures of people acting out the song. Back then there were no digital cameras or film. He printed out his pictures on glass slides. Then he showed the images on a screen. At the same time, musicians and singers performed the song.

The first show was a mess! The slides were upside-down. People in the audience screamed with laughter. Some even walked out. George was not discouraged. He fixed the problem. By the next show, no one would budge from their seats.

People packed theaters to see the new song show. "The Little Lost Child" became a gigantic hit. There were no CDs back then. Instead, people bought sheet music. They bought thousands of copies of the song. Music publishers' budgets soared.

George had a gem of an idea. Modern technology polished it to a bright shine.

WORD SORT

1–3. Write the one-syllable words that contain the /j/ sound.

4–7. Write the three-syllable words that contain the /j/ sound. Draw a line between the syllables.

8–10. Write the four-syllable words that contain the /j/ sound. Draw a line between the syllables.

 TEKS 4.22D Use spelling patterns and rules and print and electronic resources to determine and check correct spellings.

Unit 18 Assess for Transfer

Units 13–17

Assessment

Each assessment word in the box fits one of the spelling patterns and rules you have studied over the past five weeks. Read the unit descriptions. Then write each assessment word under the unit number it fits.

Unit 13

1–4. The **r-controlled vowel** sound you hear in **cart** (/är/) is spelled **ar**. The **r-controlled vowel** sound you hear in **spare** (/âr/) is spelled **are**.

Unit 14

5–8. Some words have more vowel letters than vowel sounds.

Unit 15

9–12. Some words are spelled with silent consonants: **k** in **knot** and **s** in **island**. Patterns such as **wr** and **kn** are sometimes called **complex consonants**.

Unit 16

13–16. The /**kw**/ sound is spelled **qu: quiz, squint**.

Unit 17

17–20. The /**j**/ sound can be spelled **g** followed by **e** (**gem**), **g** followed by **y** (**gym**), and **g** followed by **i** (**gigantic**). The /**j**/ sound can also be spelled **dge** (**edge**). These patterns are sometimes called **complex consonants**.

Words for Assessment

starch
deaf
bomb
squab
flare
squad
wage
leather
fudge
writer
squawk
wreck
dread
carve
mare
steady
voyage
sword
queer
urge

120

Review

Unit 13: r-Controlled Vowels: /âr/, /är/

apart	chart	parent	scare	market
compare	share	beware	mark	army

These spelling words are missing letters. Write the spelling words.

1. m __ rk

2. ch __ __ t

3. ap __ __ t

4. p __ __ ent

5. m __ __ ket

6. __ __ my

Write the spelling word that completes each sentence.

7. When you finish, _____ your answers with those in the book.

8. The sign told us to _____ of the dog.

9. Please _____ your paper with me.

10. That movie didn't _____ me.

Unit 14: More Letters Than Sounds

built	instead	meant	ready	enough
young	breakfast	already	build	touch

Write the spelling word that completes each sentence.

11. Now I am _____ to go.

12. You have taken more than _____ time.

13. Did you have a good _____ this morning?

14. That child is too _____ to play with us.

15. Have you ever _____ a sandcastle?

16. I plan to _____ a castle on the beach today.

17. Lee wants to build a sand city _____ of a castle.

18. I'm sorry, but that was not what I _____ to say.

19. If you stretch, can you _____ the top of the door?

20. I have read that book _____.

Review

Unit 15: Silent Consonants, Complex Consonants

answer	honest	often	listen	known
though	island	knee	wrong	calm

Add the missing silent consonants to write the spelling words.

1. ans __ er
2. i __ land
3. __ nee
4. __ rong
5. lis __ en

6. __ nown
7. of __ en
8. __ onest
9. thou __ __
10. ca __ m

Unit 16: Complex Consonants: qu, squ

quiet	quite	quarter	question	quilt
quit	square	squeeze	queen	quick

Write the spelling word that rhymes with the underlined word in each sentence.

11. After the new bed was <u>built</u>, they ordered a _____.
12. This doll will <u>sneeze</u> if you give her a _____.
13. The holiday <u>fair</u> was set up in the town _____.
14. That tall person has _____ a great <u>height</u>.
15. This delicious <u>bean</u> soup is fit for a _____.
16. John played the mail <u>sorter</u>, and stamps were just a _____.

Write the spelling word that has the opposite meaning of each word.

17. noisy
18. answer

19. slow
20. continue

Unit 17: Complex Consonant: Soft g

baggage	gem	judge	strange	village
edge	engine	range	dodge	bridge

1–3. Write the spelling words that have two syllables.

4–7. Write the spelling words that spell the /j/ sound **dge**.

8. Write the spelling word that means the opposite of **familiar**.

9. Write the spelling word that means "a precious stone."

10. Write the spelling word that can mean "a kitchen stove" or "open grazing country for cattle."

Spelling Study Strategy

Play Circle Dot

Practicing spelling words can be fun.

1. Choose a partner. Each of you should write a list of twenty spelling words that you find hard to spell. Trade your list with your partner. Ask your partner to read your list aloud.

2. Then your partner should read one word from your list aloud. You write that word on a piece of paper. When you finish, your partner should spell the word out loud, one letter at a time.

3. As your partner says each letter, make a dot under the correct letter on your page. If you have a letter that is not correct, draw a circle under it. If you have left out a letter, make a little circle to show where it should have been.

4. The circles will show where you have trouble. Write the word again and check the spelling.

Directions: Read the introduction and the passage that follows. Then read each question and fill in the correct answer on your answer sheet.

Josh read a book that was about Martin Luther King Jr. as a young boy. Josh wrote this book report to tell about the book and why he liked it. Here is the draft of Josh's book report. As you read it, think about the corrections and improvements Josh should make when he revises.

My Brother Martin, by Christine King Farris

(1) This book was ritten by Martin Luther King's older sister, and it relates stories of him at a young age. (2) Some stories made me smile, but one made me kind of sad. (3) It was about how Martin learned that some people thought it was rong for a black person to have a white friend.

(4) The kings lived on a quiet street quite close to a white-owned food market. (5) Martin and the owner's son played in the yard, but one day the owner told Martin to listen up and kwuit coming around or else! (6) It's stranje to imagine a threat like that happening today.

(7) Martin asked his grandmother for an explanation. (8) She gave an honest anser to the question. (9) She told Martin that some people thought that white folks and black folks were meant to be kept aparet.

(10) Martin knew this was wrong and said he ment to change it. (11) He did. (12) When he was grown, he led a march on Washington to spread the message of Equal rights. (13) His words still eko as we often quote from the speech he gave that day.

1 What change, if any, should be made in sentence 1?

   A Change *ritten* to **written**
   B Change *young* to **yung**
   C Change *age* to **aje**
   D Make no change

2 What change should be made in sentence 3?

   F Change *thought* to **thot**
   G Change *rong* to **wrong**
   H Change *friend* to **frend**
   J Change *black* to **Black**

3 What change should be made in sentence 4?

   A Change *kings* to **Kings**
   B Change *quiet* to **kwiet**
   C Change *quite* to **qwite**
   D Change *market* to **mareket**

4 What change, if any, should be made in sentence 5?

   F Change *yard* to **yared**
   G Change *listen* to **lissen**
   H Change *kwuit* to **quit**
   J Make no change

5 What change, if any, should be made to sentence 6?

   A Change *stranje* to **strange**
   B Change *imagine* to **imadgen**
   C Change *threat* to **thret**
   D Make no change

6 What change, if any, should be made in sentence 8?

   F Change *honest* to **onest**
   G Change *anser* to **answer**
   H Change *question* to **qwestion**
   J Make no change

7 What change, if any, should be made to sentence 9?

   A Change *thought* to **thot**
   B Change *meant* to **ment**
   C Change *aparet* to **apart**
   D Make no change

8 What change should be made in sentence 10?

   F Change *knew* to **new**
   G Change *wrong* to **rong**
   H Change *ment* to **meant**
   J Change *change* to **chanje**

9 What change, if any, should be made to sentence 12?

   A Change *march* to **marech**
   B Change *spread* to **spred**
   C Change *Equal* to **equal**
   D Make no change

10 What change, if any, should be made in sentence 13?

   F Change *eko* to **echo**
   G Change *often* to **ofen**
   H Change *quote* to **kwote**
   J Make no change

STOP

Grammar, Usage, and Mechanics
Linking Verbs

A **linking verb** links the subject with words that tell what the subject is like. For example, in the sentence *The carpet was dirty,* **was** is a linking verb. It links **carpet** and **dirty**. **Dirty** tells what the carpet is like. Linking verbs include **am, is, are, was, were, become,** and **seem**.

The swans **are** beautiful!   The football player **is** injured.

The icicles **were** cold.   The coaches **seem** proud.

Suddenly the room   I **am** happy.
became warm.

Practice Activity

A. Write the linking verb in each sentence.
1. My school bus was late this morning.
2. That new girl seems friendly.
3. Today I am cold and tired.
4. The twins were happy about the party.
5. After the storm, the ground soon became dry again.

B. Find the linking verb in each sentence. Then write the word in each sentence that comes after the linking verb and tells what the subject is like.
6. That picture seems strange.
7. Everyone was calm during the storm.
8. Last year those kittens were young.
9. You are wrong about that!
10. The ripe oranges tasted sweet.

The Writing Process: Expository
Writing an E-Mail

PREWRITING

Recycling is one way to protect the earth. How can your community help protect the environment? Sending e-mail to an expert or official website is a quick and easy way to find out. You can find facts about the environment in books at the library. The Internet also has helpful sites, such as the U.S. Environmental Protection Agency's website. As you research your topic, write down questions for your e-mail.

DRAFTING

Use your notes to write the e-mail. Begin with the reason you are e-mailing. Use the proper Netiquette, such as typing a clear subject line, avoiding special type features, and including a detailed salutation (full name and e-mail address). Use as many spelling words as possible.

REVISING

When you have finished your first draft, read your e-mail from beginning to end. Did you include the correct e-mail address? Did you use the proper Netiquette?

EDITING

Print out a hard copy and use the **Editing Checklist** to proofread your e-mail. Find three words that could be misspelled. Use the spell-check function in your e-mail program or an online dictionary to check your spelling. Be sure to use proofreading marks when you make corrections.

PUBLISHING

Send your e-mail to the expert or website. When you receive a response, share it with your classmates.

EDITING CHECKLIST

Spelling
- ✓ Circle words that contain the spelling patterns and rules learned in Units 13–17.
- ✓ Check the circled words in your **Spelling Dictionary**.
- ✓ Check for other spelling errors.

Capital Letters
- ✓ Capitalize important words in the title.
- ✓ Capitalize the first word in each sentence.
- ✓ Capitalize proper nouns.

Punctuation
- ✓ End each sentence with the correct punctuation.
- ✓ Use commas, apostrophes, and quotation marks correctly.

Grammar, Usage, and Mechanics
- ✓ Use linking verbs and adjectives correctly to make sentences more interesting.

TEKS 4.22D Use spelling patterns and rules and print and electronic resources to determine and check correct spellings.

Unit 19

Double Consonants, Final -le

Connections to THINKING

Read the spelling words and sentences.

#	Word	Cursive	Sentence
1.	bottle	bottle	They bought a **bottle** of juice.
2.	pebble	pebble	A **pebble** is smaller than a rock.
3.	single	single	I have only a **single** pencil left.
4.	jumble	jumble	A **jumble** of papers lay on his desk.
5.	tickle	tickle	When you **tickle** me, I have to laugh.
6.	rattle	rattle	Keys **rattle** when we unlock the door.
7.	middle	middle	She is in **middle** school.
8.	bubble	bubble	Angie blew a huge soap **bubble**.
9.	sample	sample	Taste a **sample** of my cooking.
10.	cattle	cattle	They raise **cattle** on the prairie.
11.	snuggle	snuggle	I **snuggle** under warm blankets.
12.	kettle	kettle	The hot **kettle** was whistling.
13.	jungle	jungle	He photographs many **jungle** animals.
14.	ankle	ankle	She wore a silver **ankle** bracelet.
15.	giggle	giggle	A laugh often follows a **giggle**.
16.	simple	simple	I am learning to tie **simple** knots.
17.	settle	settle	They came here to **settle** the land.
18.	temple	temple	We attend a **temple** on Main Street.
19.	battle	battle	The **battle** was fought at sea.
20.	mumble	mumble	When you **mumble,** I cannot hear you.

Think & Sort the spelling words.

1–11. Write the words that have double consonants. Draw a line between the syllables.

12–20. Write the words that do not have double consonants. Draw a line between the syllables.

Remember

Final **-le** ends many multi-syllable words. If the word has a double consonant, divide the word between the double consonants. If two different consonants precede **-le,** usually divide between the two consonants.

TEKS 4.22Aiii Spell words with more advanced orthographic patterns and rules: double consonants in middle of words. **4.22D** Use spelling patterns and rules and print and electronic resources to determine and check correct spellings.

128

Connections to VOCABULARY

Word Meanings

Write a spelling word for each definition. Circle the words that have double consonants. Use your **Spelling Dictionary** to check your answers and your spelling.

1. a small stone
2. to touch lightly to produce laughter
3. a building for worship
4. a wild, tropical land
5. a small laugh
6. the joint that connects the leg to the foot
7. a container usually made of glass or plastic
8. a round film of liquid

Word Structure

Follow the directions to write spelling words.

9–11. Change the first letter in **tattle** to write spelling words that rhyme.

12–13. Change the first letter in **nettle** to write spelling words that rhyme.

14–15. Change the first letter in **bumble** to write spelling words that rhyme.

Use the
Thesaurus

Look up these spelling words in your **Writing Thesaurus: single, middle, sample, snuggle, simple**. Write the word that goes with each group of synonyms below.

16. cuddle, curl up, nestle
17. example, specimen
18. lone, one, only, sole
19. easy, effortless, elementary
20. center, midst

 TEKS 4.22Aiii Spell words with more advanced orthographic patterns and rules: double consonants in middle of words. **4.22D** Use spelling patterns and rules and print and electronic resources to determine and check correct spellings.

bottle	pebble	single	jumble	tickle
rattle	middle	bubble	sample	cattle
snuggle	kettle	jungle	ankle	giggle
simple	settle	temple	battle	mumble

Complete the Analogies

Write the spelling word that completes each analogy.

1. **Two** is to **double** as **one** is to _____.
2. **Hard** is to **difficult** as **easy** is to _____.
3. **Large** is to **boulder** as **small** is to _____.
4. **Deer** is to **forest** as **monkey** is to _____.
5. **Education** is to **school** as **religion** is to _____.
6. **Side** is to **edge** as **center** is to _____.
7. **Hand** is to **wrist** as **foot** is to _____.
8. **Cuddle** is to **curl up** as **nestle** is to _____.

Complete the Idioms

Read the meaning of each idiom. Then write the spelling word that completes it. Circle the words with double consonants.

9. (to disappoint someone) I'm sorry to have to burst your _____.
10. (to be annoyed) She always finds a way to _____ my cage.
11. (to be quiet) Will you please _____ it up!
12. (to make someone happy) You just _____ me pink!

Use Context Clues

Write the spelling word that best completes each sentence.

13. I want to _____ the flavor before I order mango ice cream.
14. Boots and an umbrella will help us _____ the storm.
15. Do all _____ have horns and hooves?
16. It is hard to _____ down after all that excitement.
17. All our jackets are piled on the bed in a _____.
18. The _____ is whistling merrily on the stove.
19. Did she _____ that she was sorry? I couldn't hear her.
20. That joke made me _____.

TEKS 4.22Aiii Spell words with more advanced orthographic patterns and rules: double consonants in middle of words. **4.22D** Use spelling patterns and rules and print and electronic resources to determine and check correct spellings.

Connections to WRITING

Proofread a Persuasive Essay

Proofread the essay below for ten misspelled words. Then rewrite the essay. Write the spelling words correctly and make the corrections shown by the proofreading marks.

Open land is disappearing at an alarming rate. The land is nature's tempel, and we must join together in the battel to save our country's open spaces. Look at what is happening around us. Cattel have less grass for grazing. Jungel animals, such as zebras, have less space in which to roam freely. our children have hardly any space in which to play. Before long, even that space will be be the size of a pebl. This is only a small sampel of the problem The solution seems simpel and begins with a singel idea. Write our government leaders Tell them that more land must be set aside for parks and wildlife refuges. There is no midle ground in this fight. We cannot setel for less. We must act now!

Proofreading Marks

≡	Capital Letter
/	Small Letter
∧	Add
℘	Delete
⊙	Add a Period
¶	Indent

PERSUASIVE Writing Prompt

Write a Persuasive Essay

Write or type a persuasive essay about something that concerns you and that you want other people to care about, too. Tell why you are concerned, what you think should be done, and what people can do to help. Use as many spelling words as you can.

- Use the writing process: prewrite, draft, revise, edit, and publish.
- Use language that will help persuade readers that they should take action to help solve the problem.
- Use correct capitalization, punctuation, grammar, and spelling.
- Use a print or online dictionary to check your spelling.

Transfer

Write two words from your essay that have an **-le** ending and two words that have double consonants in the middle. Write the words in alphabetical order in your Spelling Journal.

TEKS 4.22Aiii Spell words with more advanced orthographic patterns and rules: double consonants in middle of words. **4.22D** Use spelling patterns and rules and print and electronic resources to determine and check correct spellings.

131

circle	tickle	battle	ankle	syllable
couple	middle	pebble	giggle	triangle
maple	sample	jumble	temple	meddle
people	cattle	rattle	mumble	wriggle
uncle	jungle	bubble	bicycle	sparkle
bottle	simple	snuggle	needle	brittle
single	settle	kettle	principle	tangle

Use words from the spelling list above to complete these exercises.

Pattern Power

1–3. Write the three rhyming words that contain double consonants.

4–5. Write the two rhyming words that differ by only one letter and contain double consonants.

6–7. Write the two rhyming words that do not contain double consonants.

8–9. Write the two rhyming words in which one word has a silent consonant. Circle the silent consonant.

Word Building

A. Write the noun that is related to each of these verbs.

10. bubbling   **12.** giggling   **14.** sampling

11. bottling   **13.** bicycling   **15.** tickling

B. Write the spelling words that are base words for these words.

16. anklet   **17.** simplicity   **18.** sampler   **19.** sparkling

Word History

20. Words such as **circus, circuit,** and **circulate** are related by the Latin root **circ,** which means "around." Write the spelling word that is also related to these words.

TEKS 4.22Aiii Spell words with more advanced orthographic patterns and rules: double consonants in middle of words.
4.22Av Spell words with more advanced orthographic patterns and rules: silent letters. **4.22B** Spell base words and roots with affixes. **4.22D** Use spelling patterns and rules and print and electronic resources to determine and check correct spellings.

Math
Word Hunt

Read the paragraphs below. Look for words that end in **-le**.

Here's a riddle. What is flat and has two long sides that match and two short sides that match? It's your spelling book—it's a geometric shape called a rectangle.

Geometric shapes are everywhere. The most familiar shape is a circle. A ring is a circle and so is a wheel. A cookie may start out as a circle until you nibble on it. When you whistle, your lips form a circle. An oval is a stretched-out circle that looks like an egg.

Circles and ovals have no straight lines, but a triangle is all straight lines with a top that looks like a steeple. The word *triangle* comes from the Greek word *tri,* which means "three"; a triangle has three sides and three angles. An angle is the place where two straight lines come together. Angles can be big or little.

A square has four straight sides that are the same length and form four angles that are the same size. Is the ceiling in your classroom a square or a rectangle? What shape is your kitchen table? What shape is a bubble?

Look in your math book for the names of other geometric shapes, and then find those shapes in the world around you.

WORD SORT

1–4. Write the words that end in **-le** and have double consonants. Draw a line between the syllables.

5–9. Write the two-syllable words that end in **-le** and do not have double consonants. Draw a line between the syllables.

10. Write the word that means "three angles." Draw lines between the syllables.

 TEKS 4.22Aiii Spell words with more advanced orthographic patterns and rules: double consonants in middle of words.
4.22D Use spelling patterns and rules and print and electronic resources to determine and check correct spellings.

133

Connections to THINKING

Read the spelling words and sentences.

1. stumble	*stumble*	It is easy to **stumble** in the dark.
2. trouble	*trouble*	When in **trouble** you need a friend.
3. eagle	*eagle*	An **eagle** builds a huge nest.
4. harden	*harden*	The candy will **harden** as it cools.
5. brighten	*brighten*	Your kindness will **brighten** my day.
6. thicken	*thicken*	Use flour to **thicken** the sauce.
7. wrinkle	*wrinkle*	Try not to **wrinkle** your clothes.
8. soften	*soften*	The sun will **soften** the ice.
9. lighten	*lighten*	Two helpers will **lighten** the load.
10. table	*table*	The children set the **table**.
11. dampen	*dampen*	Before ironing, **dampen** the cloth.
12. moisten	*moisten*	Please **moisten** the sponge with water.
13. double	*double*	Twins are **double** the pleasure.
14. weaken	*weaken*	Lack of exercise can **weaken** you.
15. tighten	*tighten*	I must **tighten** a bolt on my bike.
16. example	*example*	He set a good **example** for others.
17. darken	*darken*	Rain clouds will **darken** the sky.
18. tremble	*tremble*	The dog began to **tremble** with cold.
19. fasten	*fasten*	Be sure to **fasten** your seat belt.
20. blacken	*blacken*	Factory soot can **blacken** homes.

Think & Sort the spelling words.

1–8. Write the words that end in **-le**.

9–20. Write the words that end in **-en**.

Remember

Words often end with **-le** or **-en**. Final **-en** usually means "to make" or "to become." The word **brighten** means "to become bright."

 TEKS 4.22B Spell base words and roots with affixes. **4.22D** Use spelling patterns and rules and print and electronic resources to determine and check correct spellings.

Word Meanings

The suffix **-en** means "to make" or "to become." Write the spelling word that goes with each meaning.

1. to make light
2. to make moist
3. to become weak
4. to become dark
5. to become hard
6. to make black
7. to make thick
8. to make damp

Silent Letters

Read the following words and write the spelling word that each came from. Circle the consonants that are not pronounced.

9. softener
10. fastener
11. brightener
12. tightener

Use the Dictionary

Syllables ending with a vowel sound are called **open syllables**. Those ending with a consonant sound are called **closed syllables**. Find the following spelling words in your **Spelling Dictionary**. Write each word. Then write **o** if the first syllable is open or **c** if the first syllable is closed.

13. table
14. stumble
15. wrinkle
16. example
17. eagle
18. tremble
19. double
20. trouble

TEKS 4.22Av Spell words with more advanced orthographic patterns and rules: silent letters. **4.22B** Spell base words and roots with affixes. **4.22D** Use spelling patterns and rules and print and electronic resources to determine and check correct spellings.

stumble	trouble	eagle	harden	brighten
thicken	wrinkle	soften	lighten	table
dampen	moisten	double	weaken	tighten
example	darken	tremble	fasten	blacken

Replace the Words

For each sentence, write the spelling word that can replace the underlined word or words.

1. Watch out! Don't <u>trip</u> over that rug.
2. We <u>close firmly in place</u> our seat belts as soon as we get in the car.
3. This bread dough will soon <u>grow twice</u> in size.
4. If I don't hang up this shirt, it will <u>get creased</u>.
5. Leah's helmet strap is loose; please ask her to <u>attach</u> it to the hook on the helmet.
6. She took three of his books to <u>make less heavy</u> his heavy load.
7. The sun will soon <u>make less dark</u> this cheerless, gray day.
8. If I don't wash the glue off my fingers, it will <u>toughen</u>.

Make Inferences

Write the spelling word for each clue. Write each word once.

9. what the sky does at night
10. what the sky does before a storm
11. make something slightly damp
12. make something less strong

Use Context Clues

Write spelling words from the box to complete the story.

Seth has often helped his neighbor Mabel work on projects on a __13.__ in the basement. Mabel has made useful items. For __14.__, she made a powder to help __15.__ the sparse grass in her yard. She also made a cream to __16.__ and __17.__ dry, rough skin. The cream made Seth's skin as soft as the feather of an __18.__.

Mabel's inventions were not always useful. Seth remembers when he tried a new food she had created. He knew he was in __19.__ when his mouth began to twitch and __20.__.

thicken
moisten
trouble
tremble
example
soften
table
eagle

 TEKS 4.22D Use spelling patterns and rules and print and electronic resources to determine and check correct spellings.

Word Meanings

Write a spelling word for each definition.

1. somewhat; to a certain extent; instead
2. less important
3. having a harsh, unpleasant taste
4. to bring together in a group
5. to go into
6. excitedly wanting or expecting
7. the season between autumn and spring
8. one or the other of two
9. not one or the other

Base Words

The suffix **-ous** means "full of" or "having." Write the spelling word that is the base word for each of these words.

10. wondrous
11. dangerous
12. thunderous

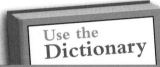
Use the Dictionary

Write the spelling words that would appear on a dictionary page with each pair of guide words.

13. verb • wed
14. Wednesday • young
15–16. loan • Mexican
17. signature • sometimes
18. scale • shy
19–20. times • tube

 TEKS 4.22B Spell base words and roots with affixes. **4.22D** Use spelling patterns and rules and print and electronic resources to determine and check correct spellings.

141

gather	winter	master	tractor	shower
major	danger	enter	whether	water
thunder	eager	bitter	silver	minor
neither	wonder	either	rather	together

Complete the Rhymes

Write the spelling word that rhymes with the underlined word and completes the sentence.

1. I _____ what is <u>under</u> the blanket.
2. Use the <u>center</u> door to _____ the store.
3. Sandy got a <u>splinter</u> while chopping firewood for the _____.
4. I could not tell _____ the suitcase was made of plastic or <u>leather</u>.
5. The park <u>ranger</u> talked about the _____ of hiking alone.
6. That beautiful <u>flower</u> got soaked in the rain _____.

Complete the Analogies

Write a spelling word to complete each analogy.

7. **Feel** is to **rough** as **taste** is to _____.
8. **Eat** is to **food** as **drink** is to _____.
9. **Street** is to **car** as **field** is to _____.
10. **See** is to **lightning** as **hear** is to _____.

Use Context Clues

Write two spelling words to complete each sentence.

11–12. If we study _____, we can help each other _____ the words.

13–14. Shannon was not _____ to begin _____ of her two chores.

15–16. In the story, _____ of the baby squirrels knew how to _____ nuts.

17–18. She would _____ have a _____ dollar than a dollar bill.

19–20. When we proofread, we correct the _____ errors as well as the _____ mistakes.

 TEKS 4.22D Use spelling patterns and rules and print and electronic resources to determine and check correct spellings.

Connections to WRITING

Proofread a Description

Proofread the description below for ten misspelled words. Then rewrite the description. Write the spelling words correctly and make the corrections shown by the proofreading marks.

Reflections on a Lake

¶While camping in the forest, Mom and I got up early one day and wandered ~~down~~ down to the lake togethur. The /sun was shining on the watter, turning it a beautiful silver color. The wintir had been long. We were enjoying the warmth of spring.

As we watched the lake, I began to wunder about the fish that lived in it and the animals that drank from it. I was in no dangir from the wildlife, so I was not eger to return to camp⊙ I would rathur have stayed where I was. All of a sudden, we heard thundr. We decided to gathur our things and head /home.

Proofreading Marks

≡	Capital Letter
/	Small Letter
∧	Add
ℯ	Delete
⊙	Add a Period
¶	Indent

DESCRIPTIVE Writing Prompt
Write a Description

Write or type a description about something you experienced. Include where you were, the season of the year, and the time of day. Use as many spelling words as you can.

- Use the writing process: prewrite, draft, revise, edit, and publish.
- Write a topic sentence that tells what you are going to describe. Then write supporting details that will help the reader see what you saw and feel as you felt. End with a concluding sentence.
- Use correct capitalization, punctuation, grammar, and spelling.
- Read your description. Circle three words that may be misspelled. Use an electronic resource to check the spelling.

Transfer
Write two words from the description you wrote that have a **schwa + r** ending spelled **er** and two words that have a **schwa + r** ending spelled **or**. Write the words in your Spelling Journal.

TEKS 4.22D Use spelling patterns and rules and print and electronic resources to determine and check correct spellings.

143

colors	whether	together	thunder	passenger
father	water	gather	eager	professor
later	silver	master	bitter	halter
mother	neither	shower	minor	barber
never	wonder	major	alligator	rubber
winter	either	danger	bother	razor
tractor	rather	enter	differ	anchor

Pattern Power

A. Use words from the spelling list to complete these exercises.

1–6. Write the three pairs of rhyming words that end in **schwa + r** spelled **er**.

7–12. Write the words with double consonants. Draw a line between the syllables.

B. Anagrams are words that have all the same letters. **Below** and **elbow** are anagrams. Write the spelling words that are anagrams of these words.

13. sliver   **14.** agree   **15.** thermo

Word Building

Replace the underlined letters in these words to make spelling words.

16. m<u>i</u>ster   **17.** <u>f</u>lower   **18.** en<u>joy</u>

Homophones

19. Write the spelling word that is a homophone for **weather**.

20. Write the spelling word that is a homophone for **miner**.

TEKS 4.22Aiii Spell words with more advanced orthographic patterns and rules: double consonants in middle of words. **4.22C** Spell commonly used homophones. **4.22D** Use spelling patterns and rules and print and electronic resources to determine and check correct spellings.

Technology
Word Hunt

Read the paragraphs below. Look for words with the **schwa-r** sound spelled **er** or **or**.

Do you like to surf the Internet? Lots of people do, but some people are there for improper reasons. Sooner or later you may encounter them.

Many kids chat online with kids their age, but not every visitor to an online chat room is like you.

Chat rooms can harbor people who just don't belong there. These people may be adults pretending to be kids. They may start a chat with you and shower you with questions, so you have to censor what you say. There is no supervisor to watch out for you in a chat room.

It's a major mistake to give your real name, your address, or the name of your parents to someone you don't know. Some people use that information to try to steal your identity. That means they'll run up a lot of bills using your name. It's a real nightmare to be a victim of identify theft, so watch out for people you don't know who ask many questions.

The Internet is a great place to get information or to talk with your friends. Don't be scared to use it. Just be smart about how you use it.

WORD SORT

1–4. Write the two- and three-syllable words that contain the **schwa + r** sound spelled **or**.

5–10. Write the two- and three-syllable words that contain the **schwa + r** sound spelled **er**. Circle the one word that has the **schwa + r** sound in the middle syllable.

 TEKS 4.22D Use spelling patterns and rules and print and electronic resources to determine and check correct spellings.

Unit 22

Base Words with Suffixes: -er, -est

Read the spelling words and sentences.

1.	cuter	*cuter*	I think kittens are **cuter** than cats.
2.	nearer	*nearer*	The house is **nearer** than the store.
3.	thinnest	*thinnest*	That was the **thinnest** tree I ever saw!
4.	kinder	*kinder*	Mel seems **kinder** than Homer.
5.	easiest	*easiest*	Jogging is the **easiest** thing I do.
6.	funnier	*funnier*	That joke was **funnier** than the other.
7.	nearest	*nearest*	The Pells are our **nearest** neighbors.
8.	happier	*happier*	I could not be **happier** for you.
9.	kindest	*kindest*	She did the **kindest** deed of the week.
10.	thinner	*thinner*	My dog is **thinner** than before.
11.	quietest	*quietest*	Monday is the **quietest** weekday.
12.	funniest	*funniest*	That is the **funniest** program on TV.
13.	safer	*safer*	You will be **safer** wearing a helmet.
14.	quieter	*quieter*	Babies are **quieter** at night.
15.	safest	*safest*	This is the **safest** smoke alarm.
16.	quicker	*quicker*	The hand is **quicker** than the eye.
17.	cutest	*cutest*	She has the **cutest** puppy in town.
18.	easier	*easier*	Studying is **easier** when we are quiet.
19.	quickest	*quickest*	Which is the **quickest** way home?
20.	happiest	*happiest*	This is the **happiest** day of my life.

Think & Sort the spelling words.

1–8. Write the words that do not change when adding **-er** or **-est**.

9–12. Write the words that drop final **e** and add **-er** or **-est**.

13–18. Write the words that change **y** to **i** when adding **-er** or **-est**.

19–20. Write the words that double the final consonant when adding **-er** or **-est**.

Remember

When adding **-er** or **-est** to a base word, follow these rules. If the word ends in **consonant** and **silent e,** drop the **e** and add the ending. If the word ends in **y,** change the **y** to **i** and add the ending. If the word ends in a single consonant, double the consonant and add the ending. If the word ends in a vowel and consonant or two consonants, add the ending.

TEKS **4.22Av** Spell words with more advanced orthographic patterns and rules: silent letters. **4.22B** Spell base words and roots with affixes. **4.22D** Use spelling patterns and rules and print and electronic resources to determine and check correct spellings.

Connections to VOCABULARY

Word Meanings

Write the correct form of the underlined word in each sentence.

1. We are the <u>quiet</u> of all the students in the school.
2. A whisper is <u>quiet</u> than a screech.
3. That was the <u>quick</u> fire drill of the three we had.
4. Beth is <u>quick</u> than the runner behind her.
5. Of all the ways to play the game, this is the <u>safe</u> way.

Word Categorization

Write the spelling word that does not belong in each group.

6. safest, funnier, nearest, quietest
7. safer, easier, kinder, cutest
8. safer, quickest, nearest, funniest

Antonyms

Write the spelling word that is the antonym of each word.

9. farther
10. thickest
11. meanest
12. hardest
13. thicker
14. saddest

Use the Dictionary

Suppose you forgot how to spell some of the words below. To find them in your **Spelling Dictionary,** you would have to look up their base words. Write each word below. Find its base word in your **Spelling Dictionary**. Circle the letters in the word you wrote that do not match the base word.

15. kinder
16. nearest
17. cuter
18. easier
19. happier
20. funniest

TEKS 4.22Av Spell words with more advanced orthographic patterns and rules: silent letters. **4.22B** Spell base words and roots with affixes. **4.22D** Use spelling patterns and rules and print and electronic resources to determine and check correct spellings.

cuter	nearer	thinnest	kinder	easiest
funnier	nearest	happier	kindest	thinner
quietest	funniest	safer	quieter	safest
quicker	cutest	easier	quickest	happiest

Replace the Words

Write a spelling word to replace each underlined group of words.

1. Your kitten is <u>more cute</u> than mine.
2. You drew the <u>most cute</u> picture of all.
3. You are the <u>most kind</u> person I have ever met.
4. Her comic book is <u>more funny</u> than mine.
5. Here is the <u>most thin</u> wire I could find.
6. Use the <u>more thin</u> board for the sign.
7. Your house is <u>more near</u> the school than mine.
8. The crosswalk is the <u>most safe</u> place to cross the street.
9. Mrs. Crosby is <u>more happy</u> working outside the house than in it.
10. The library is the <u>most quiet</u> room in the school.

Use Context Clues

Write the spelling word that best completes each sentence.

11. Wearing a seat belt while riding in a car is _____ than riding without one.
12. I find math to be _____ than science.
13. Crickets are _____ in the daytime than at night.
14. The baby smiles and acts the _____ when he is being held.
15. It would be _____ to say nothing than to say something mean.
16. The _____ library is three blocks from here.
17. That was the _____ joke I have ever heard!
18. We are in no hurry, so we do not need to go the _____ way.
19. That test was easy. In fact, it was the _____ test I ever took.
20. Sending this message by e-mail is _____ than sending a letter, which will take at least a day to arrive.

 TEKS 4.22Av Spell words with more advanced orthographic patterns and rules: silent letters. **4.22B** Spell base words and roots with affixes. **4.22D** Use spelling patterns and rules and print and electronic resources to determine and check correct spellings.

Connections to WRITING

Proofread Instructions

Proofread the instructions below for ten misspelled words. Then rewrite the instructions. Write the spelling words correctly and make the corrections shown by the proofreading marks.

How to Enjoy Backyard Camping

The qwickest way to get started is to set up a tent in your backyard⊙Try to find the easyest tent to set up. Pick a spot nearist the /House if you feel you will be happyier within shouting distance of your parents. The safist place is away from tree branches that could fall during a storm. The qwieter the place is, the better.

To make eating easyer, stock the tent with goodies. Add sleeping bags, a flashlight, and your funnyest books.

⁋Now invite friends. Your friends will think you are the kinddest person for including them! This this could be your happyest experience as you /Eat, chat, and read.

EXPOSITORY Writing Prompt

Write Instructions

Write or type instructions to help someone do something. Give a brief description of the activity and step-by-step instructions, along with safety warnings and comfort hints. Use as many spelling words as you can.

- Use the writing process: prewrite, draft, revise, edit, and publish.
- Begin with the goal of the instructions. Support the goal with a sequence of steps that shows how to complete the goal. End with a concluding sentence.
- Use clear language that makes the instructions easy to follow.
- Use correct capitalization, punctuation, grammar, and spelling.
- Use a print or online dictionary to check your spelling.

Transfer

Write two words from the instructions you wrote that have the **er** ending and two words that have the **est** ending. Write the words in your Spelling Journal. If you changed or dropped the last letter of the base word, write that letter in parentheses next to the word.

TEKS 4.22Av Spell words with more advanced orthographic patterns and rules: silent letters. **4.22B** Spell base words and roots with affixes. **4.22D** Use spelling patterns and rules and print and electronic resources to determine and check correct spellings.

Word Study

closer	kinder	easier	quicker	sunnier
hotter	nearest	thinnest	cutest	wiser
reddest	happier	easiest	quickest	bluest
sharper	kindest	funnier	happiest	healthier
widest	quietest	thinner	calmest	healthiest
cuter	funniest	safer	slimmer	heavier
nearer	safest	quieter	slimmest	heaviest

Comparative and Superlative Adjectives and Adverbs

A. Complete the chart below by adding the suffixes **-er** and **-est** to make the comparative and superlative forms of each adverb or adjective.

B. Circle the words in which you drop the **final e** before adding the ending.

C. Underline the words in which you change **y** to **i** before adding the ending.

D. Place a star by the words in which you double the final consonant before adding the ending.

Base	Comparative	Superlative
quiet	1. _____	2. _____
thin	3. _____	4. _____
safe	5. _____	6. _____
kind	7. _____	8. _____
cute	9. _____	10. _____
funny	11. _____	12. _____
quick	13. _____	14. _____
slim	15. _____	16. _____
healthy	17. _____	18. _____

TEKS 4.22Aiii Spell words with more advanced orthographic patterns and rules: double consonants in middle of words. **4.22B** Spell base words and roots with affixes. **4.22D** Use spelling patterns and rules and print and electronic resources to determine and check correct spellings.

Science
Word Hunt

Read the paragraphs below and look for words with the suffix **-er** or **-est**.

Here's a magic trick to thrill your friends. Become the greatest magic performer of all! Do this trickiest of tricks and you'll be the busiest magician in town.

First get a gallon plastic jug and wave it around to show your friends that it's empty. Then run hot water in the sink and put about half an inch of it in the jug. Put the cap on and shake the jug with vigor. Have your friends come nearer but at the safest distance to watch as the jug expands, or gets bigger. Now spill out the hot water, put in the same amount of cold water, and shake the jug again; it will contract, or get smaller!

The best magicians never share their secrets, even with their nosiest friends. However, this isn't magic; it's science.

The jug appeared empty, but it was really full of air, and air is a gas. When a gas is heated, it expands, and when it's cooled, it contracts. So the hot water caused the air to expand and make the jug get fatter. The cold water caused the air to contract, returning the jug to its normal size. It couldn't be easier to explain. That's the secret of the incredible shrinking jug.

Scientific knowledge is incredible and can introduce you to the magic of the universe.

1–5. Write the adjectives or adverbs with the **-er** suffix.
Draw a line between the syllables.

6–10. Write the words with the **-est** suffix.

 TEKS 4.22B Spell base words and roots with affixes. **4.22D** Use spelling patterns and rules and print and electronic resources to determine and check correct spellings.

Connections to THINKING

Read the spelling words and sentences.

1.	lone	*lone*	There was a **lone** clerk in the store.
2.	break	*break*	Lift but do not **break** the cover.
3.	waist	*waist*	Around his **waist** he wore a belt.
4.	passed	*passed*	We **passed** a school crossing.
5.	sore	*sore*	I hiked until my feet were **sore**.
6.	cellar	*cellar*	In the **cellar** was an old chest.
7.	roll	*roll*	Would you like a muffin or a **roll**?
8.	died	*died*	The flower **died** from lack of water.
9.	past	*past*	My father drove **past** your house.
10.	steak	*steak*	He likes his **steak** well done.
11.	role	*role*	What **role** did he play in the movie?
12.	steel	*steel*	Aluminum is lighter than **steel**.
13.	loan	*loan*	They needed a **loan** to buy the house.
14.	dyed	*dyed*	The feather had been **dyed** yellow.
15.	seller	*seller*	The buyer gave the **seller** money.
16.	brake	*brake*	Step on the **brake** to stop.
17.	soar	*soar*	Eagles **soar** across the sky.
18.	steal	*steal*	Do not **steal** or damage goods.
19.	stake	*stake*	A **stake** supports each plant.
20.	waste	*waste*	Recycling does not **waste** material.

Think & Sort the spelling words.

1–20. Write each homophone and its partner. Think about how the spelling affects meaning.

Remember

Homophones are words that sound the same but have different spellings and meanings.

TEKS 4.22C Spell commonly used homophones.

Connections to VOCABULARY

Word Meanings

Write the spelling word that goes with each meaning. Check your answers in your **Spelling Dictionary**.

1. without company; by itself or oneself
2. a slice of beef
3. the middle part of the body
4. colored with dye
5. the part played by an actor
6. earlier than the present time
7. to come apart

Word Categorization

Write the spelling word that belongs in each group of words below.

8. car, stop, _____
9. spin, turn, _____
10. lend, banker, _____
11. outraced, left behind, _____
12. failed, broke down, _____
13. meat, beef, _____
14. garbage, litter, _____

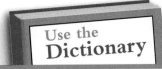

Use the Dictionary

Write two spelling words for each dictionary respelling.

   15–16. /sôr/   **19–20.** /sĕl′ər/

   17–18. /stēl/

Dictionary Check Be sure to check the respellings in your **Spelling Dictionary**.

lone	break	waist	passed	sore
cellar	roll	died	past	steak
role	steel	loan	dyed	seller
brake	soar	steal	stake	waste

Choose the Homophones

Choose the correct homophone for each sentence.

1. Please pass me a (roll, role) to eat.
2. When I go sledding, I use my foot as a (break, brake).
3. We try not to (waist, waste) the paper.
4. We need one more (steak, stake) to secure this tent.
5. She is playing the (roll, role) of the princess in the school play.
6. These paintings are on (lone, loan) from the museum.
7. Pele's knee was (sore, soar) after he fell.
8. He ate the soup before the (steak, stake).
9. A (lone, loan) horse stood in the field.
10. Please (brake, break) the seal to open the jar.
11. The dress with the black belt at the (waste, waist) looks nice.
12. Look at those seagulls (soar, sore) over the waves.

Use Context Clues

Write a homophone pair to complete each sentence.

13–14. I remember that on our _____ trips we _____ that farmhouse.
15–16. Why would anyone want to _____ a truckload of _____?
17–18. The _____ showed us what was for sale in her _____.
19–20. The flower _____ when the florist _____ it green.

 TEKS 4.22C Spell commonly used homophones.

Connections to WRITING

Proofread a Postcard

Proofread the postcard below for ten misspelled words. Then rewrite the postcard. Write the spelling words correctly and make the corrections shown by the proofreading marks.

Hi, Folks∧

    Greetings from the passed⊙ I'm in historic Williamstown, where a plate of stake and eggs once cost a few cents.?/ We pay more than that ∧Today for a buttered role. I may need a lone from you when I get back, since my waste is bigger than my wallet. But seriously, I'm having fun, although my feet are soar from walking. I bought you a steal horseshoe. The cellar said it should bring you luck. I'm trying not to waist /Money on things for myself. This was a great brake from my studies. See you soon.

l̲ove,

Ted

Proofreading Marks

≡	Capital Letter
/	Small Letter
∧	Add
ℯ	Delete
⊙	Add a Period
⁋	Indent

NARRATIVE Writing Prompt

Write a Postcard

Write a postcard about a place you have visited. Tell where you are and what you have seen or done. Tell what you like or dislike about your trip. Use as many spelling words as you can.

- Use the writing process: prewrite, draft, revise, edit, and publish.
- Be brief and to the point. Remember, there's not a lot of writing space on a postcard.
- Use correct capitalization, punctuation, grammar, and spelling.
- Use an online dictionary to check your spelling.

Transfer

Write three words from your postcard that are homophones. Next to each word, write its homophone pair.

TEKS 4.22C Spell commonly used homophones. **4.22D** Use spelling patterns and rules and print and electronic resources to determine and check correct spellings.

Word Study

its	passed	waste	dyed	vane
it's	roll	lone	seller	vein
there	past	sore	soar	mist
their	role	cellar	stake	missed
they're	steel	died	capital	guest
break	brake	steak	capitol	guessed
waist	steal	loan	vain	

Meaning Mastery

Check your answers in your **Spelling Dictionary** or a thesaurus.

A. Write a spelling word from the list that goes with each meaning.

1. part of a car that makes it stop
2. fall apart
3. stopped living
4. gave color to something
5. something borrowed
6. single

7. pointy stick
8. a slice of meat
9. strong metal
10. take without permission
11. place to wear a belt
12. use up carelessly

B. Write a spelling word from the list that is a synonym for each word. Circle the words that contain double consonants in the middle.

13. basement
14. merchant
15. fly
16. painful

17. transferred
18. earlier
19. character
20. wrap

TEKS 4.22Aiii Spell words with more advanced orthographic patterns and rules: double consonants in middle of words. **4.22C** Spell commonly used homophones.

Social Studies
Word Hunt

Read the paragraphs below and look for words that have homophones.

Barbara Jordan was the first African American woman from the South elected to Congress. In 1972, that was a historic feat. Much has changed since then, but let's look back at that time.

Barbara Jordan was born in Houston, Texas, in 1936. She was a top student in high school and college.

Jordan worked for the election of President John F. Kennedy. His election moved her to run for Texas State Senate, and she won. She was the first black woman to serve in that post.

Later she ran for Congress, and she won. "What the people want is very simple," she often said. "They want an America as good as its promise." Barbara Jordan aimed to keep that promise. She fought for fair treatment for all.

In 1979, Jordan left Congress to teach. She said, "The world is not a playground, but a schoolroom." She taught at the University of Texas. Jordan was once banned from attending that university. Black people were not allowed, but America had changed. Barbara Jordan helped the country heal past injustices.

Barbara Jordan died in 1996. Many came to mourn her. Among them was President Bill Clinton. "Barbara, we the people will miss you," he said. "We thank you, and Godspeed."

WORD SORT

Write the word in the selection that is a homophone for each word below. If you do not know the meaning of any of these words, look them up in a print or online dictionary.

1. feet
2. borne
3. four
4. one
5. fare
6. band
7. heel
8. morn
9. aloud

 TEKS 4.22C Spell commonly used homophones. **4.22D** Use spelling patterns and rules and print and electronic resources to determine and check correct spellings.

Unit 24

Units 19–23

Assessment

Each assessment word fits one of the spelling patterns and rules you have studied over the past five weeks. Write each assessment word under the unit number it fits.

Unit 19

1–6. Final **-le** ends many multi-syllable words. If the word has a double consonant, divide the word between the double consonants. If two different consonants precede **-le,** usually divide between the two consonants.

Unit 20

7–8. Words often end with **-le** or **-en**. Final **-en** usually means "to make" or "to become." The word **brighten** means "to become bright."

Unit 21

9–12. The **schwa + r** sound is spelled in different ways: **er** in **water** and **or** in **major**.

Unit 22

13–16. When adding **-er** or **-est** to a base word, follow these rules. If the word ends in **consonant** and **silent e,** drop the **e** and add the ending. If the word ends in **y,** change the **y** to **i** and add the ending. If the word ends in a single consonant, double the consonant and add the ending. If the word ends in a vowel and consonant or two consonants, add the ending.

Unit 23

17–20. Homophones are words that sound the same but have different spellings and meanings.

Words for Assessment

paddle

driven

heir

janitor

driest

trimmer

clever

handle

forever

aisle

saddle

bitten

juggle

sunniest

candle

throne

isle

anger

humble

smaller

Review

Unit 19: Double Consonants, Final -le

middle	sample	simple	single	cattle
jungle	tickle	battle	bottle	settle

These spelling words are missing letters. Write the spelling words.

1. j __ n __ le
2. cat __ __ e
3. s __ n __ le
4. bo __ __ le
5. ti __ __ le

6. mi __ dl __
7. __ et __ le
8. sam __ __ e
9. ba __ tl __
10. si __ p __ e

Unit 20: Final -le, Final -en

moisten	example	fasten	trouble	brighten
harden	table	lighten	darken	double

Write the spelling word that completes each sentence.

11. Drink some water to _____ your mouth.
12. If you _____ five, you will get ten.
13. Pull the shades down to _____ the room.
14. Put four chairs around the _____.
15. We will need to _____ the box of books before I can carry it.
16. The coach's hard work set a good _____ for his team.
17. Cold weather caused the water to _____ into ice.
18. We are having _____ with our television.
19. The morning sun began to _____ the room.
20. The sailor will _____ the boat to the dock with rope.

Review

Unit 21: Schwa + r: er, or

together	tractor	whether	wonder	either
water	rather	winter	neither	silver

Write a spelling word for each clue.

1. It is an antonym for **apart**.
2. It begins with a **long e** sound spelled **ei**.
3. Add one letter to your answer for number 2.
4. The word **won** can be found in this word.
5. Change one letter in **gather** to make this word.
6. It comes before spring.
7. A homophone for this word is **weather**.
8. Use this with soap.
9. You will find one of these on most farms.
10. Some coins contain this.

Unit 22: Base Words With Suffixes: -er, -est

cuter	easier	funniest	quietest	kindest
safest	happier	nearer	kinder	nearest

Write the spelling word that completes each group of words.

11. happy, _____ , happiest
12. near, nearer, _____
13. safe, safer, _____
14. funny, funnier, _____
15. kind, _____ , kindest

16. cute, _____ , cutest
17. kind, kinder, _____
18. easy, _____ , easiest
19. quiet, quieter, _____
20. near, _____ , nearest

Unit 23: Homophones

break	past	steel	waste	roll
passed	brake	waist	role	steal

Write the homophone that completes each sentence.

1. We (passed, past) the school on our way to the game.
2. In the (passed, past), it took weeks to cross the ocean.
3. One should never (waist, waste) food.
4. The cook tied an apron around her (waist, waste).
5. If you drop the glass, it will surely (brake, break).
6. Use the (brake, break) to stop your bicycle.
7. Heavy trucks cross the river on a (steal, steel) bridge.
8. Put your money where no one can (steal, steel) it.
9. What is your (role, roll) in the play?
10. I saw the big snowball (role, roll) down the hill.

Spelling Study Strategy

Sorting by Endings

One good way to practice spelling is to place words into groups according to some spelling pattern. Here is a way to practice some of the words you studied in the past few weeks.

1. Make five columns on a large piece of paper or on the board.
2. Write one of the following words at the top of each column: **apple, soften, sailor, power,** and **simplest**.
3. Have a partner choose a spelling word from Units 19 through 22 and say it aloud.
4. Write the spelling word under the word with the same ending.

Directions: Read the introduction and the passage that follows. Then read each question and fill in the correct answer on your answer sheet.

Shyla loves wildflowers and knows many of their names. She researched how they got some of those names and wrote a report for school. Read this draft of Shyla's report. As you read it, think about the improvements Shyla should make when she revises.

What's in a Name?

(1) Simpel wildflowers brighten the day with a jumble of color. (2) Nature plants them without a single bit of troubel. (3) But humans gave them names and stories.

(4) A tale is told of a girl who would steal onto a sailing ship and wonder whethor her sweet William was there. (5) She was Black-eyed Susan. (6) Sweet William is a wildflower. (7) It blooms when Black-eyed Susan does. (8) Nature had no trouble getting them twogether.

(9) The story of Forget-me-not is sad. (10) After a battle, a knight and his lady past a riverbank where pretty blue flowers grew. (11) The knight was so eager to pick one that he could not help but stumble over a pebble and fall into the wator. (12) He tossed the lady the flower as the current took him away. (13) "Forget me not," he called.

(14) Here's a happyier story to tickle you and make you giggle. (15) There's a wildflower called "Dutchman's Breeches," or pants. (16) It has the cutest doubel blooms that together look like a pair of pants.

(17) Wildflowers have a place in history. (18) An example is the pink Mayflower that the pilgrims named for the ship that brought them to settle in the New World.

(19) Gather some wildflowers to put in a vase in the middel of a table. (20) Talk to them. (21) You do know their names.

GO ON

1 What change, if any, should be made in sentence 1?

    A Change *simpel* to **simple**

    B Change *brighten* to **briten**

    C Change *jumble* to **jumbel**

    D Make no change

2 What change, if any, should be made in sentence 2?

    F Change *single* to **singel**

    G Change *troubel* to **troubell**

    H Change *troubel* to **trouble**

    J Make no change

3 What change, if any, should be made in sentence 4?

    A Change *steal* to **steel**

    B Change *wonder* to **wondor**

    C Change *whethor* to **whether**

    D Make no change

4 What change, if any, should be made in sentence 8?

    F Change *trouble* to **troubell**

    G Change *twogether* to **together**

    H Change *twogether* to **togethor**

    J Make no change

5 What change should be made in sentence 10?

    A Change *battle* to **battel**

    B Change *battle* to **batel**

    C Change *past* to **pased**

    D Change *past* to **passed**

6 What change should be made in sentence 11?

    F Change *eager* to **eagre**

    G Change *stumble* to **stumbel**

    H Change *pebble* to **pebel**

    J Change *wator* to **water**

7 What change, if any, should be made in sentence 14?

    A Change *happyier* to **happier**

    B Change *tickle* to **tikel**

    C Change *giggle* to **giggel**

    D Make no change

8 What change, if any, should be made in sentence 16?

    F Change *cutest* to **cuteest**

    G Change *doubel* to **double**

    H Change *together* to **twogether**

    J Make no change

9 What change should be made in sentence 18?

    A Change *example* to **exampel**

    B Change *pilgrims* to **Pilgrims**

    C Change *settle* to **settel**

    D Change *settle* to **setell**

10 What change should be made in sentence 19?

    F Change *vase* to **vace**

    G Change *gather* to **gathor**

    H Change *middel* to **middle**

    J Change *table* to **tabel**

STOP

Grammar, Usage, and Mechanics
Pronouns

Personal pronouns include the words **I, me, you, we, us, he, him, she, her, they, them,** and **it**. These words can be used in place of names for people and things.

> **Ida** is here. **She** came early.

Possessive pronouns include the words **my, your, his, her, its, their,** and **our**. These pronouns show ownership.

> Call **Greg**. **His** tickets are here.

Practice Activity

A. Write the boldfaced word in each sentence that is a pronoun.

1. The vase of **colorful** flowers made **their** table look pretty.
2. **The** players are tired, so **they** want to stop.
3. Bart and **he** are cocaptains **of** the men's team.
4. The lifeguard **put** sunscreen on **her** nose.
5. The bird **is** carrying food to **its** babies.

B. Replace the underlined word or words with a pronoun from the box.

them	he	we	its	their	she	our

6. All the cattle are waiting for <u>the cattle's</u> water.
7. Eric is late, so <u>Eric</u> may lose this seat.
8. Did you bring the lunches that <u>you and I</u> packed?
9. Mom is still at work, but <u>Mom</u> will be home soon.
10. The playful kitten tumbled around with <u>the kitten's</u> ball of yarn.

The Writing Process: Persuasive
Writing a Persuasive Essay

PREWRITING

Sometimes people copy information from books or the Internet without permission. You can convince others to respect and follow copyright rules by listing reasons in a persuasive essay. Look for facts and details about copyright in reference books at the library. On the Internet, check out the U.S. Patent and Trademark Office website. As you think about your essay, make an outline of your reasons.

DRAFTING

Use your outline to write a persuasive essay. Begin with a topic sentence, followed by supporting sentences. Be sure to provide convincing reasons why your readers should agree with you. Use as many spelling words as possible.

REVISING

When you have finished your first draft, read your essay from beginning to end. Check to see if you have included all of the reasons from your outline. Does each sentence support the topic? Now write your final draft.

EDITING

Use the **Editing Checklist** to proofread your essay. Find three words that could be misspelled. If you typed your essay, run the spell-check feature in your word processing program to check your spelling. Otherwise, use a print or online dictionary to check your spelling. Be sure to use proofreading marks when you make corrections.

PUBLISHING

Make a copy of your persuasive essay and share it with your readers.

EDITING CHECKLIST

Spelling
- ✓ Circle words that contain the spelling patterns and rules learned in Units 19–23.
- ✓ Check the circled words in your **Spelling Dictionary**.
- ✓ Check for other spelling errors.

Capital Letters
- ✓ Capitalize important words in the title.
- ✓ Capitalize the first word in each sentence.
- ✓ Capitalize proper nouns.

Punctuation
- ✓ End each sentence with the correct punctuation.
- ✓ Use commas, apostrophes, and quotation marks correctly.

Grammar, Usage, and Mechanics
- ✓ Use personal and possessive pronouns correctly.

TEKS 4.22D Use spelling patterns and rules and print and electronic resources to determine and check correct spellings.

unit 25

Plurals

Connections to THINKING

Read the spelling words and sentences.

1.	goose	*goose*	We cooked a **goose** for dinner.
2.	woman	*woman*	The **woman** held her son's hand.
3.	calf	*calf*	The **calf** stays near its mother.
4.	fish	*fish*	I saw **fish** swimming in the lake.
5.	mouse	*mouse*	The **mouse** lives in the hayfield.
6.	leaf	*leaf*	A **leaf** takes in light for a plant.
7.	children	*children*	The **children** are six years old.
8.	geese	*geese*	The **geese** fly together in flocks.
9.	calves	*calves*	Many **calves** are in the barn.
10.	leaves	*leaves*	The **leaves** fell from the elm tree.
11.	self	*self*	The restaurant had **self** service.
12.	child	*child*	The **child** is looking for her father.
13.	women	*women*	These **women** are studying law.
14.	mice	*mice*	If **mice** come inside, get a cat.
15.	selves	*selves*	The actress played two different **selves**.
16.	ox	*ox*	An **ox** is very strong.
17.	popcorn	*popcorn*	I eat **popcorn** at the movies.
18.	elf	*elf*	An **elf** is a fantasy character.
19	oxen	*oxen*	The **oxen** pulled the heavy cart.
20.	elves	*elves*	The **elves** guarded the pot of gold.

Think & Sort the spelling words.

1–2. Write two words that are both singular and plural.

3–20. Write each singular word and its plural partner. Think about how the spelling changes when you write the plural form.

Remember

Some nouns form the plural in irregular ways.

TEKS 4.22Ai Spell words with more advanced orthographic patterns and rules: plural rules. **4.22Aii** Spell words with more advanced orthographic patterns and rules: irregular plurals. **4.22D** Use spelling patterns and rules and print and electronic resources to determine and check correct spellings.

Connections to VOCABULARY

Word Building

Follow the directions to write spelling words. Circle the words whose plural is formed by changing **f** to **v** and adding **-es**.

1. leaves – ves + f = _____
2. women – en + an = _____
3. catch – tch + lf = _____
4. golf – go + se = _____
5. mountain – ntain + se = _____
6. oven – ven + x = _____

Word Structure

7–10. Write the plural forms of **calf, leaf, self,** and **elf**.
11. Change one letter in **loose** to make this word.
12. Write the spelling word that is formed by two smaller words and has the same singular and plural form.
13. Change one letter in **fist** to make this word.
14. Change two letters in **goose** to make its plural form.
15. Write the singular form of **children**.
16. Remove two letters in **shelf** to make this word.

Use the Dictionary

The dictionary lists plural forms of words that do not form the plural by adding an **-s** or **-es**. Write the plural form of the spelling word that you would find in the **Spelling Dictionary** for each of these words.

17. child
18. mouse
19. ox
20. woman

TEKS 4.22Ai Spell words with more advanced orthographic patterns and rules: plural rules. **4.22Aii** Spell words with more advanced orthographic patterns and rules: irregular plurals. **4.22D** Use spelling patterns and rules and print and electronic resources to determine and check correct spellings.

167

Connections to READING

goose	woman	calf	fish	mouse
leaf	children	geese	calves	leaves
self	child	women	mice	selves
ox	popcorn	elf	oxen	elves

Word Categorization

Write the spelling word or words that belong in each group.

1. infant, baby, _____
2. stem, twig, _____
3. hamster, gerbil, _____
4. fairies, pixies, _____
5. ladies, wives, _____
6–7. bulls, cows, _____, _____

Complete the Idioms

Read the meaning of each idiom. Then write the spelling word that completes it.

8. (You're in big trouble.) Your _____ is cooked.
9. (When the one in charge is away, others act badly.) When the cat's away, the _____ will play.
10. (Make up your mind.) _____ or cut bait!

Use Context Clues

Write the singular or plural form of the spelling word in parentheses that best completes each sentence.

11. Jimmy and Timmy are two separate _____. (self)
12. In the autumn, the _____ on the trees change color. (leaf)
13. Hal's mother is a very nice _____. (women)
14. Paul Bunyan had an animal called Babe, the Blue _____. (oxen)
15. We made _____ in the microwave before the movie started. (popcorn)
16. An _____ is a make-believe creature like a fairy. (elves)
17. The little _____ stay in the shallow end of the pool. (child)
18. The brown _____ is in the pasture with its mother. (calves)
19. The _____ fly south in the winter. (goose)
20. Rosa was angry, but now she's back to her sweet _____. (selves)

 TEKS 4.22Ai Spell words with more advanced orthographic patterns and rules: plural rules.
4.22Aii Spell words with more advanced orthographic patterns and rules: irregular plurals. **4.22D** Use spelling patterns and rules and print and electronic resources to determine and check correct spellings.

Connections to VOCABULARY

Word Meanings

The prefix **un-** means "not." The prefix **re-** means "again." The prefix **pre-** means "before." Write the spelling word that fits each definition.

1. to cover again or get back again
2. to look at before
3. not lucky
4. to read again
5. to heat beforehand
6. not fair
7. to build again
8. to pay beforehand
9. to write again
10. to check again
11. a place for children to go before they go to school

Use Synonyms

Write the spelling word that is a synonym for each word.

12. unlace
13. dangerous
14. reveal
15. sad
16. study
17. open

Use the Dictionary

Write a spelling word that would appear on a dictionary page with the following guide words.

18. player • print
19. record • ridge
20. Tues. • useless

TEKS 4.22B Spell base words and roots with affixes. **4.22D** Use spelling patterns and rules and print and electronic resources to determine and check correct spellings.

unlucky	review	preschool	unfair	reheat
prepay	untie	recover	preview	unhappy
rewrite	pretest	rebuild	uncover	recheck
unlock	preheat	unsafe	reread	unpack

Complete the Sequences

A word in each series is missing a prefix. Add the prefix and write the spelling word to complete the sequence.

1. to wrap, to bake, to _____ cover, to eat
2. to pack, to travel, to _____ pack
3. to lock, to leave, to return, to _____ lock
4. to cook, to cool, to _____ heat, to eat
5. to build, to fall apart, to _____ build
6. to put on, to tie, to _____ tie, to take off
7. to write, to proofread, to _____ write
8. to catch a cold, to be ill, to _____ cover

Replace the Words

Replace the underlined words with a spelling word that means the same.

9. I will <u>read</u> those directions <u>again</u>.
10. Please <u>look over and study</u> your notes again.
11. I will <u>pay ahead</u> for the book I ordered.
12. I have been <u>having bad luck</u> lately.
13. I am going to <u>check</u> my answers <u>again</u>.

Use Context Clues

Add the correct prefix to each word in parentheses to complete each sentence.

14. The cook will _____ the oven before he bakes the potatoes. (heat)
15. Let's _____ our home movies before we show them to friends. (view)
16. My four-year-old brother goes to _____. (school)
17. What was your score on the spelling _____? (test)
18. I will be _____ when my best friend moves. (happy)
19. Using a tool before you are taught how to use it is _____. (safe)
20. It is _____ to borrow a book and not return it. (fair)

174

TEKS 4.22B Spell base words and roots with affixes. **4.22D** Use spelling patterns and rules and print and electronic resources to determine and check correct spellings.

Connections to WRITING

Proofread a List

Proofread the list below for ten misspelled words. Then rewrite the list. Write the spelling words correctly and make the corrections shown by the proofreading marks.

Things to Do This Week

1. Study for math preatest.
2. Make list of unnsafe activities for social studies.
3. Rereed book, revue plot, and prepare book report.
   Rerite book report more neatly.
4. Finish writing story "Unluckey Me" by wednesday.
5. Help Dad rebild doghouse this weekend.
6. Unpak everything from bookbag. Re-check my school supplies
7. Ask Mom for money to to preapay this week's lunches.

Proofreading Marks

≡	Capital Letter
/	Small Letter
∧	Add
℮	Delete
⊙	Add a Period
⁋	Indent

NARRATIVE Writing Prompt

Write a List

Write a list of things to do. Include important things you need to remember to complete a task, the order in which things need to be done, and when they need to be completed. Use as many spelling words as you can.

- Use the writing process: prewrite, draft, revise, edit, and publish.
- Make sure your list includes the time frame for when you have to finish your task. When you review the list, you should be able to tell a story of what you did.
- Use correct capitalization, punctuation, grammar, and spelling.
- Read your list. Circle three words that may be misspelled. Use a dictionary to check the spelling.

Transfer

Write three words from your list that have prefixes. Circle the prefix in each word.

 TEKS 4.22B Spell base words and roots with affixes. **4.22D** Use spelling patterns and rules and print and electronic resources to determine and check correct spellings.

preslice	prepay	reread	recheck	refresh
preplan	untie	unlucky	preheat	unknown
regroup	recover	review	unsafe	uncertain
rename	unhappy	reheat	unpack	unfriendly
unkind	rewrite	preview	prehistoric	reorder
preschool	uncover	pretest	prerecorded	refill
unfair	unlock	rebuild	reform	presoak

Prefixes and Suffixes

A. Many base words can use more than one prefix. Add or change the prefix in each word below to write spelling words.

1–2. heat   7. relock   11. repack

3–4. cover   8. review   12. retest

   5. uncheck   9. repay

   6. retie   10. unread

B. The noun suffix **-ness,** which means "state or condition of," changes adjectives to nouns. Write the spelling words that are related to each noun below.

13. unhappiness   15. unkindness

14. unfairness   16. unfriendliness

Silent Letters

17–18. Write the spelling words that contain silent **w** or silent **h**.

Anagrams

19–20. Write the spelling words that are anagrams for these words.

    former   filler

TEKS 4.22Av Spell words with more advanced orthographic patterns and rules: silent letters. **4.22B** Spell base words and roots with affixes. **4.22D** Use spelling patterns and rules and print and electronic resources to determine and check correct spellings.

Art Word Hunt

Read the paragraphs below and look for words that have prefixes.

A good cook is an artist unlike any other. That's because the quicker the art disappears, the better the artist is! It is hard work to be an artist in the kitchen. Sometimes a recipe must be redone again and again until it is worthy of a good review. Who reviews it? You do!

If you watch the artist at work, you get to preview the art as well as review it. Of course, you must take some precautions. For example, it is unwise to get too close to a hot stove or to uncover a boiling pot. Also, you'd better not mess around with any of the ingredients. You wouldn't fool around with Picasso's paints, would you?

Perhaps you're unable to create art in the kitchen. You can still be the artist's assistant. You can prearrange the table where the masterpiece will be unveiled. After all, great art must be properly shown. By the way, *prearrange* is a fancy way to say, "Set the table, please."

Then, when the meal is over, you can clear the table and do the dishes!

Use a print or online dictionary to check your answers. Do not write the same word twice.

1–5. Write the words with the prefix **un-**.

6–7. Write the words with the prefix **re-**.

8–10. Write the words with the prefix **pre-**.

 TEKS 4.22B Spell base words and roots with affixes. **4.22D** Use spelling patterns and rules and print and electronic resources to determine and check correct spellings.

177

Base Words With Suffix: -er

Connections to THINKING

Read the spelling words and sentences.

1.	farmer	*farmer*	The **farmer** milked his cows.
2.	skater	*skater*	She was judged the best **skater**.
3.	painter	*painter*	The **painter** stirred his paint.
4.	camper	*camper*	We met a **camper** in the forest.
5.	listener	*listener*	Drake is a good **listener**.
6.	banker	*banker*	We got a loan from the **banker**.
7.	owner	*owner*	Who is the **owner** of this farm?
8.	learner	*learner*	A good **learner** pays attention.
9.	hiker	*hiker*	Each **hiker** wore a backpack.
10.	catcher	*catcher*	The **catcher** signaled to the pitcher.
11.	speaker	*speaker*	That **speaker** was very entertaining.
12.	climber	*climber*	A rock **climber** needs good equipment.
13.	player	*player*	The team captain is a good **player**.
14.	reader	*reader*	This book will please any **reader**.
15.	baker	*baker*	Thanks to the **baker** for this bread.
16.	dreamer	*dreamer*	He is a **dreamer** who has great ideas!
17.	reporter	*reporter*	The **reporter** covered the fire.
18.	builder	*builder*	The house was planned by the **builder**.
19.	singer	*singer*	Each **singer** used the microphone.
20.	leader	*leader*	He is the **leader** of the band.

Think & Sort the spelling words.

1–17. Write the words in which **-er** is added without changing the base word.

18–20. Write the words in which final **e** is dropped before adding **-er**.

Remember

The suffix **-er** is often added to a verb to make a noun meaning "one who." If the base word ends in silent **e**, drop the **e** and add the ending.

 TEKS 4.22B Spell base words and roots with affixes. **4.22D** Use spelling patterns and rules and print and electronic resources to determine and check correct spellings.

Connections to VOCABULARY

Word Meanings

The suffix **-er** can change a verb to a noun that means "someone who does something." Add the suffix **-er** to each underlined verb to write a noun that is a spelling word.

1. I often <u>hike</u> in the woods or hills near the park. I am a _____.
2. Missy will <u>play</u> goalie on a hockey team. She will be a _____.
3. I <u>listen</u> carefully. I am a good _____.
4. Walter likes to <u>speak</u> to large groups of people. He is a _____.
5. My cousin wants to <u>report</u> on sports for a newspaper. He wants to be a _____.
6. Mr. Brown can <u>farm</u> both his land and his father's. He is a successful _____.

Word Completion

Write a spelling word by adding the suffix **-er** to each of the following base words.

7. dream
8. lead
9. own
10. paint
11. climb
12. read

Use the
Dictionary

Write the spelling word for each of the following dictionary respellings.

13. /kăm′ pər/
14. /băng′ kər/
15. /sĭng′ ər/
16. /kăch′ ər/
17. /bā kər/
18. /skā′ tər/
19. /bĭl′ dər/
20. /lûr′ nər/

Dictionary Check Be sure to check your answers in your **Spelling Dictionary.**

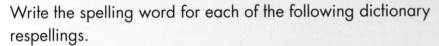

TEKS 4.22B Spell base words and roots with affixes. **4.22D** Use spelling patterns and rules and print and electronic resources to determine and check correct spellings.

farmer	skater	painter	camper	listener
banker	owner	learner	hiker	catcher
speaker	climber	player	reader	baker
dreamer	reporter	builder	singer	leader

Make Inferences

Write the spelling word that solves each riddle.

1. I go for long walks in the mountains. Who am I?
2. I spend many nights in a tent. Who am I?
3. I study hard and learn my lessons. Who am I?
4. I am a box that sound comes from. What am I?
5. I take care of my animals and plow my fields. Who am I?
6. I spend all my spare time looking at words in books. Who am I?
7. I am looking for my lost dog. Who am I?
8. I see pictures in my sleep. Who am I?
9. I handle a lot of money every day. Who am I?
10. I make fresh bread and rolls each day. Who am I?

Use Context Clues

Add **-er** to the word in parentheses to complete each sentence.

11. A monkey is a natural tree _____. (climb)
12. The _____ captured the colors of the sunset. (paint)
13. She is a _____ on a baseball team. (play)
14. Abraham Lincoln was a great _____. (lead)
15. That _____ is helping to put up the new shopping mall. (build)
16. We went to the ice arena to watch the figure _____ perform. (skate)
17. A good _____ is as important as a good speaker. (listen)
18. The local television station sent its best news _____ to cover the mayor's speech. (report)
19. She is a _____ with a beautiful soprano voice. (sing)
20. A pitcher and a _____ work together to strike out a batter. (catch)

 TEKS 4.22B Spell base words and roots with affixes. **4.22D** Use spelling patterns and rules and print and electronic resources to determine and check correct spellings.

Connections to WRITING

Proofread a Description

Proofread the description below for ten misspelled words. Then rewrite the description. Write the spelling words correctly and make the corrections shown by the proofreading marks.

A Lesson on Ice

⌙No paintir could have produced such a colorful /Picture. No reportur could have written about a more exciting show for the readr. First there was a singur who made every ~~every~~ listiner smile. Then each skatr, wearing a splendid costume, glided onto the ice. The speeker roared the name of each star as he or she whipped around the arena, following the leeder of the group. ⸱the beautiful scene was the work of a dremer, and everyone in the audience became a leerner.⊙

Proofreading Marks

≡	Capital Letter
/	Small Letter
∧	Add
ℰ	Delete
⊙	Add a Period
⌙	Indent

DESCRIPTIVE Writing Prompt
Write a Description

Write or type a description about something you have seen. Describe where you were, what you saw, and how you felt. Use as many spelling words as you can.

- Use the writing process: prewrite, draft, revise, edit, and publish.
- Use descriptive language to help the reader "see" what you saw and "feel" as you felt.
- Use correct capitalization, punctuation, grammar, and spelling.
- If you typed your description, run the spell-check feature in your word processing program to check your spelling. Otherwise, use a print or online dictionary to check your spelling.

Transfer
Write three words from the description you wrote that have the suffix **-er**. Write the words in your Spelling Journal. Circle the suffix and write the base word.

 TEKS 4.22B Spell base words and roots with affixes. **4.22D** Use spelling patterns and rules and print and electronic resources to determine and check correct spellings.

181

Extend & Transfer

Word Study

driver	listener	leader	climber	pitcher
teacher	owner	skater	baker	publisher
jumper	speaker	camper	dreamer	dancer
racer	player	banker	singer	jogger
worker	reader	learner	commander	jeweler
farmer	reporter	hiker	gardener	forester
painter	builder	catcher	homemaker	letter carrier

Pattern Power

1. Write the word with a silent consonant before the prefix **-er**.
2. Write the word with a one-syllable base word whose final consonant is doubled before the suffix **-er** is added.
3. Write the word that contains a compound word with the suffix **-er**.

Write the spelling words that are anagrams for these words.

4. reteach   5. rebuild   6. replay

Meaning Mastery

Write the spelling word that fits each meaning. Circle the word that dropped the final **e** before adding the ending.

7. a soprano
8. a person who vacations in a national forest
9. a person who grows crops
10. a person who walks on trails
11. a baseball player who stays behind home plate

Word History

12. The Latin root word **port** means "to carry." The Latin prefix **re-** means "back or again." Which spelling word means "one who carries back"?

TEKS 4.22Av Spell words with more advanced orthographic patterns and rules: silent letters. **4.22B** Spell base words and roots with affixes. **4.22D** Use spelling patterns and rules and print and electronic resources to determine and check correct spellings.

Math

Word Hunt

Read the paragraphs below and look for words that have the suffix **-er**.

Mathematics and banking are like a buyer and a seller. You can't have one without the other.

Suppose a business owner takes out a loan. The banker uses percentages to calculate the rate of interest the borrower has to pay. That calls for complicated math.

The money in savings accounts earns interest. Interest is calculated on the amount of money in the account. The longer your money stays in the account, the greater the amount of interest it earns. What could be nicer than getting more money than what you started out with?

Banks issue checking accounts. It's safer to pay bills by check than with cash. A check paid by the bank is called a canceled check. Canceled checks prove that a bill has been paid. You have to keep track of the money that goes in and out of your checking account. That's called balancing your account. The bank also has to be sure not to pay out more money than is in the account.

Bank employees are careful to check that the money you put in the bank comes and goes in the right direction. Maybe that's why a bank is quieter than most places. Everyone is concentrating on math!

WORD SORT

Use a print or online dictionary to check your answers.

1–8. Write the base words whose spelling does not change when the suffix **-er** is added.

9–10. Write the base words in which the final **e** is dropped before the suffix **-er** is added.

 TEKS 4.22B Spell base words and roots with affixes. **4.22D** Use spelling patterns and rules and print and electronic resources to determine and check correct spellings.

Connections to THINKING

Base Words With Suffixes: -ful, -less

Read the spelling words and sentences.

#			
1.	joyful	*joyful*	She sang a **joyful**, happy song.
2.	helpless	*helpless*	We untangled the **helpless** butterfly.
3.	restful	*restful*	The quietness was **restful**.
4.	careless	*careless*	She tried not to be **careless**.
5.	useful	*useful*	A pen is a **useful** writing tool.
6.	thankless	*thankless*	Cleaning is a **thankless** activity.
7.	peaceful	*peaceful*	May your day be happy and **peaceful**.
8.	hopeless	*hopeless*	Finding the lost coin was **hopeless**.
9.	thankful	*thankful*	He is **thankful** for family and friends.
10.	cloudless	*cloudless*	The sky was **cloudless** and bright.
11.	powerful	*powerful*	Kindness is a **powerful** force.
12.	helpful	*helpful*	We try to be **helpful** at home.
13.	powerless	*powerless*	They felt **powerless** against the wind.
14.	careful	*careful*	Be **careful** not to slip on the tile.
15.	restless	*restless*	He was **restless** with nothing to do.
16.	wasteful	*wasteful*	Not recycling bottles is **wasteful**.
17.	cheerful	*cheerful*	We are **cheerful** most of the time.
18.	useless	*useless*	The toy is **useless** without a battery.
19.	playful	*playful*	Kittens are young, **playful** cats.
20.	thoughtful	*thoughtful*	The decision was a **thoughtful** one.

Think & Sort the spelling words.

1–12. Write the words with the suffix **-ful**.

13–20. Write the words with the suffix **-less**.

Remember

Add a suffix to the end of a base word to make a new word with a new meaning. The suffix **-ful** means "full of." The suffix **-less** means "without."

 TEKS 4.22B Spell base words and roots with affixes. **4.22D** Use spelling patterns and rules and print and electronic resources to determine and check correct spellings.

Connections to VOCABULARY

Replace Words

Write a spelling word to replace the underlined word or words in each sentence.

1. Grandpa's 90th birthday party was a <u>happy</u> celebration.
2. It is important to look both ways and be <u>cautious</u> when crossing the street.
3. A <u>very strong</u> earthquake shook the building.
4. Rodrigo was <u>grateful</u> that his sister was able to attend his graduation.
5. The people of the village were <u>without the ability</u> to stop the river from flooding.
6. It is <u>handy</u> to have a map when you are lost.
7. It was <u>considerate</u> of Ava to send me flowers on my birthday.
8. The volunteers were <u>willing to offer aid</u> to the victims of the hurricane.

Use Antonyms

Write the spelling word that is an antonym for each word below.

9. hopeful
10. calm
11. cheerless
12. cloudy
13. thankful
14. thrifty
15. warlike
16. useful
17. careful

Use the Thesaurus

Write the following words. Beside each word, write the number of synonyms for it that are listed in your **Writing Thesaurus**.

18. restful   19. helpless   20. playful

Thesaurus Check Be sure to check for synonyms in your **Writing Thesaurus**.

TEKS 4.22B Spell base words and roots with affixes. **4.22D** Use spelling patterns and rules and print and electronic resources to determine and check correct spellings.

185

joyful	helpless	restful	careless	useful
thankless	peaceful	hopeless	thankful	cloudless
powerful	helpful	powerless	careful	restless
wasteful	cheerful	useless	playful	thoughtful

Complete the Analogies

Write the spelling word that completes each analogy.

1. Wealth is to **riches** as **cautious** is to _____.

2. Question is to **answer** as **careful** is to _____.

3. Vanish is to **appear** as **valuable** is to _____.

4. Dinner is to **supper** as **grateful** is to _____.

5. Laugh is to **cry** as **useless** is to _____.

6. Tiny is to **small** as **ungrateful** is to _____.

7. Hard is to **soft** as **patient** is to _____.

8. Work is to **labor** as **happy** is to _____.

9. Show is to **display** as **helpless** is to _____.

Use Context Clues

Write the spelling word that best completes each sentence.

10. A thrifty person is not _____.

11. That nation will not wage war; it is a _____ country.

12. Sending a get-well card was very _____ of you.

13. The sky was clear and _____.

14. The lost climbers felt _____ until they saw the search plane.

Complete the Comparisons

Choose a spelling word that best completes each comparison.

15. A kitten with a ball is as _____ as a baby with a rattle.

16. The lost puppy was as _____ as a newborn baby.

17. Your map was more _____ than mine.

18. The dinner was as _____ as a holiday celebration.

19. The engine in that machine is as _____ as the engine in a locomotive.

20. A ten-minute nap is not as _____ as a night's sleep.

helpless
restful
helpful
powerful
joyful
playful

186

Connections to VOCABULARY

Word Meanings

Write the name of the month that completes each sentence.

1. In _____ we have a parade to celebrate Independence Day.
2. We buy bright orange pumpkins at the end of _____.
3. Mom will try to fool me on the first day of _____.
4. I will send you a valentine in _____.
5. In _____ we will have a Memorial Day picnic.
6. When spring begins in _____, I will fly my kite.
7. In the Northern Hemisphere, summer begins late in the month of _____.
8. The month before the last month of the year is _____.
9. Labor Day always falls on the first Monday of _____.

Word Structure

Unscramble the letters to write spelling words. Begin the name of each month with a capital letter.

10. auyjnar
11. utgsua

12. eembrcde
13. alncedra

Use the Dictionary

Look up the names of the days of the week in your **Spelling Dictionary**. Then write the name that goes with each word history.

14. Tiu's day
15. day of the sun
16. Saturn's day
17. Thor's day

18. Woden's day
19. Freya's day
20. day of the moon

Connections to READING

January	February	March	April	May
June	July	August	September	October
November	December	calendar	Sunday	Monday
Tuesday	Wednesday	Thursday	Friday	Saturday

Complete the Poem

Write the names of the months to complete this poem.

In __1.__ the new year starts.
__2.__ brings Valentine hearts.
In __3.__ the winds will come and go.
In __4.__ we usually don't see snow.
In __5.__ the green grass grows, and soon
School will end in the month of __6.__ .
And maybe we'll watch a parade go by
On our own most special Fourth of __7.__ .
__8.__ is usually hot, not cool.
__9.__ sees us back in school.
In __10.__ the leaves turn gold,
And in __11.__ the weather turns cold.
So now let's give a little cheer
For __12.__ , which ends the year.

Use Context Clues

Write the spelling word that best completes each sentence.

13. After all the yard work I did last weekend, I was glad to go back to school on _____.
14. With three days on either side of it, _____ is the middle of the week.
15. Thanksgiving falls on the fourth _____ of November.
16. _____ is the last weekday but the first day of the weekend.
17. The last day of school each week is _____.
18. The first day of the week on many calendars is _____.
19. _____ is the day that follows Monday.
20. Jim writes the date of every away game in his _____.

Connections to WRITING

Proofread a How-To Paragraph

Proofread the how-to paragraph below for ten misspelled words.
Then rewrite the paragraph. Write the spelling words correctly and
make the corrections shown by the proofreading marks.

Gardening Hints

¶Mark your calender for Janurary 1⊙This is
a good month to buy seed. in Febuary, check
that you have all your supplies. Start your
~~your~~ seeds indoors. Take a Saterday to plan
your garden. Hardy crops may be planted in
Aprel or Mae. Know which plants like the
heat of Juli and Augist. you may be able
to harvest Crops as late as Septembir or
Oktober. Happy gardening!

Proofreading Marks

≡	Capital Letter
/	Small Letter
∧	Add
℮	Delete
⊙	Add a Period
¶	Indent

EXPOSITORY Writing Prompt
Write a How-To Paragraph

Write a paragraph telling how to make or do something.
Tell what is being made or done. Explain the advantages of
following your advice. Use as many spelling words as you can.

- Use the writing process: prewrite, draft, revise, edit, and publish.
- Write the steps involved, the order in which they should be done, and the time each will take.
- Be sure that your how-to steps are in the proper sequence.
- Use correct capitalization, punctuation, grammar, and spelling.
- Read your writing. Circle three words that may be misspelled. Use a print dictionary to check the spelling.

Transfer

Write in your Spelling
Journal three spelling
words that you used
in your paragraph.
Circle the first letter
of each word. Write
whether it is a capital
or lowercase letter
and tell why.

 TEKS 4.22D Use spelling patterns and rules and print and electronic resources to determine and check correct spellings.

Extend & Transfer
Word Study

month	April	Saturday	December	up-to-date
monthly	June	January	calendar	Fourth of July
spring	July	May	Tuesday	Memorial Day
summer	Sunday	August	Thursday	Labor Day
week	Monday	September	bimonthly	Martin Luther King Day
February	Wednesday	October	biweekly	Presidents' Day
March	Friday	November	daily	Thanksgiving

Meaning Mastery

Use these clues to write the English months and days.

A. Roman months are named for gods, rulers, and numbers.

1. *aperire*—"to open"
2. *Februus*—Roman god
3. *Maia*—goddess of spring
4. *Juno*—goddess of marriage
5. *Julius Caesar*—Roman emperor
6. *Janus*—god who looked forward and back
7. *Augustus*—first Roman emperor
8. *septem*—seven
9. *octo*—eight
10. *Mars*—god of war
11. *novem*—nine
12. *decem*—ten

B. *Tag* is German for **day**. *Woch* means "week." *Mon* means "moon." *Sonn* means "sun." *Mitt* means "mid." Use these clues to write each German word below in English. Circle the day of the week that has a silent consonant.

13. *Montag*
14. *Sonntag*
15. *Donnerstag*—after *Mittwoch*
16. *Samstag*—before *Sonntag*
17. *Freitag*—between *Donnerstag* and *Samstag*
18. *Mittwoch*
19. *Dienstag*—after *Montag*

194

 TEKS 4.22Av Spell words with more advanced orthographic patterns and rules: silent letters.

Technology
Word Hunt

Read the paragraphs below. Look for words that name the days of the week or months of the year.

A calendar is a tool. It helps you remember what you need to do and when you need to do it. You can't just hang it on the refrigerator and ignore it. You need to check it.

An online calendar won't let you ignore it. Let's say that your Mom's birthday is April 1 and you don't want to shop for a gift at the last minute. Put a reminder for March 1 on your online calendar. A pop-up window will appear on your computer on March 1. It will remind you to check your calendar.

Suppose you have a book report due on Wednesday. On Thursday, you have a spelling test, and you have a math test on Friday. A friend asks you to sleep over on Tuesday. Check your calendar! You'd better schedule that sleepover for another day, maybe Sunday. No, Sunday is October 29, pumpkin-picking day with your family.

You can keep all that information on a paper calendar, but a paper calendar doesn't give pop-up reminders. You don't have to buy a new calendar every January, and it won't fall off the refrigerator and disappear!

WORD SORT

Write the name of the month or day of the week to match each clue. Check your answers in a print or online dictionary.

1. has a silent consonant
2. can be respelled /**thûrz'** dā/
3. is a homograph; can mean "to walk in step with others"
4. has a **long i** sound
5. has a first syllable that rhymes with **man**
6. the /**k**/ sound is spelled **c**
7. looks like a compound word

 TEKS 4.22Av Spell words with more advanced orthographic patterns and rules: silent letters. **4.22D** Use spelling patterns and rules and print and electronic resources to determine and check correct spellings.

Assessment

Each assessment word in the box fits one of the spelling patterns you have studied over the past five weeks. Read the spelling patterns. Then write each assessment word below the unit number it fits.

Unit 25

1–4. Some nouns form the plural in irregular ways.

Unit 26

5–9. Prefixes, like **un-, re-,** and **pre-,** are added to the beginning of base words to make new words with different meanings: **pack, unpack; write, rewrite; pay, prepay.** The base word usually does not change.

Unit 27

10–13. The suffix **-er** is often added to a verb to make a noun meaning "one who." If the base word ends in silent **e,** drop the **e** and add the ending.

Unit 28

14–18. Add a suffix to the end of a base word to make a new word with a new meaning. The suffix **-ful** means "full of." The suffix **-less** means "without."

Unit 29

It is important to learn to spell the names of the months of the year and the days of the week. These words always begin with a capital letter.

Words for Assessment

- preset
- pajamas
- biker
- painless
- crossroads
- endless
- kicker
- unload
- retell
- keeper
- harmful
- gentleman
- unemployed
- gentlemen
- adventurer
- glassful
- preflight
- blissful

Review

Unit 25: Plurals

mice	mouse	children	self	selves
fish	leaf	leaves	child	popcorn

Write the spelling word that best completes each sentence.

1. Our cat caught a _____ yesterday.
2. Betsy is finally acting like her old _____ again.
3. Each fourth grader will help one young _____.
4. All the _____ in the play were kindergarteners.
5. Do you like to rake _____ in the fall?
6. I caught only one _____ at the lake.
7. We enjoyed eating hot _____ while watching our favorite movie.
8. "When the cat's away the _____ will play" is a popular idiom.
9. To "turn over a new _____" means to make a new start.
10. As we grow older, we learn more about our true _____.

Unit 26: Base Words With Prefixes: un-, re-, pre-

preschool	reread	rewrite	untie	prepay
unlock	recover	unfair	unhappy	uncover

Write the spelling word that fits the meaning.

11. before school
12. pay in advance
13. read again
14. get well
15. write again
16. not fair
17. not happy
18. take the cover off
19. open the lock
20. undo the knot or bow

Review

Unit 27: Base Words With Suffix: -er

builder	listener	reporter	speaker	reader
painter	player	owner	leader	farmer

Write the spelling word that best completes each sentence.

1. If you farm, you are a _____.
2. If you build things, you are a _____.
3. If you have a role in a game, you are a _____.
4. If you own a bike, you are its _____.
5. If you can read, you are a _____.
6. If you direct a band, you are its _____.
7. If you listen to a speaker, you are a _____.
8. If you report stories for a newspaper, you are a _____.
9. If you paint pictures or houses, you are a _____.
10. If you give a speech, you are a _____.

Unit 28: Base Words With Suffixes: -ful, -less

careless	thoughtful	useless	useful	helpful
cheerful	peaceful	careful	helpless	powerful

Write the spelling word that is the opposite of each of these words.

11. careful
12. powerless
13. useful
14. useless
15. helpful

16. helpless
17. cheerless
18. thoughtless
19. careless
20. warlike

Unit 29: Calendar Words

April	February	Saturday	Wednesday	Sunday
Friday	July	Monday	March	June

Write the spelling word for each clue.

1. This word ends with a **long e** sound.
2. This one-syllable word has an **r**-controlled vowel.
3. This word begins with a **long a** sound.
4. This word has a **vowel-consonant-e** spelling pattern.
5. This word ends with a **long i** sound.

6–10. List the five spelling words that name days according to their order in the week.

Spelling Study Strategy

Word Swap

Practicing spelling words can be fun if you make it into a game. Here's an idea you can try with a friend.

1. Swap spelling lists with a partner. Ask your partner to read your list and tell you if there are any words she or he doesn't know how to say. Say those words for your partner.

2. Ask your partner to read the first word on your list. Write the word on a piece of scrap paper.

3. Ask your partner to check your spelling. If you spelled the word correctly, your partner should say the next word on your list. If you did not spell the word correctly, ask your partner to spell the word out loud for you. Write the correct spelling.

4. Keep going until you have practiced five words. Then trade roles. Keep taking turns until you and your partner have practiced all the words on your lists.

Directions: Read the introduction and the passage that follows. Then read each question and fill in the correct answer on your answer sheet.

Eli is a budding photographer. He has strong opinions about digital versus film cameras. He decided to use an experience from his own life to write about why he prefers one kind of camera over another. Read this draft of Eli's writing. As you read it, think about the improvements Eli should make when he revises it.

Picture Perfect

(1) A cloudless Juli day is perfect for a student of photography to take pictures. (2) So is a September day when leafs change colors and geese fly south. (3) Maybe you'd rather shoot pictures of a powerfull skater on a cold December day, but you should decide on a camera first.

(4) You can get a film camera, but I think a digital one is better. (5) It is useful to preview a picture right away and retake it if you're unhappy with the result. (6) The owneer of a film camera is powerless to review pictures—at least not until they are developed.

(7) Last tuesday I was thankful to have a digital camera to shoot my little sister's preschool graduation. (8) The restless childrens were like mice chasing their tails. (9) It was hopeless to try to listen to the unlucky speeker.

(10) I kept snapping away. (11) Most pictures were blurry, but I got one clear shot. (12) It was of a child smiling like a joiful elf. (13) That cheerful child was my sister. (14) I would have missed that shot with a film camera, because it would have already run out of film! (15) A digital camera can hold over 100 pictures on a tiny flash card. (16) No running out of film for me! (17) I'm thankful that we have a colorfull memory of my sister's special day.

1. What change, if any, should be made in sentence 1?
   A. Change *cloudless* to **clowdless**
   B. Change *Juli* to **July**
   C. Change *student* to **studint**
   D. Make no change

2. What change, if any, should be made in sentence 2?
   F. Change *September* to **september**
   G. Change *leafs* to **leaves**
   H. Change *geese* to **gooses**
   J. Make no change

3. What change, if any, should be made in sentence 3?
   A. Change *powerfull* to **powerful**
   B. Change *skater* to **skayter**
   C. Change *December* to **Desember**
   D. Make no change

4. What change, if any, should be made in sentence 5?
   F. Change *useful* to **yuseful**
   G. Change *preview* to **preeview**
   H. Change *unhappy* to **unhappee**
   J. Make no change

5. What change should be made in sentence 6?
   A. Change *owneer* to **owner**
   B. Change *powerless* to **powrless**
   C. Change *review* to **revue**
   D. Change *review* to **reeview**

6. What change, if any, should be made in sentence 7?
   F. Change *tuesday* to **Tuesday**
   G. Change *thankful* to **thankfull**
   H. Change *preschool* to **pre-school**
   J. Make no change

7. What change, if any, should be made in sentence 8?
   A. Change *restless* to **resless**
   B. Change *childrens* to **children**
   C. Change *mice* to **myce**
   D. Make no change

8. What change should be made in sentence 9?
   F. Change *hopeless* to **hopless**
   G. Change *unlucky* to **unluckee**
   H. Change *unlucky* to **unluky**
   J. Change *speeker* to **speaker**

9. What change should be made in sentence 12?
   A. Change *child* to **childe**
   B. Change *smiling* to **smileing**
   C. Change *joiful* to **joyful**
   D. Change *elf* to **elves**

10. What change, if any, should be made in sentence 17?
    F. Change *colorfull* to **colorful**
    G. Change *memory* to **memoree**
    H. Change *sister's* to **sisters'**
    J. Make no change

STOP

Grammar, Usage, and Mechanics
Adjectives

An **adjective** usually describes a noun or a pronoun. It tells what the noun or pronoun is like. Adjectives can tell what kind, how many, or which one.

- what kind:

    The **friendly** dog wagged its **bushy** tail.

- how many:

    We ate **three** pizzas in **one** hour!

- which one:

    This computer cannot solve **that** problem.

Practice Activity

A. Write the adjective in each sentence.
1. Tara looked for the correct key.
2. Don't use a dull pencil.
3. Yesterday was a chilly day for a picnic.
4. What a delicious drink you made!
5. I snuggled in the soft blanket.

B. Fill in the blanks with other adjectives from the spelling lists in Units 25–29.
6. Jon wore a _____ smile.
7. One _____ act could ruin the project.
8. A _____ storm damaged trees and buildings.
9. Throw out that _____ lamp.
10. I appreciate your _____ act of kindness.

The Writing Process: Expository
Writing a Business Letter

PREWRITING
Does it bother you that people talk on cell phones while driving their cars? Do you think your community needs more parks? A good way to voice your complaints or opinions is to write a business letter. Your teacher can help you find addresses of community officials to whom you can write. As you think about an area of concern in your community, make an outline for your letter.

DRAFTING
Use your outline to write a business letter. As you state your case, make sure you have all six parts of a business letter: heading, inside address, salutation, body, closing, and signature. It is important to be polite in your letter, too. Use as many spelling words as possible.

REVISING
When you have finished your first draft, read your letter from beginning to end. Check to see if you have included all of the points in your outline. Did you offer a solution to the problem? Now write your final draft.

EDITING
Use the **Editing Checklist** to proofread your letter. Look for three words that could be misspelled and circle them. Use a print or online dictionary to check the spelling. Be sure to use proofreading marks when you make corrections.

PUBLISHING
Make a copy of your business letter. If you wrote about a real concern, have an adult help you mail it, or you can share it with your classmates.

EDITING CHECKLIST

Spelling
- ✓ Circle words that contain the spelling patterns and rules learned in Units 25–29.
- ✓ Check the circled words in your **Spelling Dictionary**.
- ✓ Check for other spelling errors.

Capital Letters
- ✓ Capitalize important words in the title.
- ✓ Capitalize the first word in each sentence.
- ✓ Capitalize proper nouns.

Punctuation
- ✓ End each sentence with the correct punctuation.
- ✓ Use commas, apostrophes, and quotation marks correctly.

Grammar, Usage, and Mechanics
- ✓ Use adjectives correctly to make sentences more interesting.

TEKS 4.22D Use spelling patterns and rules and print and electronic resources to determine and check correct spellings.

Connections to THINKING

Read the spelling words and sentences.

1. election	*election*	I voted in the class **election**.
2. invitation	*invitation*	I got an **invitation** to the party.
3. shadow	*shadow*	A **shadow** fell over the table.
4. motion	*motion*	Wind causes most of a wave's **motion**.
5. shoulder	*shoulder*	My **shoulder** aches this morning.
6. dictionary	*dictionary*	Look up that word in the **dictionary**.
7. fiction	*fiction*	The story is not true; it is **fiction**.
8. abolish	*abolish*	I wish we could **abolish** war.
9. division	*division*	Long **division** is hard for me.
10. multiplication	*multiplication*	I know my **multiplication** facts.
11. patient	*patient*	The **patient** tigress fed three cubs.
12. publish	*publish*	Mary will **publish** her diary.
13. shelter	*shelter*	Alex ran to the barn for **shelter**.
14. constellation	*constellation*	The big dipper is a **constellation**.
15. magician	*magician*	Houdini was a master **magician**.
16. constitution	*constitution*	I helped write our club's **constitution**.
17. imitation	*imitation*	Do your **imitation** of a lion's roar.
18. capitalization	*capitalization*	I learned when to use **capitalization**.
19. confusion	*confusion*	There was **confusion** on the long line.
20. exclamation	*exclamation*	An **exclamation** mark can express joy.

Think & Sort the spelling words.

1–5. Write the words that begin or end with **sh**.

6–16. Write the words that include **tion**.

17. Write the word that ends in **cian**.

18–19. Write the words that end in **sion**.

20. Write the word that ends in **tient**.

Remember

The /**sh**/ sound can be spelled **sh** as in **shelter**. Other ways to spell /**sh**/ appear in these patterns: **tion** (fiction), **cian** (magician), and **tient** (patient). The /**zh**/ sound appears in the **sion** pattern (division).

TEKS 4.22Aiv Spell words with more advanced orthographic patterns and rules: other ways to spell sh.
4.22D Use spelling patterns and rules and print and electronic resources to determine and check correct spellings.

Add Suffixes

Change the base words as needed to add the Latin suffix **-ion,** meaning "the result of," to write spelling words. Circle the letters that spell /**sh**/ or /**zh**/ in each word.

1. capitalize
2. elect
3. invite
4. multiply
5. exclaim
6. constitute
7. divide

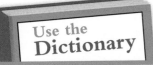

Word Meanings

Write the spelling word that has the same or almost the same meaning as each group of words.

8. the rules and laws of a government
9. use of a capital letter
10. performer of magic tricks
11. made-up story
12. result of a mix-up
13. process of separating into equal parts
14. excited declaration
15. request for someone's attendance
16. good at waiting

Use the Dictionary

Many English words come from other languages. For example, the word **election** originally came from the Latin word **ēligere,** meaning "to pick out, select." Write the spelling words that came from these words.

17. Latin **abolēre,** meaning "to die out"
18. Old English **sceadu,** meaning "shade"
19. Old English **scield,** meaning "shield"
20. Latin **constēllātiō,** meaning "set with stars"

Dictionary Check Be sure to check the word histories in your **Spelling Dictionary.**

TEKS 4.22Aiv Spell words with more advanced orthographic patterns and rules: other ways to spell sh. **4.22B** Spell base words and roots with affixes. **4.22D** Use spelling patterns and rules and print and electronic resources to determine and check correct spellings.

205

election	invitation	shadow	motion	shoulder
dictionary	fiction	abolish	division	multiplication
patient	publish	shelter	constellation	magician
constitution	imitation	capitalization	confusion	exclamation

Complete the Analogies

Write a spelling word to complete each analogy.

1. **Promote** is to **promotion** as **move** is to _____.
2. **Expect** is to **expectation** as **imitate** is to _____.
3. **Bread** is to **food** as **house** is to _____.
4. **Add** is to **addition** as **multiply** is to _____.
5. **Synonym** is to **thesaurus** as **definition** is to _____.
6. **Leg** is to **hip** as **arm** is to _____.
7. **Select** is to **selection** as **elect** is to _____.

Complete the Groups

The first two words in each group are parts of a whole. Write the spelling word that names the whole.

8. ballot, vote: _____
9. roof, walls: _____
10. print, distribute: _____
11. run, jump: _____
12. word, definition: _____
13. stars, shape: _____

Use Context Clues

Write a spelling word to complete each idiom, saying, or quote.

14. When you *put your _____ to the wheel,* you contribute to an effort.
15. Some say that _____ *is the sincerest form of flattery.*
16. In which state is everyone mixed up? It is the state of _____.
17. If something is *beyond a _____ of a doubt,* there are no doubts about it.
18. "It's no wonder that truth is stranger than _____. _____ has to make sense." —Mark Twain (American author)
19. "The end of law is not to _____ or restrain, but to preserve and enlarge freedom." —John Locke (English philosopher)
20. "If I have done the public any service, it is due to my _____ thought." —Sir Isaac Newton (English mathematician)

 TEKS 4.22Aiv Spell words with more advanced orthographic patterns and rules: other ways to spell sh.
4.22D Use spelling patterns and rules and print and electronic resources to determine and check correct spellings.

Plurals

1. Write the spelling word with the plural formed by adding **-es**.

2–3. Write the spelling words with the plural formed by changing **f** to **v** and adding **-es**.

4. Write the spelling word in which the plural form does not end in **s** or **sh**.

5. Write the word in which the plural and singular forms are the same.

Plural Possessives

Each word below is the singular possessive form of a noun. Write the spelling word that is the plural possessive form of the same noun.

6. wife's

7. poet's

8. couple's

9. son's

10. father's

11. sister's

Singular Possessives

Each word below is the plural possessive form of a noun. Write the spelling word that is the singular possessive form of the same noun.

12. herds'

13. wives'

14. groups'

15. poems'

16. calves'

17. mothers'

18. brothers'

19. daughters'

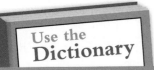

Use the Dictionary

20. Which spelling word can be used as a singular possessive and a plural possessive?

Dictionary Check Check your answer by finding the base word and a plural form of the word in your **Spelling Dictionary**.

TEKS 4.22Ai Spell words with more advanced orthographic patterns and rules: plural rules. **4.22Aii** Spell words with more advanced orthographic patterns and rules: irregular plurals. **4.22D** Use spelling patterns and rules and print and electronic resources to determine and check correct spellings.

Connections to READING

farmer's	poets'	group's	calf's	watches'
fish's	poem's	calves'	brother's	herd's
couples'	mother's	wives'	child's	fathers'
daughter's	sisters'	children's	wife's	sons'

Form the Possessives

Write the spelling word that is the possessive form of each word.

1. the lines of the poem; the _____ lines
2. the project of the group; the _____ project
3. the idea of the wife; the _____ idea
4. the crop of the farmer; the _____ crop
5. the feed for the calves; the _____ feed
6. the faces of the children; the _____ faces
7. the fins of the fish; the _____ fins
8. the meeting of the wives; the _____ meeting

Use Context Clues

Complete each sentence by writing the correct possessive form of each of the words in parentheses.

9. This is the spotted _____ collar. (calf)
10. All the _____ names are on this list. (father)
11. The farmer painted the _____ barn. (herd)
12. Thursday was the sick _____ last day of school. (child)
13. Three _____ works were read at the library program. (poet)
14. All the _____ bands are made of the same fabric. (watch)
15. Both of my _____ rooms are decorated differently. (sister)
16. His only _____ birthday is in June. (daughter)
17. I laughed at my _____ joke when he told it. (brother)
18. My _____ car is in the driveway. (mother)
19. Her two _____ toys were put away neatly. (son)
20. My mom and dad went to the _____ picnic. (couple)

TEKS 4.22Ai Spell words with more advanced orthographic patterns and rules: plural rules. **4.22Aii** Spell words with more advanced orthographic patterns and rules: irregular plurals. **4.22D** Use spelling patterns and rules and print and electronic resources to determine and check correct spellings.

Connections to WRITING

Proofread an Ad

Proofread the ad below for ten errors in the spelling words. Then rewrite the ad. Write the spelling words correctly and make the corrections shown by the proofreading marks.

Inexpensive Travel

¶Got the winter doldrums? Don't know how to spend the long, Dark nights? Why not curl up with a good book? reading is a farmers' escape, a wifes tropical trip, a childs' adventure, and a daughters dream. Between the covers of a book lie a poems appeal and a fathers tender tale. Best books has it all—even a childrens' section and two poets corners. Also, our book groups meetings are many couples night out.

Proofreading Marks

≡	Capital Letter
/	Small Letter
∧	Add
℮	Delete
⊙	Add a Period
¶	Indent

PERSUASIVE Writing Prompt
Write a Newspaper Ad

Write or type an ad offering something for sale. Think of people who would want to buy your item. Include a description of the item and the advantages to the reader of buying your product. Use as many spelling words as you can.

- Use the writing process: prewrite, draft, revise, edit, and publish.
- Include at least three reasons to buy the item.
- Use persuasive language to make the reader want to buy the item.
- Use complete sentences with correct capitalization, punctuation, grammar, and spelling.
- Read your writing. Circle three words that could be misspelled. Use an electronic spell checker to check the spelling.

Transfer
Write three possessive plurals from your ad in your Spelling Journal. Next to each word, write its possessive singular form.

 TEKS 4.22Ai Spell words with more advanced orthographic patterns and rules: plural rules. **4.22Aii** Spell words with more advanced orthographic patterns and rules: irregular plurals. **4.22D** Use spelling patterns and rules and print and electronic resources to determine and check correct spellings.

Extend & Transfer

Word Study

city's	brother's	sons'	herd's	youth's
geese's	mother's	farmer's	couples'	tourists'
grandmother's	child's	poets'	wives'	infant's
grandfather's	fathers'	group's	daughter's	nephew's
pies'	sisters'	calf's	actors'	crowd's
watches'	children's	poem's	artist's	umpires'
fish's	wife's	calves'	company's	runners'

Meaning Mastery

1–12. Write the words that tell that a single person owns something.

Plurals

13–14. Write the spelling words whose plurals are formed by changing **y** to **i** and adding **-es**.

15–16. Write the plural possessive form of **goose** and **child**.

Homophones

Write the spelling words whose base words are homophones of these words.

17. sun   **18.** heard

Silent Letters

19. Write the two possessive spelling words with silent **l**.

Word History

20. The Old English word **wif** meant "wife." Write the spelling word you would use to translate into modern English the possessive plural of **wif**.

TEKS 4.22Ai Spell words with more advanced orthographic patterns and rules: plural rules. **4.22Aii** Spell words with more advanced orthographic patterns and rules: irregular plurals. **4.22Av** Spell words with more advanced orthographic patterns and rules: silent letters. **4.22C** Spell commonly used homophones. **4.22D** Use spelling patterns and rules and print and electronic resources to determine and check correct spellings.

Language Arts

Word Hunt

Read the paragraphs below and look for words that show possession.

The Grimm brothers and the Brontë sisters are alike in some ways and different in other ways. They were all writers. The Brontë sisters' stories are found in the adults' section of the library. Each sister wrote her own books. The Grimm brothers' stories are fairy tales that are found in the children's section of the library. The brothers wrote their books together.

Charlotte, Emily, and Anne Brontë grew up in England. Jacob and Wilhelm Grimm grew up in Germany.

The Grimms' collection of fairy tales was first published in 1812. It contained such favorites as "Cinderella," "Sleeping Beauty," and "Snow White." Walt Disney's movies added to the popularity of these tales. Mrs. Grimm would have been surprised at her sons' success. She expected them to become lawyers.

The Brontë sisters' stories were published in the mid-1800s. Charlotte's most well-known book is *Jane Eyre*. Emily's *Wuthering Heights* has many fans. The least known of the Brontës' books is Anne's *The Tenant of Wildfell Hall*.

There is one really big difference between the Grimms and the Brontës. Jacob and Wilhelm used their own names. The Brontës had to use men's names. There was a prejudice against women writers in the Brontës' time. Thank goodness that has changed!

WORD SORT

1–8. Write the singular possessive form of each plural possessive in the selection.

9–10. Write the plural nouns in the selection that do not end in **s** and are written as plural possessives.

 TEKS 4.22Ai Spell words with more advanced orthographic patterns and rules: plural rules. **4.22Aii** Spell words with more advanced orthographic patterns and rules: irregular plurals.

Base Words With Suffixes: -ness, -ment

Read the spelling words and sentences.

1. kindness — *kindness* — He always treats people with **kindness**.
2. treatment — *treatment* — When you are ill, you need **treatment**.
3. stillness — *stillness* — I left in the **stillness** of the night.
4. apartment — *apartment* — She lives in a large **apartment**.
5. fitness — *fitness* — They use **fitness** equipment at home.
6. pavement — *pavement* — The **pavement** was wet with rain.
7. weakness — *weakness* — Arriving late is his **weakness**.
8. shipment — *shipment* — A **shipment** of goods arrived today.
9. brightness — *brightness* — The sun's **brightness** made me squint.
10. agreement — *agreement* — We will try to reach an **agreement**.
11. placement — *placement* — Father works at a **placement** bureau.
12. illness — *illness* — He is at home because of **illness**.
13. enjoyment — *enjoyment* — Her **enjoyment** of the movie was clear.
14. darkness — *darkness* — I stumbled in the **darkness**.
15. movement — *movement* — We studied the **movement** of the stars.
16. softness — *softness* — The blanket's **softness** was comforting.
17. boldness — *boldness* — The **boldness** of his plan surprised us.
18. payment — *payment* — Expect the first **payment** next week.
19. thickness — *thickness* — She measured the **thickness** of the wall.
20. sadness — *sadness* — He has known great **sadness** and joy.

Think & Sort the spelling words.

1–11. Write the words with the suffix **-ness**.

12–20. Write the words with the suffix **-ment**.

Remember

The suffix **-ness** means "a condition or quality": **kindness**. The suffix **-ment** means "the result of an action": **enjoyment**. The base word usually does not change.

 TEKS 4.22B Spell base words and roots with affixes. **4.22D** Use spelling patterns and rules and print and electronic resources to determine and check correct spellings.

Connections to VOCABULARY

Add Suffixes

The suffix **-ness** means "a condition or quality." Add **-ness** to each word below to change it from an adjective to a noun.

1. fit
2. kind
3. sad
4. bold
5. bright

6. soft
7. still
8. weak
9. thick

The suffix **-ment** means "the result of an action." Add **-ment** to each word below to change it from a verb to a noun. Circle the **e** or **y** at the ending of any of the base words. Notice that the ending does not change when the suffix is added because the suffix does not start with a vowel.

10. agree
11. place
12. pay
13. pave

14. move
15. treat
16. enjoy

Use the Thesaurus

Write a spelling word for each pair of synonyms below.

17. gloom; blackout
18. flat; suite

19. cargo; freight
20. ailment; malady

Thesaurus Check Be sure to check the synonyms in your **Writing Thesaurus**.

TEKS 4.22B Spell base words and roots with affixes. **4.22D** Use spelling patterns and rules and print and electronic resources to determine and check correct spellings.

217

kindness	treatment	stillness	apartment	fitness
pavement	weakness	shipment	brightness	agreement
placement	illness	enjoyment	darkness	movement
softness	boldness	payment	thickness	sadness

Make Inferences

Write a spelling word by adding **-ness** or **-ment** to each underlined word.

1. The <u>ship</u> is carrying a large _____.
2. When they <u>pave</u> this road, the _____ will be easier to ride on.
3. <u>Kind</u> people bring out _____ in others.
4. This <u>thick</u> board is the same _____ as those other boards.
5. As you <u>move</u> your arms, follow the _____ of the dance director.
6. Please <u>pay</u> your bill by sending your _____ by mail.
7. We <u>agree</u> that he should sign the _____ today.
8. His <u>bold</u> words match the _____ of his personality.
9. The doctors will <u>treat</u> certain injuries at a special _____ center.
10. As you <u>place</u> the pieces in the jigsaw puzzle, their _____ will help create a picture.

Write the Antonyms

Write the spelling word that is an antonym of each of the following words.

11. hardness
12. health
13. dimness
14. happiness
15. brightness

Use Context Clues

Write the spelling words that complete the paragraph.

The accident left Martha weak. Each day, in the __16.__ of her small __17.__, she worked with physical __18.__ equipment to overcome her __19.__ Although it was hard work, she felt much __20.__ because she knew that one day she would be strong again.

| fitness |
| weakness |
| stillness |
| enjoyment |
| apartment |

218

Connections to WRITING

Proofread a Note

Proofread the note below for ten misspelled words. Then rewrite the note. Write the spelling words correctly and make the corrections shown by the proofreading marks.

Dear Maria,   October 12, 2012

 Cindy's apartmint is beautiful. The briteness and warmth of the sun streaming through her windows are comforting. At night, the stilness of the Street lulls me to sleep. I try to repay her kindniss by going with her to her fitnes class. We get a lot of enjoiment from each other's company. You were were right. This is good treatmint for my saddness. cindy's nice not to expect any paymennt while I stay here. We made an agreemint that I would help with the cooking and cleaning. I'll call you this weekend.

love,

Sharon

Proofreading Marks

 Capital Letter

/ Small Letter

∧ Add

℘ Delete

 Add a Period

⌗ Indent

EXPOSITORY Writing Prompt

Write a Note

Write or type a note to a friend with some news about what you are doing. Include the date, a greeting, and your news. Write a closing with your signature. Use as many spelling words as you can.

- Use the writing process: prewrite, draft, revise, edit, and publish.
- Use descriptive details to help the reader visualize what you are doing and feeling.
- Use complete sentences with correct capitalization, punctuation, grammar, and spelling.
- Read your writing. Circle three words that could be misspelled. Use an electronic spell checker to check the spelling.

Transfer

Choose two words from your note that have the suffix **-ness** and two words that have the suffix **-ment**. Write the words in your Spelling Journal. Circle each suffix and underline the base words.

TEKS 4.22B Spell base words and roots with affixes. **4.22D** Use spelling patterns and rules and print and electronic resources to determine and check correct spellings.

Word Study

highness	agreement	treatment	softness	tardiness
rightness	illness	fitness	boldness	smoothness
roundness	enjoyment	pavement	payment	restfulness
mildness	darkness	weakness	argument	happiness
kindness	movement	shipment	employment	emptiness
stillness	thickness	brightness	government	wonderment
apartment	sadness	placement	sickness	

Pattern Power

Write words from the spelling list above to answer the questions.

1–2. Which spelling words have base words with the **long e** sound spelled **ea** in the middle?

3–8. Which spelling words have base words ending in **y**?

9–12. Which spelling words have base words that end in silent **e** and have a long vowel sound?

Suffixes

A. Add the suffix **-ness** or **-ment** to each word below. Circle the word in which the silent **e** is dropped before adding the suffix.

13. govern   **15.** thick   **17.** ship

14. ill   **16.** argue

B. The suffix **-ly** means "like." Write the spelling words that are forms of these words.

18. darkly   **19.** boldly   **20.** softly

TEKS 4.22Av Spell words with more advanced orthographic patterns and rules: silent letters. **4.22B** Spell base words and roots with affixes. **4.22D** Use spelling patterns and rules and print and electronic resources to determine and check correct spellings.

Science
Word Hunt

Read the paragraphs below. Look for words with the suffix **-ness** or **-ment**.

Scientists are detectives. They don't investigate crimes, but they have a commitment to investigate the world around them.

First, they ask a question. Next, they hypothesize, or make a good guess, about the answer. Then they experiment to test the correctness of their guess.

Let's suppose we are botanists, or scientists who study plants. Hydroponics is the process in which seeds sprout in water. Our awareness of this process leads us to see if we can improve it. We want to make an assessment of liquids in which seeds can grow.

Our hypothesis, or guess, is that since seeds grow in water, they can grow in other liquids. We might try orange juice, milk, or even club soda. We will test each liquid. A requirement is that the management of the test is controlled. To guarantee fairness, each liquid will receive the same treatment. We will use the same amount in the same size containers. The same type of seed will be placed in each liquid.

We will record what happens to the seeds. At the end of the experiment, the question of whether seeds can grow in liquids other than water might be answered. What will the answer be? I don't know. Try the experiment yourself to find out. Join in on the excitement of scientific discovery.

1–3. Write each base word to which the suffix **-ness** has been added.

4–9. Write each base word to which the suffix **-ment** has been added.

10. Write the word that has the same root word as **experience** to which the suffix **-ment** has been added.

 TEKS 4.22B Spell base words and roots with affixes. **4.22D** Use spelling patterns and rules and print and electronic resources to determine and check correct spellings.

Connections to THINKING

Read the spelling words and sentences.

1. tablecloth	*tablecloth*	We use a red and white **tablecloth**.
2. everyone	*everyone*	Was **everyone** at the soccer game?
3. nearby	*nearby*	We walk to school, which is **nearby**.
4. outdoors	*outdoors*	We play **outdoors** when it is warm.
5. high school	*high school*	My older brother is in **high school**.
6. anywhere	*anywhere*	You may sit **anywhere** you wish.
7. flashlight	*flashlight*	I need a **flashlight** to find my way.
8. air mail	*air mail*	A plane carrying **air mail** landed.
9. whenever	*whenever*	We can go **whenever** he is ready.
10. driveway	*driveway*	The car is parked in the **driveway**.
11. sometimes	*sometimes*	I walk to school **sometimes**.
12. seat belt	*seat belt*	Use your **seat belt** when in a car.
13. basketball	*basketball*	She is our new **basketball** coach.
14. mailbox	*mailbox*	I dropped the letter in the **mailbox**.
15. babysitter	*babysitter*	She is a **babysitter** for the twins.
16. upstairs	*upstairs*	My bedroom is **upstairs**.
17. everyday	*everyday*	That is one of my **everyday** chores.
18. alarm clock	*alarm clock*	I set the **alarm clock** for 7:30.
19. newspaper	*newspaper*	We read a **newspaper** every day.
20. weekend	*weekend*	The **weekend** at the lake will be fun.

Think & Sort the spelling words.

1–16. Write the compound words that are written as one word.

17–20. Write the compound words that are written as two words.

Remember

A **compound word** is formed from two or more smaller words. Closed compounds are written as one word. Open compounds are written as two separate words.

 TEKS 4.22D Use spelling patterns and rules and print and electronic resources to determine and check correct spellings.

Connections to VOCABULARY

Word Meanings

Write the spelling word that is made by combining each of the following definitions.

1. an infant/one who rests on the lower part of the body
2. information/a sheet of processed wood or vegetable fibers
3. a container usually made of straw or rope/a round object
4. tall/a place of learning
5. a period of seven days in a month/final
6. almost/close
7. top/a series of steps
8. apart from the boundaries/openings to a structure
9. all inclusive/single
10. not particular/a location

Plurals

11. Write the spelling word whose plural is formed by adding **-es**.
12. Write the open compound that is the same in singular and plural form.

Use the
Dictionary

Find the following words in your **Spelling Dictionary**. Write each word. Then write **n., adj., adv.,** or **conj.** after it to name the part of speech it usually has.

13. whenever
14. seat belt
15. tablecloth
16. everyday

17. flashlight
18. sometimes
19. driveway
20. alarm clock

TEKS 4.22Ai Spell words with more advanced orthographic patterns and rules: plural rules. **4.22D** Use spelling patterns and rules and print and electronic resources to determine and check correct spellings.

Connections to READING

tablecloth	high school	whenever	basketball	everyday
everyone	anywhere	driveway	mailbox	alarm clock
nearby	flashlight	sometimes	babysitter	newspaper
outdoors	air mail	seat belt	upstairs	weekend

Replace the Words

Replace the underlined part of each sentence with a spelling word.

1. <u>Every person</u> can be seated now.
2. The <u>person who takes care of children</u> arrived.
3. Some post offices used to have a special slot for <u>mail that is sent by air</u>.
4. We subscribe to a daily <u>news printed on sheets of paper</u>.
5. I <u>now and then</u> listen to the radio.

Use Context Clues

Write the spelling word that completes each sentence and contains the word in parentheses.

6. I always wear a _____ when riding in a car. (seat)
7. We have old dishes that Mom calls her _____ tableware. (day)
8. I was late yesterday because my _____ did not ring. (clock)
9. I would rather be _____ than indoors. (doors)
10. My father parks his car in our _____. (way)
11. Was there a letter in the _____? (mail)
12. I need a bright _____ for my camping trips. (flash)
13. Please put the lace _____ on the table. (table)
14. Our school will have a _____ game tonight. (basket)
15. I squint _____ the sun is in my eyes. (when)

Complete the Analogies

Write spelling words to complete the analogies.

16. **Wednesday** is to **weekday** as **Saturday** is to _____.
17. **Fourth grade** is to **elementary school** as **tenth grade** is to _____.
18. **Distant** is to **faraway** as **close** is to _____.
19. **First floor** is to **downstairs** as **second floor** is to _____.
20. **No one** is to **anyone** as **nowhere** is to _____.

224

 TEKS 4.22D Use spelling patterns and rules and print and electronic resources to determine and check correct spellings.

Connections to VOCABULARY

Word Meanings

Write the name of the nationality that goes with the name of each of the following countries. Circle the letters that spell /**sh**/.

1. China
2. Russia
3. Ireland
4. France
5. America
6. Mexico
7. Great Britain

Beginnings and Endings

8–12. Write the names of the continents that begin and end with the letter **a**.

Suffixes

The adjective suffixes **-ish, -an, -ian** and **-ese** mean "like." Write the spelling word with the correct suffix to describe each nation. Circle any letters that spell /**sh**/.

13. Japan
14. Germany
15. Spain
16. Canada

Use the Dictionary

17–20. Write the following spelling words in alphabetical order.

Italian   Greek   Europe   Indian

Dictionary Check Be sure to check the alphabetical order of the words in your **Spelling Dictionary**.

 TEKS 4.22Aiv Spell words with more advanced orthographic patterns and rules: other ways to spell sh. **4.22B** Spell base words and roots with affixes. **4.22D** Use spelling patterns and rules and print and electronic resources to determine and check correct spellings.

Connections to READING

Greek	Europe	French	Mexican	Italian
Russian	Indian	Antarctica	Spanish	British
Africa	Japanese	Canadian	America	Asia
American	Australia	Chinese	German	Irish

Word Categorization

Write the spelling word that is suggested by each of the following groups of words.

1. panda bears, chopsticks, Great Wall
2. maple leaf, hockey, provinces
3. shamrocks, Blarney Stone, green fields
4. snow, ice, whales, penguins
5. kangaroos, koala bears, boomerangs
6. Paris, Louvre Museum, Eiffel Tower
7. Big Ben, London, Buckingham Palace
8. Olympics, mythology, Athens

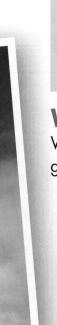

Use Context Clues

Write the spelling word that completes each sentence. Use a print or online encyclopedia to check your answers.

9. The largest continent in the world is _____.
10. The United States is in North _____.
11. A sari is a dress worn by many _____ women.
12. Rome is an _____ city.
13. _____ festivals in Mexico are called fiestas.
14. Madrid is a _____ city.
15. *Sputnik I* was a _____ spacecraft, the first to orbit Earth.
16. France and Spain are countries in _____.
17. Origami is the _____ art of folding paper.
18. The two _____ continents are South America and North America.
19. Berlin is a large _____ city.
20. You can go on a desert safari in _____.

Connections to WRITING

Proofread a Newspaper Ad

Proofread the ad below for ten misspelled words. Then rewrite the ad. Write the spelling words correctly and make the corrections shown by the proofreading marks.

Omniworld Offers It All

¶ Do you want to sweat in a jungle in Affrica, shiver in Antartica, visit europ, photograph kangaroos in Austraalia, or explore South Americka? We have it all: Greak food, Irrish hospitality, the Chineese Great Wall! Visit or call our canadien or Ammerican offices today.

Proofreading Marks

≡	Capital Letter
/	Small Letter
∧	Add
ℰ	Delete
⊙	Add a Period
¶	Indent

PERSUASIVE Writing Prompt

Write a Newspaper Ad

Write or type a travel ad to persuade the reader to visit a place you have visited or would like to visit. Give the name of the travel agency, what it offers, and the suggested prices. Use as many spelling words as you can.

- Use the writing process: prewrite, draft, revise, edit, and publish.
- Use descriptive words in your ad to help the reader visualize the places advertised and why the reader should choose to go there.
- Use complete sentences with correct capitalization, punctuation, grammar, and spelling.
- Read your writing. Circle three words that could be misspelled. Use an electronic spell checker to check the spelling.

Transfer

Choose the names of two countries people might like to visit. Next to each country name, write the spelling word that names the people who live in that country.

 TEKS 4.22D Use spelling patterns and rules and print and electronic resources to determine and check correct spellings.

231

street	Indian	Irish	Canadian	Texas
east	French	Greek	German	Washington
earth	Chinese	Russian	Italian	yen
west	Mexican	Europe	British	Euro
south	Spanish	Japanese	California	peso
Africa	America	Australia	Colorado	Australian
American	Asia	Antarctica	New York	dollar

Meaning Mastery

Complete the chart with the description and currency for each country below. Today, European nations use the Euro as currency.

Country	People	Currency
Japan	1. _____	2. _____
Italy	3. _____	4. _____
Mexico	5. _____	6. _____
France	7. _____	8. _____
Great Britain	9. _____	10. _____

Plurals

11–23. Write the spelling words that are proper nouns and have no plural form. If a word has already been used on this page, do not write it again.

TEKS 4.22Ai Spell words with more advanced orthographic patterns and rules: plural rules. **4.22D** Use spelling patterns and rules and print and electronic resources to determine and check correct spellings.

Social Studies

Word Hunt

Read the paragraphs below and look for the names of continents and nationalities.

There are seven continents. The largest is Asia. About 4 billion people live there. Chinese people, Japanese people, and Russian people live there. So do people of lots of other nationalities.

Russians also live in Europe. Europe is the sixth-largest continent. About one-fifth of the world's people live there. That's very crowded.

Australia is the smallest continent. About 20 million people live there. Antarctica is the fifth-largest continent. No one lives there all the time. It's too cold. About 4,000 researchers go there in the summer. Maybe 1,000 of them stay through the icy cold winters.

India is part of Asia. It is often called the Indian subcontinent. That means it's a large part of a continent. Continents! Subcontinents! It's pretty confusing. Here's another fact: Some 15 million people don't live on any continent! They live in island countries.

Imagine that you had a world of your own. What would it be like?

WORD SORT

Write the spelling word that names the nationality of people from each country below.

1. Russia   2. China   3. India

Write the spelling word that names the continent that each nationality comes from.

4. Europeans   5. Australians   6. Asians

7–8. Write the words that have the /**sh**/ sound.

9–10. Write the words that have the suffix **-ese**.

 TEKS 4.22Aiv Spell words with more advanced orthographic patterns and rules: other ways to spell sh. **4.22B** Spell base words and roots with affixes. **4.22D** Use spelling patterns and rules and print and electronic resources to determine and check correct spellings.

Units 31–35

Assessment

Each assessment word in the box fits one of the spelling patterns and rules you have studied over the past five weeks. Read the unit descriptions. Then write each assessment word under the unit number it fits.

Unit 31

1–4. The /**sh**/ sound can be spelled **sh** as in **shelter**. Other ways to spell /**sh**/ appear in these patterns: **tion (fiction), cian (magician),** and **tient (patient)**. The /**zh**/ sound appears in the **sion** pattern (**division**).

Unit 32

5–8. Add **'s** to show ownership when a noun is singular. Add **s'** to show ownership when a plural noun ends in **-s**. When a plural noun does not end in **-s**, add **'s** to show ownership (**children's**).

Unit 33

9–12. The suffix **-ness** means "a condition or quality": **kindness**. The suffix **-ment** means "the result of an action": **enjoyment**. The base word usually does not change.

Unit 34

13–16. A **compound word** is formed from two or more smaller words. Closed compounds are written as one word. Open compounds are written as two separate words.

Unit 35

17–20. It is important to be able to spell words that name and describe places in our world.

Words for Assessment

shallow

parents'

Dutch

prepayment

home run

turtleneck

cheerfulness

Korean

friend's

action

decision

teacher's

Portuguese

peacefulness

meantime

Cuban

beautician

aunt's

swiftness

applesauce

Review

Unit 31: Consonant Sounds: /sh/, /zh/

dictionary	fiction	abolish	division	multiplication
invitation	election	shadow	motion	magician

Change each base word as needed to add the suffix **-ion, -ian,** or **-ary** to form a spelling word. Circle the spelling for /**sh**/ or /**zh**/ in each word.

1. diction
2. multiply
3. fictitious
4. elect

5. magic
6. mobile
7. divide
8. invite

9. Write the word that begins with /**sh**/.
10. Write the word that ends with /**sh**/.

Unit 32: Possessives

brother's	children's	fathers'	mother's	watches'
fish's	sisters'	wife's	child's	sons'

Write the spelling word that completes the phrase.

11. the faces of two watches: the _____ faces
12. the eyes of one fish: the _____ eyes
13. the shoes of my sisters: my _____ shoes
14. the name of his wife: his _____ name
15. the interests of my mother: my _____ interests
16. the grades of her brother: her _____ grades
17. the toys of the children: the _____ toys
18. the tricycle of the child: the _____ tricycle
19. the lawn mowers of our fathers: our _____ lawn mowers
20. the paintings of her sons: her _____ paintings

Review

Unit 33: Base Words With Suffixes: -ness, -ment

agreement	enjoyment	kindness	thickness	stillness
movement	apartment	illness	sadness	darkness

Write the spelling word whose base word rhymes with the word below.

1. mind
2. sick
3. smart
4. spark

5. free
6. mad
7. prove
8. employ

Write the spelling word that goes with each base word.

9. ill
10. still

Unit 34: Compounds

basketball	everyday	everyone	sometimes	newspaper
outdoors	nearby	anywhere	whenever	upstairs

Change one word in each compound word below to form a spelling word.

11. nowhere
12. anyone
13. softball
14. outside
15. paperback

16. evergreen
17. weekday
18. downstairs
19. pastimes
20. near miss

Unit 35: Words About Our World

Africa	American	Chinese	Spanish	Asia
Mexican	Indian	America	Irish	French

Write the word that fits the description.

1. a child born in Ireland
2. a type of food eaten in Mexico
3. the language spoken in China
4. the music and dance of Spain
5. the continent that includes China and Vietnam
6. the continent where Ethiopia and South Africa are
7. a woman born in the United States of America
8. the language spoken in France
9. someone from India
10. South _____, the continent south of North America

Spelling Study Strategy

Sorting by Endings

One good way to practice spelling words is to place words into groups according to some spelling pattern.

1. Make six columns across a large piece of paper.

2. Write one of these words, including the underlined parts, at the top of each column: **lunches, friends, brother's, fathers', darkness, enjoyment**.

3. Have a partner choose a spelling word from Unit 31, 32, or 33 and say it aloud.

4. Write the spelling word in the column under the word with the same ending.

Directions: Read the introduction and the passage that follows. Then read each question and fill in the correct answer on your answer sheet.

Ramona wants to travel around the world when she grows up. She has been reading travel books and has some ideas about where she'd like to go. She wrote an essay about her travel ideas. Read this draft of Ramona's essay. As you read it, think about the improvements Ramona should make when she revises.

Great Travel Tips

(1) A travel book is the tourist's invitashun to travel anywhere. (2) Every one can mention a place they have a desire to see. (3) I have two. (4) They are both great. (5) One is the Great Barrier Reef. (6) The other is the Great Wall of China.

(7) The Great Barrier Reef in Australia is a fishs' paradise and a source of enjoyment for divers. (8) It is the largest coral reef in the world. (9) It is larger than the Great Wall of China. (10) This constellation of reefs and islands is the only living thing on Earth visible from the darkness of space.

(11) It is fiction that the Great Wall can be seen from space, but it is fact that millions of Chineze workers died to finish the Wall. (12) It was started almost 3,000 years ago and took several centuries to build. (13) The Wall was 4,000 miles long when it was done. (14) Only about half is still standing.

(15) People from Europe, Aisha, Africa, and other places visit us. (16) They travel Amereeca from east to west. (17) They marvel at New York City's bright lights and the stilness of our redwood forests.

(18) Sometimes I think I'll stay nearbye and see America, too. (19) I'll go to Washington, D.C., to see our founding father's greatest work, our Constitution. (20) It's true. (21) This land was made for you and me.

1 What change, if any, should be made in sentence 1?

   A Change *tourist's* to **toorist's**
   B Change *invitashun* to **invitation**
   C Change *anywhere* to **anyware**
   D Make no change

2 What change, if any, should be made in sentence 2?

   F Change *Every one* to **Everyone**
   G Change *mention* to **mencion**
   H Change *place* to **playce**
   J Make no change

3 What change, if any, should be made in sentence 7?

   A Change *Australia* to **Australya**
   B Change *fishs'* to **fish's**
   C Change *enjoyment* to **enjoiment**
   D Make no change

4 What change, if any, should be made in sentence 10?

   F Change *constellation* to **constellasion**
   G Change *Earth* to **Erth**
   H Change *darkness* to **darkiness**
   J Make no change

5 What change, if any, should be made in sentence 11?

   A Change *fiction* to **fikshun**
   B Change *Chineze* to **Chinese**
   C Change *finish* to **finash**
   D Make no change

6 What change should be made in sentence 15?

   F Change *Europe* to **Yurope**
   G Change *Aisha* to **Asha**
   H Change *Aisha* to **Asia**
   J Change *Africa* to **Afrika**

7 What change should be made in sentence 16?

   A Change *Amereeca* to **Amereeka**
   B Change *Amereeca* to **America**
   C Change *east* to **eest**
   D Change *west* to **wests**

8 What change, if any, should be made in sentence 17?

   F Change *New York* to **Nu York**
   G Change *City's* to **Sity's**
   H Change *stilness* to **stillness**
   J Make no change

9 What change, if any, should be made in sentence 18?

   A Change *Sometimes* to **Sumtimes**
   B Change *nearbye* to **nearby**
   C Change *America* to **Ameerica**
   D Make no change

10 What change should be made in sentence 19?

   F Change *Washington* to **Washingten**
   G Change *father's* to **fathers'**
   H Change *Constitution* to **Constitushun**
   J Change *Constitution* to **Constitucion**

STOP

Grammar, Usage, and Mechanics
Adverbs

An **adverb** that ends in **-ly** usually tells about a verb. It tells how something is done or how often it is done.

The actor walked **quietly** across the stage.

The hare ran **quickly**.

Slowly but **surely,** the tortoise won the race.

Practice Activity

A. Write the adverb in each sentence below.
   1. Someone carelessly left a shoe on the floor.
   2. Tawana smiled cheerfully at the audience.
   3. People are sleeping, so talk softly.
   4. George packed his suitcase carefully.
   5. With trembling hands, I excitedly opened the huge envelope.

B. Which sentences contain adverbs? Write the adverb you see in each sentence. Write **no** if a sentence has no adverb.
   6. The audience cheered loudly for both teams.
   7. I love staying in this quiet library.
   8. Your brother's watch ticks noisily.
   9. The door slammed suddenly and startled me.
   10. The delicious aroma filled the room completely.

The Writing Process: Persuasive
Writing a Letter to the Editor

PREWRITING
One way to share your opinions about current events is to write a letter to the editor of a newspaper. Think about an article you have read. Why did you agree or disagree with the information presented? Be sure to research and organize your response with facts to support your opinion. As you think about your letter, make an outline of the facts you learn.

DRAFTING
Use your outline to write a letter to the editor. Begin with a topic sentence that presents the main idea. Follow your outline as you write supporting sentences. Use as many spelling words as possible. If you don't know how to spell a word, make your best guess. You will be able to revise your letter later.

REVISING
When you have finished your first draft, read your letter from beginning to end. Check to see if you have included all of the points in your outline. Does each sentence support the topic? Now use a word processor to key your final draft.

EDITING
Use the **Editing Checklist** to proofread your letter to the editor. Circle three words that may be misspelled. Use an electronic resource to check the spelling.

PUBLISHING
Make a copy of your letter and share it with your readers. Have an adult help you mail it to the editor of a newspaper.

EDITING CHECKLIST

Spelling
- ✓ Circle words that contain the spelling patterns and rules learned in Units 31–35.
- ✓ Check the circled words in your **Spelling Dictionary**.
- ✓ Check for other spelling errors.

Capital Letters
- ✓ Capitalize important words in the title.
- ✓ Capitalize the first word in each sentence.
- ✓ Capitalize proper nouns.

Punctuation
- ✓ End each sentence with the correct punctuation.
- ✓ Use commas, apostrophes, and quotation marks correctly.

Grammar, Usage, and Mechanics
- ✓ Use adverbs that end in **-ly** correctly to tell about verbs.

TEKS 4.22D Use spelling patterns and rules and print and electronic resources to determine and check correct spellings.

Spelling and the
Writing Process

Writing anything—a friendly letter, a paper for school—usually follows a process. The writing process has five steps. It might look like this if you tried to draw a picture of it:

Part of the writing process forms a loop. That is because not every writing task is the same. It is also because writers often jump back and forth between the steps as they change their minds and think of new ideas.

Here is a description of each step:

PREWRITING This is thinking and planning ahead to help you write.

DRAFTING This means writing your paper for the first time. You usually just try to get your ideas down on paper. You should spell correctly those words that you do know. Attempt to spell those that you don't. You can fix them later.

REVISING This means fixing your final draft. Here is where you rewrite, change, and add words.

EDITING This is where you feel you have said all you want to say. Now you proofread your paper for spelling errors and errors in grammar and punctuation. Be sure to use a print or online dictionary to check your spelling.

PUBLISHING This is making a copy of your writing and sharing it with your readers. Put your writing in a form that your readers will enjoy.

Confident spellers are better writers. Confident writers understand their own writing process better. Know how the five steps best fit the way you write.

Spelling and
Writing Ideas

Being a good speller can help make you a more confident writer. Writing often can make you a better writer. Here are some ideas to get you started.

Descriptive writing describes something.
You might...
- describe something very, very small and something very, very big.
- describe something from the point of view of one of your favorite book characters.
- describe a national monument you've seen.

Narrative writing tells a story.
You might...
- write a story about your first visit to someplace new.
- pretend to be a famous American and write a journal or diary entry as that person.
- write a friendly letter to your best friend.
- write a mystery story. Use an empty mansion as the setting for the events.

Persuasive writing tries to persuade the reader to think or do something.
You might...
- try to persuade your parents to get an exotic pet, such as a snake or a ferret.
- try to persuade your mayor to change a town law.
- try to persuade your classmates that the Internet is the best thing to happen to education and explain why.

Expository writing explains something.
You might...
- write a report about the cause and effect of watching television while studying.
- use the Internet to research and write a report about healthy eating habits.
- write a clear and detailed explanation of how to plan for a vacation.

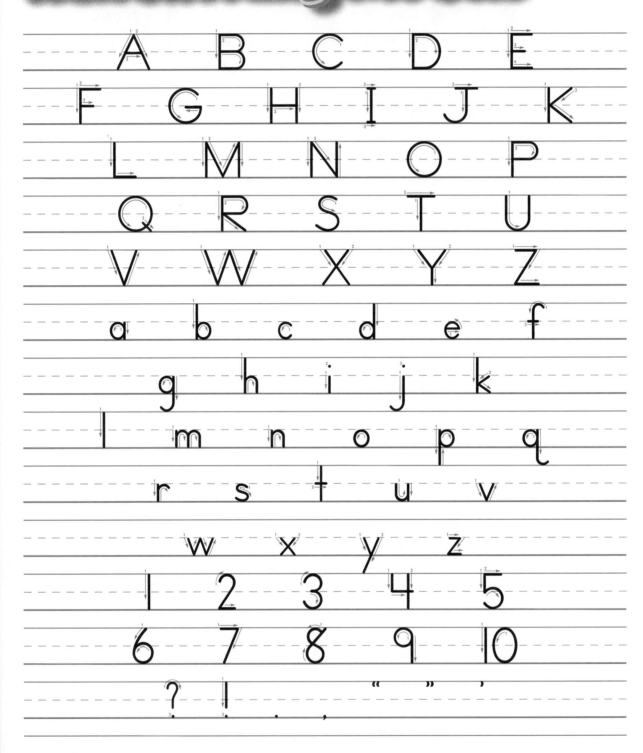

A B C D E
F G H I J K
L M N O P
Q R S T U
V W X Y Z

a b c d e f
g h i j k
l m n o p q
r s t u v
w x y z

1 2 3 4 5
6 7 8 9 10

? ! . , " " ,

Cursive Handwriting Models

A B C D E
F G H I J
K L M N O
P Q R S T
U V W X Y Z
a b c d e f
g h i j k
l m n o p q
r s t u v
w x y z
1 2 3 4 5
6 7 8 9 10
? ! . , " " '

High Frequency Writing Words

A

a
about
afraid
after
again
air
all
almost
also
always
am
America
an
and
animal
animals
another
any
anything
are
around
as
ask
asked
at
ate
away

B

baby
back
bad
ball
balloons
baseball

basketball
be
bear
beautiful
because
become
bed
been
before
being
believe
best
better
big
bike
black
boat
book
books
both
boy
boys
bring
broke
brother
build
bus
but
buy
by

C

call
called
came
can
candy

can't
car
care
cars
cat
catch
caught
change
charge
children
Christmas
circus
city
class
clean
clothes
come
comes
coming
could
couldn't
country
cut

D

Dad
day
days
decided
did
didn't
died
different
dinner
do
does
doesn't

dog
dogs
doing
done
don't
door
down
dream

E

each
earth
eat
eighth
else
end
enough
even
every
everybody
everyone
everything
except
eyes

F

family
fast
father
favorite
feel
feet
fell
few
field
fight

finally
find
fire
first
fish
five
fix
food
football
for
found
four
free
Friday
friend
friends
from
front
fun
funny
future

G

game
games
gas
gave
get
gets
getting
girl
girls
give
go
God
goes
going

good
got
grade
grader
great
ground
grow

 H

had
hair
half
happened
happy
hard
has
have
having
he
head
heard
help
her
here
he's
high
hill
him
his
hit
home
homework
hope
horse
horses
hot
hour
house

how
hurt

 I

I
I'd
if
I'm
important
in
into
is
it
its
it's

 J

job
jump
just

 K

keep
kept
kids
killed
kind
knew
know

 L

lady
land
last
later
learn
leave

left
let
let's
life
like
liked
likes
little
live
lived
lives
long
look
looked
looking
lost
lot
lots
love
lunch

 M

mad
made
make
making
man
many
math
may
maybe
me
mean
men
might
miss
Mom
money

more
morning
most
mother
mouse
move
Mr.
Mrs.
much
music
must
my
myself

 N

name
named
need
never
new
next
nice
night
no
not
nothing
now

 O

of
off
oh
OK
old
on
once
one

only
or
other
our
out
outside
over
own

P

parents
park
party
people
person
pick
place
planet
play
played
playing
police
president
pretty
probably
problem
put

R

ran
read
ready
real
really
reason
red
responsibilities

rest
ride
riding
right
room
rules
run
running

 S

said
same
saw
say
scared
school
schools
sea
second
see
seen
set
seventh
she
ship
shot
should
show
sick
since
sister
sit
sleep
small
snow
so

some
someone
something
sometimes
soon
space
sport
sports
start
started
states
stay
still
stop
stopped
store
story
street
stuff
such
sudden
suddenly
summer
sure
swimming

 T

take
talk
talking
teach
teacher
teachers
team
tell
than

Thanksgiving
that
that's
the
their
them
then
there
these
they
they're
thing
things
think
this
thought
three
through
throw
time
times
to
today
together
told
too
took
top
tree
trees
tried
trip
trouble
try
trying
turn
turned

TV
two

 U

united
until
up
upon
us
use
used

 V

very

 W

walk
walked
walking
want
wanted
war
was
wasn't
watch
water
way
we
week
weeks
well
went
were
what
when

where
which
while
white
who
whole
why
will
win
winter
wish
with
without
woke
won
won't
work
world
would
wouldn't

 Y

yard
year
years
yes
you
your
you're

Using the
Dictionary

Guide Words

The **guide words** at the top of each dictionary page can help you find the word you want quickly. The first guide word tells you the first word on that page. The second guide word tells you the last word on that page. The entries on the page fall in alphabetical order between these two guide words.

Entries

Words you want to check in the dictionary are called **entries**. Entries provide a lot of information besides the correct spelling. Look at the sample entry below.

Tips for Finding a Word in a Dictionary

- Practice using guide words in a dictionary. Think of words to spell. Then use the guide words to find each word's entry. Do this again and again until you can use guide words easily.

- Some spellings are listed with the base word. To find **easiest,** you would look up **easy.** To find **remaining,** you would look up **remain.** To find **histories,** you would look up **history.**

- If you do not know how to spell a word, guess the spelling before looking it up. Try to find the first three letters of the word. (If you use just the first letter, it will probably take too long to find the word.)

- If you can't find a word, think of how else it might be spelled. For example, if a word starts with the /**k**/ sound, the spelling might begin with **k, c,** or even **ch.**

entry the correct spelling, sometimes broken into syllables

pronunciation

other spellings other word forms, including plurals, that change the spelling of the base word

po•ny /pō′ nē/ *n.* (**po•nies** *pl.*) a kind of horse that is small in size when fully grown. *Children ride a pony at an amusement park.*

definition to be sure you have the correct entry word

sample sentence to make the definition clearer

-able or **-ible** a Latin suffix that means "capable of": *arguable.*

a•ble /ā′ bəl/ *adj.* having power, skill, or talent. *With practice you will be able to play the piano.*

a•bol•ish /ə bŏl′ ĭsh/ *v.* to put an end to. *The speaker urged us to abolish poverty.* [Latin *abolescere* die out]

a•bout /ə bout′/ *adv.* somewhere near. *She guessed it was about seven o'clock.*

ac•tor /ăk′ tər/ *n.* a person who acts on the stage, in motion pictures, on radio, or on television. *A good actor can make people laugh or cry.*

ad•di•tion[1] /ə dĭsh′ ən/ *n.* the adding of one number to another to get a total. *2 + 2 = 4 is an example of addition.*

ad•di•tion[2] /ə dĭsh′ ən/ *adj.* having to do with adding numbers: *an addition problem.*

Af•ri•ca /ăf′ rĭ kə/ *n.* a large continent that lies south of Europe. *The explorer visited jungles and deserts in Africa.*

age /āj/ *n.* number of years old. *The baby's age is now two years.*

a•gree /ə grē′/ *v.* to have the same opinion. *We all agree that Mr. Jansen would make a good mayor.*

a•gree•ment /ə grē′ mənt/ *n.* an arrangement or understanding between two persons or groups. *The students came to an agreement about the best day for the litter cleanup.*

a•head /ə hĕd′/ *adv.* in advance; in front. *Dad walked ahead to look for a campsite.*

aim /ām/ *v.* to point at; to direct toward. *Aim the arrow at the center of the target.*

air•less /âr′ lĭs/ *adj.* having no air. *They sealed the important document in airless packaging.*

air mail /âr′ māl′/ *n.* mail carried by airplanes. *The air mail is placed in special bags.*

a•larm /ə lärm′/ *n.* a warning signal that danger is near. *The alarm went off moments after the fire started.*

a•larm clock /ə lärm′ klŏk′/ *n.* a clock that can be set to ring or buzz at a certain time. *My alarm clock wakes me up at seven every morning.*

a•live /ə līv′/ *adj.* living; not dead. *People sometimes forget that trees are alive.*

al•li•ga•tor /ăl′ ĭ gā′ tər/ *n.* a large reptile with a narrow body, short legs, long tail, and thick skin. *Alligators live in warm, swampy areas.* [Spanish *el lagarto,* the lizard.]

al•low•ance /ə lou′ əns/ *n.* a definite amount of money given regularly for spending. *Chang is saving his allowance to buy a basketball.*

a•lone /ə lōn′/ *adv.* without anyone else. *The box was too heavy for one person to lift alone. adj.* apart from others. *I am alone.*

al•read•y /ôl rĕd′ ē/ *adv.* by this time; before. *We stopped to visit, but they had already left.*

al•so /ôl′ sō/ *adv.* too; in addition; likewise. *Geraniums grow well not only in flowerpots, but also in gardens.*

A•mer•i•ca /ə mĕr′ ĭ kə/ *n.* the continents of the western hemisphere; North and South America. *The United States of America is often called America.*

A•mer•i•can[1] /ə mĕr′ ĭ kən/ *n.* one born or living in America. *A citizen of the United States is an American.*

A•mer•i•can[2] /ə mĕr′ ĭ kən/ *adj.* of or from the United States. *The American flag is red, white, and blue.*

a•mount /ə mount′/ *n.* the total or sum. *We raised the amount of money needed for the books.*

a•muse /ə myōōz′/ *v.* **a.** to entertain. *Parents can amuse their children by reading them stories.* **b.** to cause to laugh or smile. *The monkey's antics amused the passers-by.*

-an a Latin suffix that means "of, relating to, or resembling": *Mexican.*

an•chor /ăng′ kər/ *n.* a heavy object that keeps boats from drifting away. *We lowered the anchor so our boat wouldn't drift overnight.*

anchor

an•gle /ăng′ gəl/ *n.* the figure formed by two lines that come together in a point. *The teacher drew an angle on the chalkboard.*

an•kle /ăng′ kəl/ *n.* the joint connecting the foot with the leg. *My new sneakers are high enough to cover my ankles.*

an•swer /ăn′ sər/ *n.* **a.** a reply. *I must send my answer to her letter quickly.* **b.** a solution. *I know the answer to that math problem.*

Ant•arc•ti•ca /ănt ärk′ tĭ kə/ *n.* the continent at the South Pole. *The coldest continent on the earth is Antarctica.*

an•te•lope /ăn′ tl ōp′/ *n.* (**an•te•lope** or **an•te•lopes** *pl.*) an animal with horns that face upward and backward. *While we were in Montana, we saw an antelope roaming.*

an•y•bod•y /ĕn′ ē bŏd ē/ or /ĕn′ ē bŭd ē/ *pron.* any person. *Did you see anybody that I know at the meeting?*

an•y•thing /ĕn′ ē thĭng′/ *pron.* any thing; something. *We couldn't find anything for Grandma's birthday.*

an•y•way /ĕn′ ē wā/ *adv.* no matter what may happen; anyhow. *It may rain tomorrow, but we are going to have the picnic anyway.*

an•y•where /ĕn′ ē hwâr′/ *adv.* at or to any place. *If you're going anywhere near a hardware store, bring me some nails.*

a•part /ə pärt′/ *adv.* to pieces; in separate pieces. *The puzzle fell apart when it slipped off the table.*

a•part•ment /ə pärt′ mənt/ *n.* a group of rooms to live in, generally in a building housing more than one family. *They live in an apartment on the second floor.*

a•pol•o•gy /ə pŏl′ ə jē/ *n.* (**a•pol•o•gies** *pl.*) words saying one is sorry; asking pardon. *Please accept my apology for coming so late; I was delayed by heavy traffic.*

ap•pear /ə pîr′/ *v.* **a.** to show up; to be seen. *He appeared for breakfast promptly at seven o'clock.* **b.** to seem; to give an appearance. *She appeared to like the suggestion.*

Apr. April.

A•pril /ā′ prəl/ *n.* the fourth month of the year. *We should have some warmer weather in April.*

a•quar•i•um /ə kwâr′ ē əm/ *n.* (**a•quar•i•ums** or **a•quar•i•a** *pl.*) a tank or bowl in which fish, water animals, or water plants are kept. *Jordan bought live plants for his aquarium.*

Pronunciation Key

ă	pat	ŏ	pot	th	thin
ā	pay	ō	toe	*th*	*th*is
âr	care	ô	paw, for	hw	which
ä	father	oi	noise	zh	vision
ĕ	pet	ou	out	ə	about,
ē	be	ŏŏ	took		item,
ĭ	pit	ōō	boot		pencil,
ī	pie	ŭ	cut		gallop,
îr	pier	ûr	urge		circus

arch /ärch/ *n.* (**arch•es** *pl.*) **a.** a curved opening or structure that looks like an upside-down **U**. *The arch in the window is a design feature.* **b.** the curved section of the foot. *The arch of the foot is formed by a band of tissue that connects the heel bone to the toes.*

ar•gue /är′ gyōō/ *v.* (**ar•gues, ar•gued, ar•gu•ing**) **a.** to disagree; to dispute; to quarrel. *Tanya often argues with Michael.* **b.** to give reasons for or against. *The lawyer argued her case effectively.* (**ar•gu•a•ble** *adj.*)

ar•gu•ment /är′ gyə mənt/ *n.* **a.** a quarrel or disagreement. *Rob had an argument with his coach.* **b.** a statement that is supposed to prove a point. *Carmen's last argument was the most convincing.*

ar•my /är′ mē/ *n.* (**ar•mies** *pl.*) a large body of people organized and trained for warfare or a task. *There was an army of teachers to help with the science fair.*

ar•rive /ə rīv′/ *v.* (**ar•rives, ar•rived, ar•riv•ing**) **a.** to come to a particular place; to reach a destination. *When will you arrive at the airport?* **b.** to come. *The big day finally arrived.*

art•ist /är′ tĭst/ *n.* **a.** a person who is skilled in any of the fine arts, especially painting or music. *Picasso was a great artist.* **b.** any skillful or creative person. *A gourmet cook is an artist in the kitchen.*

A•sia /ā′ zhə/ *n.* the large continent that lies east of Europe. *The largest continent on Earth is Asia.*

at•ten•tion /ə tĕn′ shən/ *n.* **a.** staying alert to what is happening. *Always pay attention in class.* **b.** thoughtfulness; consideration. *Rhonda gives her grandparents a lot of attention.*

auc•tion /ôk′ shən/ *n.* a public sale at which property is sold to the highest bidder. *Mrs. Evans bought an antique vase at the auction.*

au•di•ence /ô′ dē əns/ *n.* **a.** a number of people who come together to see or hear something: *the audience in the theater.* **b.** all of the persons who can see or hear something: *television audience.* [Latin *audire,* to hear.]

au•di•o¹ /ô′ dē ō′/ *adj.* relating to sound. *Because of a problem with the audio equipment, we missed the last song.*

au•di•o² /ô′ dē ō′/ *n.* (**au•di•os** *pl.*) the sending, copying, or receiving of sounds. *The new speakers improved the audio of my stereo.*

Aug. August.

Au•gust /ô′ gəst/ *n.* the eighth month of the year. *August has thirty-one days.*

Aus•tra•lia /ô strāl′ yə/ *n.* (**Aus•tra•li•an** *n.*) the island continent between the Pacific and Indian oceans. *At the zoo we saw a kangaroo from Australia.*

au•thor /ô′ thər/ *n.* the writer of a book, story, article, etc.; a writer. *The author sent us a copy of her book.*

av•er•age /ăv′ ər ĭj/ or /ăv′ rĭj/ *adj.* common; ordinary; usual. *Today was just an average day; nothing exciting happened.*

a•void /ə void′/ *v.* to stay away from; to keep from meeting. *I avoided him when he had the measles.*

a•ware /ə wâr′/ *adj.* alert to; knowing; conscious of. *Are you aware that you are late to school?*

a•way /ə wā′/ *adv.* **a.** from a place; to a different place. *Our dog ran away last week.* **b.** aside; out of the way. *He put the dishes away after supper.*

aw•ful /ô′ fəl/ *adj.* very bad; very ugly; unpleasant. *That was an awful movie.*

a•while /ə hwīl′/ *adv.* for a short time. *Let's rest awhile before we continue driving.*

ba•by•sit•ter /bā′ bē sĭt′ ər/ *n.* one who takes care of young children. *John's mother called a babysitter to stay with him while she was out.*

badge /băj/ *n.* something worn to show that a person is a member of a group or organization. *Each firefighter wore a badge.*

bag•gage /băg′ ĭj/ *n.* suitcases; luggage. *Airline passengers may pick up their baggage inside the terminal.*

bak•er /bā′ kər/ *n.* a person who makes and sells breads and pastries. *We ordered a special birthday cake from the baker.*

baker

bal•loon /bə lo͞on′/ *n.* a brightly colored rubber bag that can be filled with air or gas and used as a toy. *Can you blow up this balloon?*

ban•jo /băn′ jō/ *n.* (**ban•jos** or **ban•joes** *pl.*) a musical instrument with a drumlike body, a long neck, and usually, four or five strings which may be plucked or strummed. *A banjo is similar to a guitar.*

bank•er /băng′ kər/ *n.* a person who owns or runs a bank. *We talked to the banker about opening a savings account.*

bar•ber /bär′ bər/ *n.* a person who cuts and trims hair. *My brother went to the barber to get his hair cut today.*

bare /bâr/ *adj.* **a.** not wearing clothes; not covered. *Should you be walking outside in your bare feet?* **b.** without a covering. *The floor is bare because the rug is being cleaned.*

➤ **Bare** sounds like **bear.**

bas•ket•ball /**băs′** kĭt bôl′/ *n.* **a.** a game in which points are scored by throwing a ball through a basket. *Basketball is usually played indoors.* **b.** the ball used in this game. *Our basketball had lost all its air.*

bat•tle /**băt′** l/ *n.* a fight between armies, navies, etc., during a war. *That battle was the turning point of the war.*

beat•en /**bēt′** n/ *v.* (beats, beat, beat•en, beat•ing) mixed rapidly with a utensil. *The eggs were beaten for the recipe.*

beau•ti•ful /**byoo′** tə fəl/ *adj.* having beauty; pleasing to the eye, ear, or mind; lovely: *a beautiful painting.*

beau•ty /**byoo′** tē/ *n.* (beau•ties *pl.*) the quality that makes a person or thing pleasing to the senses. *The beauty of the music made us forget everything else.*

be•came /bĭ **kām′**/ *v.* past tense of **become**.

be•cause /bĭ **kôz′**/ *conj.* for the reason that. *I study because I want to learn.*

be•come /bĭ **kŭm′**/ *v.* (be•comes, be•came, be•come, be•com•ing) to come to be. *The weather will become warmer in spring.*

be•fore /bĭ **fôr′**/ *prep.* at an earlier time than. *I had to be home before six o'clock.*

be•gan /bĭ **găn′**/ *v.* past tense of **begin**.

be•gin /bĭ **gĭn′**/ *v.* (be•gins, be•gan, be•gun, be•gin•ning) to start. *We will begin our school day with a math lesson.*

be•gun /bĭ **gŭn′**/ *v.* past participle of **begin**; started. *We waited to be seated because the play had already begun.*

be•lief /bĭ **lēf′**/ *n.* something accepted as true. *It was a common belief that Earth was flat.*

beliefs /bĭ **lēfs′**/ *n.* plural of **belief**.

be•lieve /bĭ **lēv′**/ *v.* (be•lieves, be•lieved, be•liev•ing) to accept something as true or real. *Do you believe that cats have nine lives?*

be•low /bĭ **lō′**/ *prep.* in a lower place than; to a lower place than. *Kansas is below Nebraska on the map.*

be•neath /bĭ **nēth′**/ *prep.* under; lower than. *I sat beneath the tree.*

be•ret /bə **rā′**/ *n.* a round, soft, flat cap of wool or felt. *She wore her beret tilted at a jaunty angle.* [French *béret*.]

be•side /bĭ **sīd′**/ *prep.* at the side of; near to. *The carton was left beside the trash can.*

be•tween /bĭ **twēn′**/ *prep.* in the space that separates two things. *There were four people between me and the door.*

bev•er•age /**bĕv′** ər ĭj/ or /**bĕv′** rĭj/ *n.* something to drink. *Does a beverage come with our meal?*

be•ware /bĭ **wâr′**/ *v.* to be cautious of. *Beware of the undertow when you swim in the ocean.*

bi•cy•cle[1] /**bī′** sĭk′ əl/ or /-sĭ kəl/ *n.* a vehicle having two wheels mounted on a light metal frame with a seat for the rider, a bar for steering, and pedals turned by the feet. *Riding a bicycle requires a good sense of balance.*

bi•cy•cle[2] /**bī′** sĭk′ əl/ or /-sĭ kəl/ or /-**sī′** kəl/ *v.* (bi•cy•cles, bi•cy•cled, bi•cy•cling) to ride or travel by bicycle. *How far can you bicycle?*

bi•month•ly /bī **mŭnth′** lē/ *adj.* **a.** occurring once every two months: *a bimonthly magazine.* **b.** occurring twice a month: *bimonthly meetings.*

bis•cuit /**bĭs′** kĭt/ *n.* a type of bread that is often hard and crisp. *Would you like toast or a biscuit with your tea?*

bit•ter /**bĭt′** ər/ *adj.* tasting sharp and unpleasant. *Do you think black walnuts have a bitter taste?*

bi•week•ly /bī **wēk′** lē/ *adj.* **a.** occurring once every two weeks: *a biweekly paycheck.* **b.** occurring twice a week: *biweekly classes.*

black•en /**blăk′** ən/ *v.* to make black or dark. *Use a pencil to blacken the circle that matches the correct answer.*

blame[1] /blām/ *v.* (blames, blamed, blam•ing) to put the responsibility for something bad on a person or thing. *Don't blame yourself; it wasn't your fault.*

blame² /blām/ *n.* responsibility for a fault. *The pilot put the blame for the delay on the fog.*

blan•ket /**blăng′** kĭt/ *n.* a heavy woven piece of cloth used to keep one warm. *I sleep under a wool blanket in the winter.*

blight /blīt/ *n.* a disease or injury to plants. *The blight killed our crop last year.*

blue•ber•ry /**bloo′** bĕr′ ē/ *n.* (**blue•ber•ries** *pl.*) the edible blue or blackish berry of any of several plants of the heath family. *A blueberry is a type of fruit.*

blu•est /**bloo′** ĭst/ *adj.* (**blue, blu•er**) the superlative form of **blue**. being of the truest shade of blue. *Her eyes are the bluest I have ever seen.*

blush /blŭsh/ *v.* to become red in the face. *Your flattery makes me blush.*

boast /bōst/ *v.* to brag; to talk too much about yourself and about what you can do. *Judy likes to boast about how fast she can run.*

boast•ful /bōst′ fəl/ *adj.* liking to brag. *It is better to be humble than it is to be boastful.*

boil /boil/ *v.* **a.** to bubble and send out steam. *When water is heated enough, it boils.* **b.** to heat a liquid until bubbles rise. *He boiled the soup.* **c.** to cook in boiling water. *My mother boiled eggs for breakfast.*

bold /bōld/ *adj.* not afraid to face danger; brave and daring. *The bold gymnast attempted a difficult vault.* (**bold•ly** *adv.*)

bold•ness /bōld′ nĭs/ *n.* the state of being bold; bravery; daring. *We were surprised by the boldness of the fawn in leaving its safe hiding place.*

bo•nus /bō′ nəs/ *n.* (**bo•nus•es** *pl.*) something given in addition to what is usual or expected. *Students who read extra books were given a bonus.*

both•er /bŏth′ ər/ *v.* to give trouble to. *Don't bother me while I am writing.*

bot•tle¹ /bŏt′ l/ *n.* a holder for liquids. *I think juice tastes better from a glass bottle than from a can.*

bot•tle² /bŏt′ l/ *v.* (**bot•tles, bot•tled, bot•tling**) to put into bottles. *Milk must be bottled under very clean conditions.* —**idiom. bottle up.** to remain quiet and restrained.

bought /bôt/ *v.* past tense of **buy**.

boun•ti•ful /**boun′** tə fəl/ *adj.* given or provided abundantly. *Our Thanksgiving meal was quite bountiful.*

bowl /bōl/ *n.* a round, deep dish. *Soup is usually served in a bowl.*

brag /brăg/ *v.* (**brags, bragged, brag•ging**) to boast; to talk too much about how good you are or how much you have. *Charles often brags about his new radio.*

brain /brān/ *n.* the mass of nerve tissue in the skull that controls the body and stores knowledge. *Your brain constantly tells your heart to beat.*

brake /brāk/ *n.* a thing that slows down or stops a car, a machine, a bicycle, etc. *The driver pressed on the brake when the traffic light turned red.*
➤ **Brake** sounds like **break**.

bread /brĕd/ *n.* a food baked from dough made with flour or meal. *Sandwiches are made with bread.*

break /brāk/ *v.* (**breaks, broke, bro•ken, break•ing**) to come apart; to separate into pieces. *The dish will break if it falls on the floor.*
➤ **Break** sounds like **brake**.

break•fast /brĕk′ fəst/ *n.* the first meal of the day. *Jim ate a good breakfast of orange juice, cereal, toast, and milk.*

breakfast

breed /brēd/ *n.* a group of related animals or plants with visibly similar characteristics. *Our dog is of pure breed; he is one hundred percent Labrador.*

breeze /brēz/ *n.* a light, gentle wind. *The flag barely moved in the breeze.*

brick /brĭk/ *n.* a block of baked clay used for building or paving. *Many houses and apartment buildings are built with bricks.*

bridge /brĭj/ *n.* a structure built over a river or a valley for people or vehicles to cross. *Thousands of cars cross the Golden Gate Bridge every day.*

brief /brēf/ *adj.* short; quick; direct. *Our meeting was brief.*

bright•en /brīt′ ən/ *v.* to lighten; to make or become bright. *The lamp will brighten the living room.*

bright•ness /brīt′ nĭs/ *n.* the state or quality of shining or giving light. *The moon's brightness made it easy to see at night.*

bring /brĭng/ *v.* (**brings, brought, bring•ing**) to take along. *Be sure to bring a gift to our party.*

Brit•ain /brĭt′ ən/ *n.* the country that includes England, Scotland, and Wales. *Britain is separated from the rest of Europe by the English Channel.*

Brit•ish[1] /brĭt′ ĭsh/ *adj.* of or from Britain. *British woolens are famous for their fine quality.*

Brit•ish[2] /brĭt′ ĭsh/ *n.* the people of Britain. *The British drive on the left side of the road.*

brit•tle /brĭt′ l/ *adj.* (**brit•tler, brit•tlest**) easily broken, cracked, or snapped. *Leaves are very brittle in the autumn.*

broth•er /brŭth′ ər/ *n.* a boy or man having the same parents as another person. *The girl had three older brothers and one younger sister.*

brought /brôt/ *v.* past tense of **bring**.

bub•ble[1] /bŭb′ əl/ *n.* a thin, round film of liquid that forms a ball around a pocket of gas or air. *The slightest touch can pop a bubble.*

bub•ble[2] /bŭb′ əl/ *v.* (**bub•bles, bub•bled, bub•bling**) to form bubbles. *The soup will bubble when it is hot.*

build /bĭld/ *v.* (**builds, built, build•ing**) to make; to put together. *Doug wants to build a model house out of toothpicks.*

build•er /bĭl′ dər/ *n.* a person whose business is putting up buildings. *My uncle is a builder working on the new school buildings.*

built /bĭlt/ *v.* past tense of **build**.

buoy•ant /boi′ ənt/ or /bōō′ yənt/ *adj.* capable of floating. *You should wear a life jacket because it is buoyant; it will help you float.*

bur•den /bûr′ dn/ *n.* something that is carried; a load. *Carrying all of these books to school every day is a burden on my back.*

burnt /bûrnt/ *v.* (**burns, burned** or **burnt, burning**) was on fire; affected by or as if by fire; blazed. *I burnt my hand on the hot stove.*

burst /bûrst/ *v.* (**bursts, burst, burst•ing**) to break open suddenly. *The balloon will burst if it touches the hot light.* —*idiom.* **burst a bubble**. to correct an innocent falsehood.

but•ton[1] /bŭt′ n/ *n.* a small, flat, hard, round piece used to fasten two parts of a garment by fitting through a slit. *The top button on my coat is loose.*

but•ton[2] /bŭt′ n/ *v.* to fasten with buttons. *I buttoned my shirt.*

buy /bī/ *v.* (**buys, bought, buy•ing**) to purchase. *Sally needs to buy a new pair of shoes before winter.*

cab•bage /kăb′ ĭj/ *n.* a vegetable with thick leaves growing tightly together in a solid ball. *Cabbage can be eaten raw or cooked.*

cal•en•dar /kăl′ ən dər/ *n.* a table or chart used to keep track of days, weeks, and months. *We must remember to change our classroom calendar on the first day of the month.*

calf /kăf/ *n.* (**calves** *pl.*) a young cow or bull. *A calf can walk soon after it is born.*

Cal•i•for•nia /kăl′ ə fôr′ nyə/ or /-fôr′ nē ə/ *n.* a state in the southwestern United States. *California borders on the Pacific Ocean; its capital is Sacramento.*

calm /käm/ *adj.* quiet; peaceful; motionless. *There wasn't even a breeze on that calm evening.*

calm•est /käm′ əst/ *adj.* (**calm, calmer**) quietest, most peaceful, or most motionless. *The baby was calmest when her mother held her.*

cam•er•a /kăm′ ər ə/ or /kăm′ rə/ *n.* a machine for taking photographs or motion pictures. *Is there film in your camera?*

camp•er /kăm′ pər/ *n.* **a.** a person who lives outdoors for a period of time, usually in a tent. *The campers pitched their tent next to a stream.* **b.** a van or trailer equipped for camping. *The family moved into the camper as the storm approached.*

Can•a•da /kăn′ ə də/ *n.* the country north of the United States. *Canada is larger than the United States, but it has fewer people.*

Ca•na•di•an¹ /kə nā′ dē ən/ *adj.* of or from Canada. *Many U.S. hockey teams have Canadian players.*

Ca•na•di•an² /kə nā′ dē ən/ *n.* one born or living in Canada. *Many Canadian people speak French.*

cap•i•tal /kăp′ ĭ tl/ *n.* **a.** the city or town where the government of a country or a state is located. *Washington, D.C., is the capital of the United States.* **b.** an uppercase letter in writing or printing. *You begin a sentence with a capital.*

➤ **Capital** sounds like **capitol**.

cap•i•tal•i•za•tion /kăp′ ĭ tl ĭ zā′ shən/ *n.* the process of writing or printing in capital letters. *Do you know the rules of punctuation and capitalization?*

cap•i•tol /kăp′ ĭ tl/ *n.* a building in which the representatives and senators of a state or country meet. *A committee of senators and representatives met in the capitol to discuss the tax plan.*

➤ **Capitol** sounds like **capital**.

ca•reer /kə rîr′/ *n.* a profession; a chosen occupation. *She hopes to pursue a career in marine biology.*

care•ful /kâr′ fəl/ *adj.* cautious; full of care. *Be careful when you cross the busy street.*

care•less /kâr′ lĭs/ *adj.* reckless; not cautious. *You can't afford to be careless with matches.*

car•pet /kär′ pĭt/ *n.* a thick, heavy fabric for covering a floor. *I have a new carpet in my room.*

cart /kärt/ *n.* **a.** a two-wheeled vehicle pulled by a horse or other animal. *The pony pulled a cart in the parade.* **b.** a small vehicle moved by hand. *I will push the grocery cart.*

case /kās/ *n.* a large box; a container. *The music teacher carries her violin in a case.*

catch /kăch/ *or* /kĕch/ *v.* (**catch•es, caught, catch•ing**) **a.** to capture. *I can catch the kitten before it runs outside.* **b.** to reach in time. *We can catch the train at the next stop.*

catch•er /kăch′ ər/ *n.* one who catches, especially the player behind home plate in a baseball game. *The catcher can tell the pitcher which pitch to throw.*

cat•fish /kăt′ fĭsh′/ *n.* (**cat•fish** or **cat•fish•es** *pl.*) a fish that has long whiskerlike feelers around its mouth. *We caught a catfish in the lake in the park.*

cat•tle /kăt′ l/ *n.* cows, bulls, or oxen. *The cattle eat grass in the pasture.*

cattle

caught /kôt/ *v.* past tense of **catch**.

cau•tion /kô′ shən/ *n.* careful attention to avoid risk or danger. *Everyone should cross a busy street with caution.*

cell /sĕl/ *n.* the smallest part of an organism. *The human body is made up millions of cells.*

cel•lar /sĕl′ ər/ *n.* an underground room, used for storage. *The family next door fixed up the cellar as a playroom for their children.*

➤ **Cellar** sounds like **seller**.

cer•tain /sûr′ tn/ *adj.* confident; sure; convinced. *She was certain you would win.* (**cer•tain•ly** *adv.*)

change /chānj/ *v.* (**chang•es, changed, chang•ing**) to make or become different. *She changed her mind.*

charge¹ /chärj/ *v.* **a.** to ask for as payment. *That store will charge two dollars for that notebook.* **b.** to postpone payment on by recording the amount owed. *Charge the groceries to my account.*

charge² /chärj/ *n.* **a.** an amount asked or made as payment. *There is no charge for this service.* **b.** care; supervision: the scientist in charge of the project.

charm /chärm/ *v.* to delight; to please. *The child's smile charmed the audience.*

chart[1] /chärt/ *n.* information given in the form of graphs, maps, and tables. *Newspapers often print weather charts.* (**chart•a•ble** *adj.*)

chart[2] /chärt/ *v.* to make a map or diagram of. *My job is to chart our class's spelling progress.*

cheer[1] /chîr/ *n.* happiness; comfort. *A fire in the fireplace brings warmth and cheer to the room.*

cheer[2] /chîr/ *v.* to shout words of approval; to encourage by yelling. *We all cheered for our star player as he came on the field.*

cheer•ful /chîr′ fəl/ *adj.* happy; joyful. *Kari gave a cheerful smile.*

cheese /chēz/ *n.* a food made from the thick part of milk. *I like sandwiches made with cheese.*

chief /chēf/ *n.* a leader; a head of a tribe or group. *The chief leads the tribal council.*

child /chīld/ *n.* (**chil•dren** *pl.*) a young boy or girl. *Corey is the only child absent today.*

chil•dren /chĭl′ drən/ *n.* plural of **child**.

Chi•nese[1] /chī nēz′/ *adj.* of or from China. *Our city's zoo has a Chinese panda.*

Chi•nese[2] /chī nēz′/ *n.* **a.** the people of China. *Many Chinese live in rural areas.* **b.** the language of China. *Mr. Chang can speak Chinese.*

choice /chois/ *n.* a decision; a selection. *For dinner we will go to a restaurant of your choice.*

choose /chōōz/ *v.* (**choos•es, chose, cho•sen, choos•ing**) to select; to decide upon; to pick. *I will let you choose which color you would like.*

chose /chōz/ *v.* past tense of **choose**.

cho•sen /chō′ zən/ *v.* past participle of **choose**.

circ a Latin root that means "around": *circulate.*

cir•cle /sûr′ kəl/ *n.* a closed curve that forms a perfectly round figure. *Every part of a circle is the same distance from the center.*

cir•cu•late /sûr′ kyə lāt′/ *v.* (**cir•cu•lates, cir•cu•lat•ed, cir•cu•lat•ing**) to move in a regular path back to a starting point. *The blood circulates throughout the body and returns to the heart.*

cit•y /sĭt′ ē/ *n.* (**cit•ies** *pl.*) a large and important town. *Some large cities in the United States are New York, Chicago, Los Angeles, Philadelphia, and Detroit.*

clear[1] /klîr/ *adj.* **a.** having no clouds; bright. *The sun shone in the clear sky.* **b.** distinct; not fuzzy. *I cannot get a clear picture on this TV station.*

clear[2] /klîr/ *v.* (**clears, cleared, clear•ing**) **a.** to get approval. *Let me clear that idea with the boss.* **b.** to get rid of obstructions. *Please clear the table before we eat.*

Pronunciation Key

ă	pat	ŏ	pot	th	**thin**
ā	pay	ō	toe	*th*	**this**
âr	care	ô	paw, for	hw	**which**
ä	father	oi	noise	zh	vision
ĕ	pet	ou	**out**	ə	about,
ē	be	ŏŏ	took		item,
ĭ	pit	ōō	boot		pencil,
ī	pie	ŭ	cut		gallop,
îr	pier	ûr	**ur**ge		circus

climb /klīm/ *v.* to go up, often using both hands and feet; to move on a steep slope. *The club members climb mountains all over the state.*

climb•er /klī′ mər/ *n.* one who climbs. *Her goal was to become a mountain climber.*

close /klōz/ *v.* (**clos•es, closed, clos•ing**) to shut. *Close the door when you leave.*

clos•er /klōs′ ər/ *adj.* (**close, clos•est**) nearer to something or someone than something else. *Let's go to the closer restaurant so we don't have to walk as far.*

clothes /klōz/ or /klō*th*z/ *n. pl.* garments; articles of dress; clothing. *Some people order all their clothes through a catalog.*

cloud•less /kloud′ lĭs/ *adj.* free of clouds; without clouds. *The cloudless sky was a brilliant blue.*

clue /klōō/ *n.* a piece of information that helps solve a problem or mystery. *In this game we use word clues to solve the puzzle.*

coast /kōst/ *n.* the seashore; land along the sea or ocean. *There are many beaches along the coast of the Pacific Ocean.*

coil /koil/ *v.* to wind in spirals or rings; to wind around and around. *The snake coiled around the log.*

col•lar /kŏl′ ər/ *n.* the part of a shirt or coat that circles the neck. *He loosened his tie and his collar.*

Col•o•ra•do /kŏl′ ə rä′ dō/ or /kol′ ə rä′ də/ *n.* a state in the western United States. *Colorado is in the heart of the Rocky Mountains.*

col•or•ful /kŭl′ ər fəl/ *adj.* having striking colors. *The colorful afghan has all my favorite colors: blue, red, and green.*

col•ors /kŭl′ ərz/ *n. pl.* (**col•or** *sing.*) hues, tints, or shades caused by the effect of light rays on the eyes. *All colors are combinations of red, yellow, and blue.*

comb¹ /kōm/ *n.* a tool with teeth, used to smooth or arrange the hair. *Most people carry a brush or comb.*

comb² /kōm/ *v.* to search carefully. *We will comb the room to find the contact lens.*

com•mand•er /kə măn′ dər/ *n.* a person who commands. *The superintendent of police is the commander of the police force.*

com•pa•ny /kŭm′ pə nē/ *n.* (**com•pa•nies** *pl.*) **a.** a group of people joined together for a common purpose; especially, a business. *Mr. Steel's company makes tractors.* **b.** friendship; society; association. *We enjoy each other's company.* **c.** guests. *We are having company for dinner.*

com•pare /kəm pâr′/ *v.* (**com•pares, com•pared, com•par•ing**) to examine things for similarities or differences. *If you compare prices, you can save money when you shop.* (**com•par•a•ble** *adj.*)

com•plete /kəm plēt′/ *adj.* **a.** having no parts lacking; full: *a complete set.* **b.** ended; finished. *The report will be complete tomorrow.* **c.** thorough; perfect: *a complete surprise.*

con•clu•sion /kən klōō′ zhən/ *n.* **a.** the end. *We left in a hurry at the conclusion of the dinner.* **b.** an opinion arrived at by thinking carefully. *The judge's conclusion was that Mr. Benson was innocent.*

con•fu•sion /kən fyōō′ zhən/ *n.* **a.** an act or instance of disorder. *Toby tried to find his mother in the confusion after the fire.* **b.** a mistaking of a person or thing for another. *We could see her confusion in the expression on her face.*

con•stel•la•tion /kŏn′ stə lā′ shən/ *n.* a group of stars with a name. *Many constellations were named after the animals they seemed to form in the sky.* [Latin *constellare* set with stars]

con•sti•tu•tion /kŏn′ stĭ tōō′ shən/ *n.* the rules, laws, and principles by which a nation, state, club, etc., is governed. *The constitution of our club states that we must have a new president every year.*

con•tain /kən tān′/ *v.* **a.** to have or include as contents. *Each box of dishes contains four bowls.* **b.** to have as a capacity; to be able to hold.

con•test /kŏn′ tĕst′/ *n.* a test, struggle, game, etc., to determine a winner. *Who won the prize in the art contest?*

con•ti•nent /kŏn′ tə nənt/ *n.* one of the seven main masses of land in the world. *We live on the continent of North America.*

con•tin•ue /kən tĭn′ yōō/ *v.* (**con•tin•ues, con•tin•ued, con•tin•u•ing**) **a.** to go on without stopping. *We continued walking until we reached the camp.* **b.** to go on again after stopping; to resume. *The story will be continued next week.*

cord•less /kôrd′ lĭs/ *adj.* having no cord and usually operated by battery. *We can talk on our cordless phone anywhere in the house.*

cot•tage /kŏt′ ĭj/ *n.* a small house. *We spent our vacation in a cottage near the beach.*

cottage

couch /kouch/ *n.* (**couch•es** *pl.*) a piece of furniture that can seat several people; a sofa. *My friends and I sit on the couch to watch TV.*

cou•ple /kŭp′ əl/ *n.* **a.** two of anything. *They will have to wait a couple of hours for the train.* **b.** two people together. *That couple dances well together.*

cray•on /krā′ ŏn′/ *n.* a stick of colored wax or chalk used for drawing. *The children used crayons to add details to their paintings.*

crop /krŏp/ *n.* food plants that are grown and harvested. *The farmer plants crops in the spring.*

crowd¹ /kroud/ *n.* many people gathered together. *I lost my brother in the crowd.*

crowd² /kroud/ *v.* to push or squeeze together in a small space. *The people crowded into the small room.*

crust /krŭst/ *n.* the outer surface of a loaf of bread. *Rye bread often has a dark crust.*

cube /kyōōb/ *n.* a solid figure with six square sides. *Not all ice cubes are actually in the shape of a cube.* (**cu•bic** *adj.*)

curl /kûrl/ *v.* **a.** to twist or turn into rings or spirals. *She curls her hair every night.* **b.** to coil. *The cowboy's lasso was curled around the saddle.*

cute /kyo͞ot/ *adj.* delightfully attractive or appealing. *The child looked cute in her rabbit costume.*

cut•er /kyo͞o′ tər/ *adj.* the comparative form of **cute**; being more appealing that someone or something else. *The brown puppy is cuter than the white one.*

cut•est /kyo͞o′ tĭst/ *adj.* the superlative form of **cute**; being the most appealing of anyone or anything else. *The cutest kitten is the one with the orange and white fur.*

cy•cle /sī′ kəl/ *n.* a series of events that occur over and over in the same order. *The seasons of the year form a cycle.*

dai•ly /dā′ lē/ *adj.* appearing, done, or occurring every day. *He takes a daily walk in the park.*

damp•en /dăm′ pən/ *v.* to make moist or wet. *Dampen the cloth before you begin cleaning.*

danc•er /dăns′ ər/ *n.* a person who participates in the various forms of dance. *The ballet dancer twirled on stage.*

dan•ger /dān′ jər/ *n.* peril; chance of injury or harm. *Learning safety rules can help you avoid danger.* (**dan•ger•ous** *adj.*)

dark•en /där′ kən/ *v.* to make dark. *He darkened the room by pulling down the shades.*

dark•ness /därk′ nĭs/ *n.* the state or quality of being without light or brightness. *The darkness of the sky told us a storm was coming.* (**dark•ly** *adv.*)

daugh•ter /dô′ tər/ *n.* a female child. *A princess is the daughter of a king or a queen.*

dead /dĕd/ *adj.* (**dead•er, dead•est**) no longer living. *The flowers in the vase are dead.*

deal /dēl/ *v.* (**deals, dealt, deal•ing**) to handle in a certain way; to cope. *It is important to know how to deal with emergencies.*

death /dĕth/ *n.* a dying; the ending of life or existence. *The movie ended with the death of the villain.*

Dec. December.

De•cem•ber /dĭ sĕm′ bər/ *n.* the twelfth and final month of the year. *The shortest day of the year comes in December.*

Pronunciation Key

ă	pat	ŏ	pot	th	thin
ā	pay	ō	toe	*th*	this
âr	care	ô	paw, for	hw	which
ä	father	oi	noise	zh	vision
ĕ	pet	ou	out	ə	about,
ē	be	o͝o	took		item,
ĭ	pit	o͞o	boot		pencil,
ī	pie	ŭ	cut		gallop,
îr	pier	ûr	urge		circus

de•clare /dĭ klâr′/ *v.* (**de•clares, de•clared, de•clar•ing**) **a.** to announce publicly and formally; to make known to others. *Only Congress can declare war.* **b.** to say positively and surely; to state openly. *Mark declared he would never again be late for school.* (**de•clar•a•ble** *adj.*)

de•crease /dē′ krēs′/ *n.* a growing less; a decline; a reduction. *There was a sharp decrease in interest after we lost seven games in a row.*

de•gree /dĭ grē′/ *n.* a unit used to measure temperature. *Water freezes at thirty-two degrees Fahrenheit.*

de•light /dĭ līt′/ *n.* enjoyment; pleasure; joy; something delightful. *Her sense of humor is a delight.*

de•serve /dĭ zûrv′/ *v.* (**de•serves, de•served, de•serv•ing**) to be worthy of; to have earned as a reward, punishment, right, etc. *Your suggestion deserves further consideration.*

de•sign[1] /dĭ zīn′/ *v.* to draw or sketch something to be done; to plan the details. *The builder designed a new shopping center.*

de•sign[2] /dĭ zīn′/ *n.* **a.** a drawing or plan. *The design for the building called for an elevator.* **b.** a pattern or arrangement of colors, materials, etc. *The blanket was woven in an intricate design.*

des•sert /dĭ zûrt′/ *n.* a food, usually sweet, served at the end of a meal. *I had an apple for dessert.*

dew /do͞o/ or /dyo͞o/ *n.* water droplets that form at night on cool surfaces. *In the morning you may see dew on the leaves.*

➤ **Dew** sounds like **due**.

di•al /dī′ əl/ *n.* a device that operates a television, radio, telephone, or other machine. *Before our television had a remote, we had to use the dial to change channels.*

dic•tion•ar•y /dĭk′ shə nĕr′ ē/ *n.* (**dic•tion•ar•ies** *pl.*) a book that explains the words used in a language. *A dictionary gives definitions, pronunciations, and word histories.*

die /dī/ *v.* (**dies, died, dy•ing**) to stop living or existing. *The tree will die if it is not watered.*

➤ **Die** sounds like **dye**.

dif•fer /dĭf′ ər/ *v.* to be unlike. *The two nations differ in their languages and customs.*

din•ner /dĭn′ ər/ *n.* the main meal of the day. *Some people have dinner at noon, and other people have dinner in the evening.*

di•no•saur /dī′ nə sôr′/ *n.* any of the group of extinct reptiles of the Mesozoic era. *Tyrannosaurus rex was a type of meat-eating dinosaur.*

di•rec•tion /dĭ rĕk′ shən/ *n.* **a.** act of directing. **b.** an instruction for doing something. **c.** the course along which something moves. **d.** a point on a magnetic compass. *If you take the road in that direction, you will be traveling south.*

dirt /dûrt/ *n.* **a.** mud, dust, soot, or any other thing that can soil skin, clothes, and furniture. *You have a smudge of dirt on your face.* **b.** earth; soil. *We put some dirt into the flowerpot.*

dis- a Latin prefix that means "apart, away, or not": *disagree.*

dis•cuss /dĭ skŭs′/ *v.* to talk seriously about. *The committee discussed possible solutions to the traffic problem.*

di•vi•sion /dĭ vĭzh′ ən/ *n.* the act or process of dividing. *Division is the opposite of multiplication.*

dodge /dŏj/ *v.* (**dodg•es, dodged, dodg•ing**) to try to avoid; to stay away from. *The batter stepped back from the plate to dodge the bad pitch.*

dol•lar /dŏl′ ər/ *n.* a coin or note used in several countries for currency. *In the United States a dollar is worth 100 cents.*

dou•ble /dŭb′ əl/ *v.* (**dou•bles, dou•bled, dou•bling**) to make or become twice as great. *The bread dough will double in size as it rises.*

doubt /dout/ *v.* to be unsure or uncertain. *I doubt that the Cortez family will be home from vacation before Friday.*

down•stairs /doun′ stârz′/ *adj.* on the lower floor: *a downstairs patio.*

downstairs

drag /drăg/ *v.* (**drags, dragged, drag•ging**) to pull slowly along the ground; to haul. *They drag the sled to the top of the hill and then slide down.*

dream•er /drē′ mər/ *n.* one who dreams; one who has visions of the future. *Dreamers often have the ideas that make inventions possible.*

drew /drōō/ *v.* (**draws, drew, drawn, draw•ing**) made a design, picture, etc. *The artist drew an outline before he painted the picture.*

drive /drīv/ *v.* (**drives, drove, driv•en, driv•ing**) to operate a vehicle. *Marsha's uncle drives a school bus.*

driv•er /drī′ vər/ *n.* any person who drives a vehicle or an animal. *The bus driver collected our fares when we got on.*

drive•way /drīv′ wā/ *n.* a road connecting a building to the street. *We park our car in our driveway.*

drove /drōv/ *v.* past tense of **drive**.

due /dōō/ or /dyōō/ *adj.* expected; scheduled to arrive. *The bus is not due for two hours.*

➤ **Due** sounds like **dew**.

du•ty /d$\overline{oo}$′ tē/ or /dy$\overline{oo}$′ tē/ *n.* (**du•ties** *pl.*) obligatory task or responsibility. *For this cleaning job, your duty will include sweeping.*

dye /dī/ *v.* (**dyes, dyed, dye•ing**) to give color to something or change its color. *Today we learned to dye fabric in art class.*

➤ **Dye** sounds like **die.**

ea•ger /ē′ gər/ *adj.* excitedly or impatiently wanting or expecting something. *We were eager for school to begin that day.*

ea•gle /ē′ gəl/ *n.* a large bird of prey with a hooked beak. *The bald eagle is the symbol of the United States.*

ear /îr/ *n.* **a.** the organ by which animals and humans hear. *Parts of the ear are located both inside and outside the head.* —**idiom. keep your ear to the ground.** to stay informed. **b.** the seed-bearing spike of a cereal plant, such as corn. *Please husk this ear of corn.*

ear•rings /îr′ rĭngz/ or /îr′ ĭngz/ *n. pl.* (**ear•ring** *sing.*) jewelry worn on the ears. *My favorite earrings are in my jewelry box.*

earth /ûrth/ *n.* **a.** the third planet from the sun; the planet on which we live. *Earth revolves around the sun.* **b.** ground; soil. *Plant these seeds in black earth.*

eas•i•er /ē′ zī ər/ *adj.* the comparative form of **easy**, being the least hard or difficult of two actions. *It is easier for me to write with my left hand than my right hand.*

eas•i•est /ē′ zē ĭst/ *adj.* the superlative form of **easy**; being the least hard or difficult of more than two actions. *The easiest way to get to my house is to take the number 7 bus.*

east[1] /ēst/ *n.* the direction to your right as you face north; the direction from which the sun rises. *We saw a glow of light in the east before dawn.*

east[2] /ēst/ *adv.* to the east. *We walked east until we came to the hotel.*

east[3] /ēst/ *adj.* from the east. *An east wind brought rain and colder temperatures.*

ea•sy /ē′ zē/ *adj.* (**eas•i•er, eas•i•est; eas•i•ly** *adv.*) not hard or difficult. *The quiz was easy for me because I had studied hard.*

ech•o[1] /ĕk′ ō/ *n.* (**ech•oes** *pl.*) a repeated sound caused by sound waves bouncing off a surface. *We heard an echo when we shouted into the cave.*

ech•o[2] /ĕk′ ō/ *v.* to send back a sound. *Tunnels often echo.*

edge /ĕj/ *n.* border; side. *The cup fell from the edge of the table.*

ei•ther /ē′ thər/ or /ī′-/ *adj.* one or the other of two. *I couldn't run faster than either one of my friends.*

e•lec•tion /ĭ lĕk′ shən/ *n.* a choosing or selecting by voting. *We held an election to choose a class president.*

e•lec•tri•cian /ĭ lĕk trĭsh′ ən / or /ē lĕk-/ *n.* a person who installs and repairs electrical equipment. *The electrician rewired the old house.*

elf /ĕlf/ *n.* (**elves** *pl.*) a tiny, make-believe being that is full of mischief. *The elf wore a green, pointed hat.*

elk /ĕlk/ *n.* (**elk** or **elks** *pl.*) another name for a moose. *The elk had large antlers.*

else /ĕls/ *adj.* other; different. *Would you rather ride with someone else?*

e•mo•tion /ĭ mō′ shən/ *n.* a strong reaction or feeling. *Anger is a common emotion.*

em•ploy /ĕm ploi′/ *v.* to have in one's business as paid workers; to hire. *Factories employ hundreds of people.*

em•ploy•ment /ĕm ploi′ mənt/ *n.* **a.** one's work or occupation. *Mrs. O'Connor found employment as an accountant.* **b.** the hiring of people to do work. *The new computer firm provides employment for more than seventy people.*

emp•ti•ness /ĕmp′ tē nĭs/ *n.* the condition of having nothing. *Our voices echoed in the emptiness of the abandoned house.*

-en a suffix that means "to cause to be," used to form verbs: *tighten.*

en•gage /ĕn gāj′/ *v.* (**en•gag•es, en•gaged, en•gag•ing**) to keep busy or to hire. *I will engage you to wash my car.*

en•gine /ĕn′ jĭn/ *n.* a machine that changes fuel and energy into motion. *Most automobile engines use gasoline.*

en•joy /ĕn joi′/ *v.* to get pleasure from. *Did you enjoy the movie last night?*

en•joy•ment /ĕn joi′ mənt/ *n.* the state of enjoying. *Her enjoyment of the play was evident from her delighted smile.*

e•nor•mous /ĭ nôr′ məs/ *adj.* very large. *The whale is an enormous sea animal.*

e•nough /ĭ nŭf′/ *adj.* as much or as many as needed. *The campers had enough food and water for three days.*

en•ter /ĕn′ tər/ *v.* to come or go into. *The students enter the school through the doorway closest to their classrooms.*

e•qual /ē′ kwəl/ *adj.* of the same value, size, rank, amount, etc. *The two boys are of equal weight; they both weigh seventy pounds.*

-er[1] a suffix, used to form nouns, that means: **a.** "one who": *swimmer.* **b.** "thing that": *toaster.*

-er[2] an adjective or adverbial suffix that means "more": *lazier, faster.*

e•ro•sion /ĭ rō′ zhən/ *n.* process of slowly wearing away. *The erosion of the cliffs took thousands of years.*

-ese a Latin suffix that means "of, relating to, or characteristic of": *Chinese.*

-est an adjective or adverbial suffix that means "most": *cutest, easiest.*

eu•ro or **Eu•ro** /yŏŏr′ ō/ *n.* (**eu•ros** or **eu•ro's** *pl.*) the basic unit of currency among participating European countries. *The sandwich cost a euro.*

Eu•rope /yŏŏr′ əp/ *n.* the continent east of the Atlantic Ocean and west of Asia. *Our teacher visited France and Spain on her trip to Europe.*

eve•ry•day /ĕv′ rē dā′/ *adj.* ordinary; all right for the usual day or event. *You should wear your everyday clothes to play outside.*

eve•ry•one /ĕv′ rē wŭn′/ *pron.* each person; everybody. *Everyone in the class received a permission slip for the field trip.*

eve•ry•thing /ĕv′ rē thĭng′/ *pron.* all things; each thing. *Everything is going right for me.*

ex•am•ple /ĭg zăm′ pəl/ *n.* a sample; a model; something that may be imitated. *If you don't understand how to do the problems, look at the example.*

ex•cla•ma•tion /ĕk′ sklə mā′ shən/ *n.* an excited utterance. *When Marcy saw the puppy, she let out an exclamation of delight.*

ex•plain /ĭk splān′/ *v.* **a.** to make something clear; to tell what something means. *The teacher explained the difference between nouns and verbs.* **b.** to give a reason for; to tell the cause of. *Can you explain why you didn't do your homework?* (**ex•pla•na•tion** *n.*)

eyes /īz/ *n.* the parts of the body with which humans and animals see. *Tears keep your eyes moist.*

face /fās/ *n.* the front part of the head; that part of the head on which the eyes, nose, and mouth are located. *Her face was covered by a funny mask.*

fail /fāl/ *v.* to be unsuccessful. *The pirates failed to find the treasure they had hidden.*

fame /fām/ *n.* the state of being well-known; respect; recognition. *George Washington was a man of great fame.*

fare /fâr/ *n.* money charged for a trip. *You pay a fare to ride in a bus, taxi, train, or airplane.*

farm•er /fär′ mər/ *n.* a person who owns or operates a farm. *Farmers often store chopped corn in tall towers called silos.*

fas•ten /făs′ ən/ *v.* to join; to attach. *We can fasten this lamp to the wall over my desk.*

fa•ther /fä′ thər/ *n.* the male parent. *My father helped me study my spelling.*

fa•vor /fā′ vər/ *n.* **a.** a kind or thoughtful act. *We did him a favor by mowing his lawn.* **b.** a small gift. *Each child received a balloon as a party favor.*

fear[1] /fîr/ *n.* a feeling of fright or alarm. *Dogs show fear by putting their tails between their legs.* (**fear•ful** *adj.*, **fear•less** *adj.*, **fear•less•ly** *adv.*)

fear[2] /fîr/ *v.* to be afraid of. *My little sister fears thunder and lightning.*

Feb. February.

Feb•ru•ar•y /fĕb′ rŏŏ ĕr′ ē/ *n.* the second month of the year. *February is the shortest month.*

feel /fēl/ *v.* (**feels, felt, feel•ing**) **a.** to sense by touch. *Feel how soft this cloth is!* **b.** to have a feeling or emotion. *I feel happy.*

felt /fĕlt/ *v.* past tense of **feel**.

fe•male /fē′ māl′/ *n.* a girl; a woman. *The conductor of the orchestra was a female.*

few /fyōō/ *adj.* not many. *Few copies of this rare book are available.*

fic a Latin root that means "to make": *fiction*.

fic•tion /fĭk′ shən/ *n.* writings about imaginary events and people. *Short stories and novels are types of fiction.*

field /fēld/ *n.* a piece of open land, usually part of a farm, often used for planting crops. *Some wheat fields are several miles wide.*

field trip /fēld trĭp/ *n.* a visit made by students and teachers for the purposes of firsthand observation. *Our field trip to the zoo was very interesting.*

fight /fīt/ *v.* (**fights, fought, fight•ing**) to oppose strongly, especially in battle. *Our team tried to fight well, but the other team won.*

find /fīnd/ *v.* (**finds, found, find•ing**) **a.** to come upon accidentally; to locate an object by chance. *You may find my brother at the supermarket.* **b.** to look for and get back a lost object. *We will find my watch.*

fin•ish /fĭn′ ĭsh/ *v.* to reach the end. *The important part of a marathon is to finish the race.*

firm¹ /fûrm/ *adj.* hard; solid. *They left the muddy road and walked on firm ground.* (**firm•ly** *adj.*)

firm² /fûrm/ *n.* a business partnership of two or more persons. *Samuel got a job with a law firm.*

fish /fĭsh/ *n.* (**fish** or **fish•es** *pl.*) an animal that lives in water, has fins, and breathes through gills. *Most fish have scales covering their bodies.* —***idiom.*** **fish or cut bait**. take action.

fit•ness /fĭt′ nĭs/ *n.* the state of being in good physical condition. *Many people exercise for greater fitness.*

flash•light /flăsh′ līt′/ *n.* a small light powered by batteries. *Campers carry flashlights to find their way in the dark.*

fla•vor /flā′ vər/ *n.* a particular taste. *Lemonade can have a sweet or tart flavor.*

flight /flīt/ *n.* a scheduled trip on an airplane. *The next flight to Chicago departs at 3:05.*

flood /flŭd/ *n.* water that flows over normally dry land. *The low bridge was under water for an hour after the flash flood.*

flood•light /flŭd′ līt′/ *n.* a lighting unit for projecting a beam of light. *The rescuers used a floodlight to find the lost dog.*

floun•der /floun′ dər/ *n.* a flat fish. *Baked flounder is a popular item on the menu.*

flour /flour/ *n.* a fine powder of ground grain, usually wheat. *Flour is used in making breads.*

➤ **Flour** sounds like **flower**.

flow•er /flou′ ər/ *n.* the blossom of a plant. *Many flowers bloom in the spring.*

➤ **Flower** sounds like **flour**.

flower

flute /flōōt/ *n.* a woodwind instrument with a side opening across which a player blows. *The flute makes a high, soft sound.*

foil /foil/ *n.* a sheet of metal so thin it seems like paper. *The sandwiches are wrapped in aluminum foil.*

fold /fōld/ *v.* to close or bend parts of something together in order to fit it into a smaller space. *When we take down the flag, we fold it into the shape of a triangle.*

fol•low•ing /fŏl′ ō ĭng/ *v.* (**fol•lows, fol•lowed, fol•low•ing**) going, proceeding, or coming after. *I don't know how to get there, so we are following you.*

foot /fŏot/ *n.* (**feet** *pl.*) **a.** the part of the body at the end of the leg. *Start the dance with your left foot.* **b.** a measure of length. *Twelve inches make a foot.*

for•est /fôr′ ĭst/ *n.* an area covered with trees; woods. *We found pine cones in the forest.*

for•est•er /fôr′ ĭ stər/ or /fŏr′ ĭ stər/ *n.* a person trained in caring for the forest. *The park manager hired a forester to help care for the trees.*

for•get /fôr gĕt′/ or /fər-/ *v.* (**for•gets, for•got, for•got•ten, for•get•ting**) to fail to remember. *He sometimes forgets his umbrella on rainy days.*

for•got /fôr gŏt′/ or /fər-/ *v.* past tense of **forget.**

for•got•ten /fər gŏt′ ən/ *v.* past participle of **forget.**

form /fôrm/ *v.* to give a shape to something. *Potters form dishes out of clay.*

forth /fôrth/ or /fōrth/ *adv.* forward; onward. *From that day forth the princess lived happily.*

for•ty /fôr′ tē/ *n.* one more than thirty-nine; four times ten; 40. *Her father's age is forty.*

fought /fôt/ *v.* past tense of **fight.**

found /found/ *v.* (**finds, found, find•ing**) came upon accidentally; located an object by chance. *I found my favorite ice cream at the store.*

four•teenth¹ /fôr tēnth′/ or /fōr-/ *adj.* next after the thirteenth. *This is the store's fourteenth year in business.*

four•teenth² /fôr tēnth′/ or /fōr-/ *n.* one of fourteen equal parts. *Two is one fourteenth of twenty-eight.*

Fourth of July *n.* United States Independence Day that celebrates the adoption of the Declaration of Independence in 1776. *We watch fireworks on the Fourth of July.*

frac•tion /frăk′ shən/ *n.* one or more of the equal parts into which a thing is divided. *The fraction $\frac{3}{4}$ represents three of four equal parts.*

franc /frăngk/ *n.* the currency used in France before the euro was introduced. *The toy cost one franc.*

France /frăns/ *n.* a country in western Europe. *The Eiffel Tower is in Paris, France.*

free•dom /frē′ dəm/ *n.* the state of being free; liberty. *The Revolutionary War was fought to gain freedom for our country.*

freeze /frēz/ *v.* (**freez•es, froze, froz•en, freez•ing**) **a.** became ice; turn to ice. *The lake will freeze during the night.* **b.** chill to make something cold and as hard as ice. *We will freeze the vegetables from our garden so we can eat them all year.*

freeze

French¹ /frĕnch/ *adj.* of or from France. *A beret is a soft French cap.*

French² /frĕnch/ *n.* **a.** the national language of France, also spoken in other parts of the world. *Can you speak French?* **b.** the people of France. *The French consider cooking an art.*

fresh•en /frĕsh′ ən/ *v.* to make fresh. A light shower freshens the garden.

Fri. Friday.

Fri•day /frī′ dē/ or /-dā/ *n.* the sixth day of the week. *Friday is the end of the school week.* [Old English *Frigedæg,* Freya's day.]

friend /frĕnd/ *n.* a person whom one knows, likes, and trusts. *My best friend and I went camping.*

fright /frīt/ *n.* a sudden fear. *The village was filled with fright when the forest fire started.*

fright•en /frīt′ n/ *v.* **a.** to make afraid; to scare. *The actors' costumes frightened the little girl.* **b.** to cause to move by making afraid. *The campfire frightened away the wolves.*

froze /frōz/ *v.* past tense of **freeze.**

fruit /frōot/ *n.* (**fruit** or **fruits** *pl.*) the part of certain plants that contains seeds and is good to eat. *Oranges, grapes, and pears are types of fruit.*

fu•el /fyōo′ əl/ *n.* a material burned to produce heat or power. *Most cars use unleaded fuel.*

-ful an English suffix that means: **a.** full of or having, used to form adjectives: *meaningful*. **b.** the amount that fills, used to form nouns: *cupful*.

fun•ny /fŭn′ ē/ *adj.* (**fun•ni•er, fun•ni•est**) causing laughter or amusement. *The joke was funny.*

fur /fûr/ *n.* the thick, soft hair that is on the bodies of many animals. *We brush the dog's fur to keep it shiny.*

fuse /fyo͞oz/ *n.* a strip of metal in an electrical circuit that interrupts the circuit if the current becomes too strong. *I think we blew a fuse because the lights are out!*

gadg•et /găj′ ĭt/ *n.* a small mechanical object with a practical use but often thought of as a novelty. *With this gadget you don't need your hands to open a can.*

gar•den•er /gärd′ nər/ *n.* a person who takes care of a garden or does gardening. *Sharon worked as a gardener last summer.*

gath•er /găth′ ər/ *v.* to bring or come together. *When clouds gather it often means rain.*

geese /gēs/ *n. pl.* (**goose** *sing.*) swimming birds that look like ducks but have larger bodies and longer necks. *Male geese are called ganders.*

gel•a•tin /jĕl′ ə tn/ *n.* a jellylike substance. *The gelatin had fruit in it.*

gem /jĕm/ *n.* a precious stone. *Diamonds and emeralds are gems.*

gen•er•al /jĕn′ ər əl/ *n.* a top army officer, in command of many troops. *There are five ranks of general, who wear from one to five stars.*

gen•tle /jĕn′ tl/ *adj.* light; soft. *The gentle breeze rustled through the leaves.*

Ger•man¹ /jûr′ mən/ *adj.* of or from Germany. *Oktoberfest is a German festival.*

Ger•man² /jûr′ mən/ *n.* **a.** one born or living in Germany. *The composer Bach was a famous German.* **b.** the language spoken in Germany, Austria, and parts of Switzerland. *Many English words come from German.*

Ger•ma•ny /jûr′ mə nē/ *n.* a country in north-central Europe. *Between 1949 and 1989, Germany was divided into East Germany and West Germany.*

gi•gan•tic /jī găn′ tĭk/ *adj.* extremely large. *Elephants and whales are gigantic.*

gig•gle¹ /gĭg′ əl/ *n.* a short laugh. *Hearing her giggle made everyone smile.*

gig•gle² /gĭg′ əl/ *v.* (**gig•gles, gig•gled, gig•gling**) to give repeated high-pitched laughs. *The children giggle when they watch cartoons.*

glare /glâr/ *n.* **a.** an angry or fierce stare. *When he upsets me, I give him a glare.* **b.** a brilliant light. *The sun's glare made driving difficult.*

glow¹ /glō/ *v.* to give off light; to shine. *Fireflies glow in the dark.*

glow² /glō/ *n.* a soft light. *You can see the glow of the lamp through the window.*

glue /glo͞o/ *n.* a sticky liquid that hardens to hold things together. *Broken toys can be mended with glue.*

gnat /năt/ *n.* a very small fly. *Rotten fruit may attract a gnat.*

gnaw /nô/ *v.* to bite or chew on persistently. *That dog is hungry; we will give him a bone to gnaw.*

goal /gōl/ *n.* a purpose; an aim. *Mark's goal is to play the double bass in a symphony orchestra.*

good-bye or good-by /go͝od bī′/ *n.* an expression of farewell. *We said our good-byes on the railway platform.*

goose /go͞os/ *n.* (**geese** *pl.*) a swimming bird that looks like a duck, but has a larger body and a longer neck. *The male goose is called a gander.* —*idiom.* **goose is cooked.** big trouble.

gov•ern•ment /gŭv′ ərn mənt/ *n.* **a.** a system of ruling or managing. *Our American government is a democracy, which means that the power to make laws comes from the citizens.* **b.** the people in charge of such a system. *The government has approved the new dam.*

grand•fa•ther /grănd′ fä′ *th*ər/ or /grăn′ fä′ *th*ər/ *n.* the father of one's mother or father. *One of my grandfathers lives here in town; my other grandfather lives in the country.*

grand•moth•er /grănd′ mŭ*th*′ ər/ or /grăn′ mŭ*th*′ ər/ *n.* the mother of one's father or mother. *My grandmother is coming to my birthday party.*

gray also **grey** /grā/ *adj.* (**gray•er, gray•est**) **a.** of or relating to the color between the extremes of black and white. *Her new gray skirt was a real bargain.* **b.** dull or dark. *It was a gray, rainy afternoon.* **c.** having gray hair. *My father turned gray when he was in his twenties.* **d.** lacking in cheer; gloomy. *He was in a gray mood until the movie started.*

gray•est /grā′ ĭst/ *adj.* (**gray, gray•er**) having the most gray of anything else. *That is the grayest sky I've seen this summer.*

Greece /grēs/ *n.* a country in southeastern Europe that borders on the Mediterranean Sea. *Corinth and Athens are cities in Greece.*

Greek[1] /grēk/ *n.* **a.** one born or living in Greece. *The ancient Greeks were the first people to stage plays.* **b.** the language of Greece. *Greek uses a different alphabet from English.*

Greek[2] /grēk/ *adj.* of or from Greece. *We saw Greek sculpture at the museum.*

gro•cer•y /grō′ sə rē/ *n.* (**gro•cer•ies** *pl.*) a store selling food and household supplies. *We carried two bags of groceries home from the grocery store.*

group /gro͞op/ *n.* a gathering or arranging of people or objects. *There is a large group of people in the hotel lobby.*

grow /grō/ *v.* (**grows, grew, grown, grow•ing**) to expand or increase in size. *Trees grow slowly.*

grown /grōn/ *v.* a form of **grow**.

growth /grōth/ *n.* **a.** the process of growing. *Social scientists are looking for ways to control population growth.* **b.** the development achieved by growing. *Some plants reach full growth in a single season.*

guess /gĕs/ *v.* (**guess•es, guessed, guess•ing**) form an opinion with little or no evidence. *Tom is running out of time, so he will guess the rest of the answers on the test.*

➤ **Guessed** sounds like **guest**.

guest /gĕst/ *n.* a person entertained in one's house. *Our guest will stay in our spare room this weekend.*

➤ **Guest** sounds like **guessed**.

gym /jĭm/ *n.* a gymnasium. *The teams practice in the gym.*

half /hăf/ *n.* (**halves** *pl.*) one of two equal parts. *Which half of the sandwich do you want?*

hal•ter /hôl′ tər/ *n.* the leather headgear for leading a horse or other animal. *Be careful as you place the halter on the horse.*

hap•pi•er /hăp′ ē ər/ *adj.* the comparative form of **happy**; being the more joyful than someone or something else.

hap•pi•est /hăp′ ē ĭst/ *adj.* the superlative form of **happy**; being the most joyful of anyone or anything else. *The A on his spelling test made Enrique the happiest person in the whole class.*

hap•pi•ness /hăp′ ē nĭs/ *n.* the condition of feeling glad. *Here's a toast to your good fortune and happiness!*

hap•py /hăp′ ē/ *adj.* (**hap•pi•er, hap•pi•est; hap•pi•ly** *adv.*) feeling or showing pleasure; joyful. *The happy man whistled as he worked.*

hard•en /här′ dn/ *v.* to make or become hard. *The ground hardens during cold weather.*

hare /hâr/ *n.* an animal like a rabbit, but much larger. *A hare has strong legs and can run fast.*

hare

har•ness /här′ nĭs/ *n.* (**har•ness•es** *pl.*) the set of leather straps and bands with which an animal pulls a plow or other vehicle. *Gently tug the harness to have the horse stop.*

haul /hôl/ *v.* to pull with force; to drag. *The girls hauled their rowboat out of the water.*

head /hĕd/ *n.* **a.** the uppermost part of the body of a vertebrate, containing the brain and the eyes, ears, nose, mouth, and jaws. *My new hat covered my head and my ears.* **b.** authority; the one in charge or in the lead. *The head of the band marched in front.*

health•i•er /hĕl′ thē ər/ *adj.* the comparative form of **healthy**; being of better health than someone or something else. *If you eat more vegetables, you will be healthier.*

health•i•est /hĕl′ thē ĭst/ *adj.* the superlative form of **healthy**; being of the best health of anyone or anything else. *The healthiest person is one who exercises and eats well.*

hear /hîr/ *v.* (**heard, hear•ing**) **a.** take in sound through the ears. *We hear every word clearly.* **b.** listened to; paid attention to. *Our teacher quizzed us on what we could hear her say.*

heav•i•er /hĕv′ ē ər/ *adj.* the comparative form of **heavy**; having more weight than someone or something else. *This box is heavier than that one.*

heav•i•est /hĕv′ ē ĭst/ *adj.* the superlative form of **heavy**; having the most weight of anyone or anything else. *This box is the heaviest of all of them.*

heav•y /hĕv′ ē/ *adj.* (**heav•i•er, heav•i•est; heav•i•ly** *adv.*) hard to move because of its weight; not light. *The maple tree's heavy trunk will need two people to lift it.*

hedge /hĕj/ *n.* a thick row of bushes planted as a fence or boundary. *A hedge should be trimmed evenly.*

held /hĕld/ *v.* past tense of **hold**.

hel•lo /hĕ lō′/ *interj.* (**hel•los** *pl.*) something said to express greeting. *The crossing guard always says "Hello" as we go by.*

help•ful /hĕlp′ fəl/ *adj.* giving aid; useful. *It was really helpful of you to do the dishes for me.*

help•less /hĕlp′ lĭs/ *adj.* not able to help oneself or others. *We felt helpless to stop the school's litter problem until we planned a recycling program.*

herd /hûrd/ *n.* a number of animals that feed and move about together. *The herd of deer was hard to spot in the dim forest.*

Pronunciation Key

ă	pat	ŏ	pot	th	thin
ā	pay	ō	toe	th	this
âr	care	ô	paw, for	hw	which
ä	father	oi	noise	zh	vision
ĕ	pet	ou	out	ə	about,
ē	be	ŏŏ	took		item,
ĭ	pit	ōō	boot		pencil,
ī	pie	ŭ	cut		gallop,
îr	pier	ûr	urge		circus

he•ro /hîr′ ō/ *n.* (**he•ros** or **he•roes** *pl.*) a person admired for bravery or fine qualities. *Abraham Lincoln is a national hero.*

her•self /hər sĕlf′/ *pron.* **a.** her own self. *Jennifer fell down and hurt herself.* **b.** the person or self she usually is. *Beth isn't acting like herself today.*

high /hī/ *adj.* tall; far above the ground. *Eagles build nests on high cliffs.* (**high•ness** *n.*)

high•er /hī′ ər/ *adj.* the comparative form of **high**; being the more tall or high off the ground than anyone or anything. *The top of the cabinet is higher than the bookcase.*

high school /hī′ skōōl′/ *n.* a level of school that follows elementary school; secondary school. *High school usually includes grades nine through twelve.*

high•way /hī′ wā′/ *n.* a main road. *Highways are usually numbered to simplify maps and road signs.*

hike /hīk/ *v.* (**hikes, hiked, hik•ing**) to take a long walk for exercise or pleasure. *We sang marching songs as we hiked up the trail.*

hik•er /hī′ kər/ *n.* one who hikes. *Sturdy, comfortable shoes are a must for every hiker.*

hire /hīr/ *v.* (**hires, hired, hir•ing**) to employ; to pay a person for working. *Because of good business, the store hired three more clerks.*

hoist /hoist/ *v.* to lift; to raise. *We hoist the flag every morning before noon.*

hold /hōld/ *v.* (**holds, held, hold•ing**) to have or take and keep; to grasp. *Hold tightly to the dog's leash.*

hol•i•day /hŏl′ ĭ dā′/ *n.* a day on which a special event is celebrated. *Independence Day is the favorite holiday of many people.* [Middle English *holidai*, holy day]

home•less /hōm′ lĭs/ *adj.* without a home. *Our community center provides a shelter for homeless people.*

home•mak•er /hōm′ mā′ kər/ *n.* a person with the responsibility of managing a household, including cooking, cleaning, and caring for children. *Being a homemaker is a demanding job.*

home•work /hōm′ wûrk/ *n.* work for school that is done at home. *Our class has ten arithmetic problems for homework.*

hon•est /ŏn′ ĭst/ *adj.* tending not to lie, cheat, or steal; able to be trusted. *An honest person always tells the truth.*

hoof /hŏŏf/ or /hōŏf/ *n.* (**hooves** or **hoofs** *pl.*) the horny covering of the toes or lower part of the foot of a mammal, such as a horse, ox, or deer. *The horse's hoof was muddy.*

hooves /hōŏvz/ or /hŏŏvz/ *n. pl.* (**hoof** *sing.*) the curved coverings of horn that protect the feet of animals. *The cow's hooves were muddy.*

hope•less /hōp′ lĭs/ *adj.* having very little chance of working out right. *After darkness fell, they decided the search for the ball was hopeless.*

ho•tel /hō tĕl′/ *n.* a place that provides guests with lodging and usually meals and other services. *Our grandparents stayed in a hotel near the beach in Florida.*

hot•ter /hŏt′ ər/ *adj.* (**hot, hot•test**) **a.** warmer than something or someone else; having a higher temperature than something or someone else. *You feel hotter when you have a fever.* **b.** sharper to the taste than something else; more peppery or more spicy. *This salsa is hotter than the salsa I make at home.*

hour•ly[1] /our′ lē/ *adv.* every hour. *The bells in our school ring hourly.*

hour•ly[2] /our′ lē/ *adj.* for every hour. *She receives an hourly wage of six dollars.*

house /hous/ *n.* a building in which to live. *The fine old house is for sale.*

how•ev•er /hou ĕv′ ər/ *conj.* nevertheless. *I've never tasted eggplant before; however, it looks delicious.*

huge /hyōōj/ *adj.* very large. *A skyscraper is a huge building.*

hu•man /hyōō′ mən/ *adj.* of or relating to persons. *It is a human weakness to put things off.*

hurt•ful /hûrt′ fəl/ *adj.* causing pain or injury. *Your hurtful behavior will not help you make friends.*

hy•drant /hī′ drənt/ *n.* a discharge pipe with a valve and a spout at which water may be drawn from a water main; a fireplug. *The fire hydrant in front of our house is yellow.*

-ian an English suffix that means "one who, of or relating to": *electrician.*

i•ci•cle /ī′ sĭ kəl/ *n.* a pointed, hanging piece of ice, formed by the freezing of dripping water. *Icicles hung from the roof of the house.*

i•de•a /ī dē′ ə/ *n.* a thought; a plan. *Bringing plants to decorate the room was Kristin's idea.*

i•mag•ine /ĭ măj′ ĭn/ *v.* (**i•mag•ines, i•mag•ined, i•mag•in•ing**) **a.** to make up an idea or a picture in the mind. *I can imagine all the things I would do if I had the time.* **b.** to suppose. *I imagine they'll be there soon.*

im•i•ta•tion /ĭm′ ĭ tā′ shən/ *n.* something copied from the original. *Jaime's imitation of Luis was perfect.*

im•por•tant /ĭm pôr′ tnt/ *adj.* **a.** meaning a great deal; serious. *Your birthday is important to you.* **b.** having power or authority. *These parking places are reserved for important officials.*

in•clude /ĭn klōōd′/ *v.* (**in•cludes, in•clud•ed, in•clud•ing**) **a.** to contain; to cover. *The price of the radio includes the tax.* **b.** to put in as part of the total. *Don't forget to include the guests in the other room.*

In•di•a /ĭn′ dē ə/ *n.* a large country in southern Asia. *Only China has more people than India.*

In•di•an[1] /ĭn′ dē ən/ *n.* one born or living in India. *He met an Indian from Bombay.*

In•di•an[2] /ĭn′ dē ən/ *adj.* of or from India. *She was wearing an Indian sari.*

in•fant /ĭn′ fənt/ *n.* baby. *The infant is riding in the stroller.*

in•fect /ĭn fĕkt′/ *v.* to make ill by the introduction of germs. *A wound can become infected if it is not kept clean.*

in•stead /ĭn stĕd′/ *adv.* in place of. *Since the manager wasn't in, we talked to her assistant instead.*

in•vi•ta•tion /ĭn′ vĭ tā′ shən/ *n.* a spoken or written request for someone's attendance. *I sent Lucy an invitation to my birthday party.*

in•vite /ĭn vīt′/ *v.* (**in•vites, in•vit•ed, in•vit•ing**) to ask a person to go somewhere or do something. *My mother invited my friends to lunch.*

-ion a Latin noun suffix that means "being, condition of, or result of": *explanation, relation.*

Ire•land /īr′ lənd/ *n.* the island country west of Britain. *The shamrock is an emblem of Ireland.*

I•rish¹ /ī′ rĭsh/ *n.* the people of Ireland. *The Irish are known for their lilting accent.*

I•rish² /ī′ rĭsh/ *adj.* of or from Ireland. *The Irish countryside is green and beautiful.*

i•ron /ī′ ərn/ *v.* to press with an iron to remove wrinkles. *Most fabrics today do not need to be ironed.*

-ish an English suffix that means "of, relating to, or being": *Spanish.*

is•land /ī′ lənd/ *n.* a piece of land with water all around it. *People must take a boat or an airplane to get to an island.*

island

I•tal•ian¹ /ĭ tăl′ yən/ *adj.* of or from Italy. *"Pizza" is an Italian word.*

I•tal•ian² /ĭ tăl′ yən/ *n.* **a.** one born or living in Italy. *Many Italians live in Rome.* **b.** the language of Italy. *Many operas are sung in Italian.*

It•a•ly /ĭt′ ə lē/ *n.* a country in southern Europe bordering on the Mediterranean. *Italy is shaped like a boot.*

its /ĭts/ *pron.* of or belonging to it. *The bird left its nest.*

it's it is.

it•self /ĭt sĕlf′/ *pron.* **a.** its own self. *The bird cleaned itself in the puddle.* **b.** a word used to make a statement stronger. *No wonder the house is expensive; the land itself cost thousands of dollars.*

Jan. January.

Jan•u•ar•y /jăn′ yo͞o ĕr′ ē/ *n.* the first month of the year. *January has thirty-one days.*

Ja•pan /jə păn′/ *n.* a small country of islands to the east of China. *Tokyo is the capital of Japan.*

Ja•pan•ese¹ /jăp′ ə nēz′/ *adj.* of or from Japan. *Japanese writing is very different from ours.*

Ja•pan•ese² /jăp′ ə nēz′/ *n.* **a.** the people of Japan. *Many Japanese live in apartments.* **b.** the language of Japan. *Japanese is an interesting language to learn.*

jew•el•er /jo͞o′ ə lər/ *n.* a person who makes, repairs, or deals in jewelry, precious stones, or watches. *I took my broken watch to the jeweler for repair.*

jog /jŏg/ *v.* (**jogs, jogged, jog•ging**) to run at a slow, regular pace. *She likes to jog early in the morning.*

jog•ger /jŏg′ ər/ *n.* a person who runs or rides at a slow trot. *We watched the jogger jog three laps around the track.*

join /join/ *v.* to become a member of. *Next year I am going to join the chess club.*

joint /joint/ *n.* a place where two bones are connected, allowing motion. *Your leg bends at the knee joint.*

joy /joi/ *n.* a feeling of happiness or pleasure. *Imagine my joy when I received Sandy's letter.*

joy•ful /**joi′** fəl/ *adj.* full of joy. *The first and last days of school are always joyful.*

judge /jŭj/ *n.* one who presides over a court of law by hearing cases and making decisions. *A judge must be completely fair.*

judg•ment /**jŭj′** mənt/ *n.* **a.** a decision reached through careful thought. *The final judgment of the class was in favor of a picnic rather than a trip to the zoo.* **b.** opinion. *In my judgment such a plan will never succeed.* **c.** the ability to make wise decisions. *Consuela has excellent judgment concerning horses.*

juice /jo͞os/ *n.* the liquid that can be squeezed out of fruits, meat, or vegetables. *He has a glass of orange juice every morning.*

Ju•ly /jo͞o **lī′**/ *n.* the seventh month of the year. *July is usually hot in Texas.*

jum•ble /**jŭm′** bəl/ *v.* (**jum•bles, jum•bled, jum•bling**) to mix up. *The letters of the word were jumbled in the puzzle.*

jump•er /**jŭm′** pər/ *n.* one that jumps. *The basketball player is a good jumper.*

June /jo͞on/ *n.* the sixth month of the year. *June has thirty days.*

jun•gle /**jŭng′** gəl/ *n.* wild land near the equator with thickly grown tropical plants. *Parrots and monkeys live in the jungle.*

keen•ly /**kēn′** lē/ *adv.* with sharpness or quickness in seeing, hearing, or thinking. *The expert detective keenly solved the crime.*

keep /kēp/ *v.* (**keeps, kept, keep•ing**) **a.** to store; to put away; to save. *I keep all my old homework.* **b.** to continue. *Let's keep looking until we find it.*

kept /kĕpt/ *v.* past tense of **keep**.

ket•tle /**kĕt′** l/ *n.* a pot used for heating liquids. *Put the kettle on the stove.*

kind /kīnd/ *adj.* friendly; thoughtful of others. *Everyone likes kind persons.*

kind•er /**kīnd′** ər/ *adj.* the comparative form of **kind**; being the more thoughtful of and helpful to others than anyone. *He is kinder to his little brother now.*

kind•est /**kīnd′** ĭst/ *adj.* the superlative form of **kind**; being the most thoughtful of and helpful to others than anyone else. *Marco's mother is the kindest person I know.*

kind•ness /**kīnd′** nĭs/ *n.* friendly or helpful behavior. *His kindness earned him the respect of the whole class.*

knap•sack /**năp′** săk/ *n.* a canvas or leather bag worn or carried on the back and used to hold food, clothing, equipment, etc. *The hikers carried knapsacks and sleeping bags.* [German *knappsack.*]

knee /nē/ *n.* the joint in the middle of the leg. *You bend your knees when you walk.*

knew /no͞o/ or /nyo͞o/ *v.* (**knows, knew, known, know•ing**) **a.** understood; had information about. *You knew where our car was?* **b.** was aware; was sure. *We knew we had heard a noise.* **c.** was acquainted with. *I knew them for years.* **d.** had skill in. *You knew how to write your name before you were four years old?*

knife /nīf/ *n.* (**knives** *pl.*) a flat cutting instrument with a sharp blade. *Jean sliced the carrots with a knife.*

knight /nīt/ *n.* during the Middle Ages, a warrior who was honored with a military rank by a king or lord. *The king called his knights together to plan the battle.*

knock /nŏk/ *v.* to strike with the fist or with a hard object. *I knocked on the door, but no one answered.*

knot /nŏt/ *n.* a fastening made by tying. *We joined the two ropes with a square knot.*

know /nō/ *v.* (**knows, knew, known, know•ing**) **a.** to have the facts about; to understand. *Do you know how hail is formed?* **b.** to be acquainted with. *I know the Bakers, but I'm not sure where they live.*

known /nōn/ *v.* a form of **know**.

knuck•le /**nŭk′** əl/ *n.* a joint in a finger. *I broke my knuckle playing baseball.*

La•bor Day *n.* holiday on the first Monday in September to honor working people in the United States and Canada. *We like to have a picnic on Labor Day.*

la•dy /lā′ dē/ *n.* (**la•dies** *pl.*) a polite term for a woman. *Ladies and gentlemen, may I have your attention?*

lamb /lăm/ *n.* a young sheep. *The lamb ran playfully in the field.*

lamb

land /lănd/ *v.* to set down on the ground or other surface. *This plane is able to land on water.*

land•less /lănd′ lĭs/ *adj.* having no property or land. *Because of the Great Depression, many people were left landless.*

large /lärj/ *adj.* (**larg•er, larg•est; large•ly** *adv.*) big. *A whale is large.*

larg•er /lärj′ ər/ *adj.* the comparative form of **large**. *Your bedroom is larger than mine is.*

larg•est /lärj′ ĭst/ *adj.* the superlative form of **large**. *That is the largest whale I have ever seen!*

lat•er /lā′ tər/ *adj.* (**late, lat•est**) coming or occurring a longer time after the correct or usual time. *We arrived at the party later than we wanted to arrive.*

laugh /lăf/ *v.* to make sounds with the voice that show amusement. *Everyone laughed at the funny movie.*

laugh•ter /lăf′ tər/ *n.* the noise of laughing. *Laughter filled the classroom during the puppet show.*

launch /lônch/ or /länch/ *v.* to start; to begin. *Our school will launch a cleaning and painting drive next week.*

la•va /lä′ və/ *n.* the hot, melted rock that comes from a volcano. *The lava flowed down the mountain.*

law•ful /lô′ fəl/ *adj.* obeying the law. *I am a lawful citizen in my community.*

lay /lā/ *v.* (**lays, laid, lay•ing**) **a.** put or placed. *You laid your book on the table.* **b.** produced eggs. *The hens laid three eggs each.*

la•zy /lā′ zē/ *adj.* (**laz•i•er, la•zi•est**) not wanting to work. *He was too lazy to help us.*

lead[1] /lēd/ *v.* (**leads, led, lead•ing**) to direct or show the way. *She will lead the hikers home.*

lead[2] /lĕd/ *n.* **a.** a soft mineral used in some pipes. *He put a weight made of lead on the fishing line.* **b.** graphite used to make the writing substance in a pencil. *My fingers had black smudges from the pencil lead.*

lead•er /lē′ dər/ *n.* one who leads. *The Scout troop needs a new leader.*

leaf /lēf/ *n.* (**leaves** *pl.*) a flat, green part of a plant or tree. *The caterpillar was eating a leaf.*

learn•er /lûr′ nər/ *n.* one who learns; a student. *A good learner listens carefully.*

least /lēst/ *adj.* smallest in size or amount. *Which game costs the least money?*

leave /lēv/ *v.* (**leaves, left, leav•ing**) to go away; to go from. *The train will leave in five minutes.*

length /lĕngkth/ *n.* the distance from end to end. *The length of the boat is forty feet.*

length•en /lĕngk′ thən/ or /lĕng′-/ *v.* to make or become longer. *This road has been lengthened since I last drove on it.*

-less an English suffix that means "without," used to form adjectives: *endless.*

let•ter car•ri•er /lĕt′ ər kăr′ ē ər/ *n.* a person who delivers mail. *Our letter carrier delivers our mail every day at ten o'clock.*

light•en /līt′ n/ *v.* **a.** to make brighter; to add light to. *The new paint lightens the room.* **b.** to make less heavy. *Taking out the books lightened my suitcase.*

light•ly /līt′ lē/ *adv.* **a.** with little weight or pressure. *Lightly press the button to ring the doorbell.* **b.** in a worry-free manner. *She took the news lightly.*

limb /lĭm/ *n.* a branch of a tree. *We hung the swing from a strong limb.*

lis•ten /lĭs′ n/ *v.* to pay attention; to try to hear. *The audience listened closely to the speaker.*

lis•ten•er /lĭs′ ə nər/ *n.* one who listens. *A good listener remembers what is said.*

loaf /lōf/ *n.* (**loaves** *pl.*) the shape of bread in which each one is baked as one piece. *The bakery sells them a loaf of rye bread every day.*

loaf

loan /lōn/ *n.* an amount of money lent or borrowed. *Banks charge interest on loans.*

➤ **Loan** sounds like **lone.**

lo•cate /lō′ kāt/ or /lō kāt′/ *v.* (**lo•cates, lo•cat•ed, lo•cat•ing**) **a.** to find the position or place of. *Can you locate your town on the map?* **b.** to establish in a certain place. *The store is located in the shopping center.*

lone /lōn/ *adj.* alone; single. *A lone cloud floated in the blue sky.*

➤ **Lone** sounds like **loan.**

lose /lo͞oz/ *v.* (**los•es, lost, los•ing**) **a.** to be unable to find; to misplace. *Put the key in your pocket so you won't lose it.* **b.** to fail to win. *She lost the race by less than a second.*

love•less /lŭv′ lĭs/ *adj.* having no kindness or love. *The loveless kitten was adopted by the caring family.*

lug•gage /lŭg′ ĭj/ *n.* baggage; the suitcases, trunks, bags, or boxes that are taken on a trip. *We took extra luggage for our long vacation.*

lunch /lŭnch/ *n.* meal eaten at midday. *I had soup and salad for lunch.*

-ly a Latin suffix, used to form adverbs, that means: **a.** like; in the manner of: *finally.* **b.** at certain intervals: *weekly.*

ma•gi•cian /mə jĭsh′ ən/ *n.* one who performs magic for the entertainment of others. *The magician performed amazing tricks.*

mail /māl/ *n.* packages, letters, postcards, etc., that are delivered through the post office. *Has the mail come yet?*

mail•box /māl′ bŏks′/ *n.* (**mail•box•es** *pl.*) **a.** a public box into which people put items to be delivered by mail. *The contents of a mailbox are taken to the post office.* **b.** a private box for a home or business to which mail is delivered. *Check the mailbox to see if you got a letter.*

ma•jor /mā′ jər/ *adj.* larger; greater; primary. *He played a major role in the project's success.*

make-be•lieve /māk′ bĭ lēv/ *adj.* playful or fanciful. *Some children talk to make-believe friends.*

ma•ple /mā′ pəl/ *n.* a tree with hard wood and a thin sap that is sometimes used in making syrup and sugar. *Maples are grown for both beauty and shade.*

Mar. March.

march /märch/ *v.* (**march•es, marched, march•ing**) to walk with even, steady steps. *The band marched in the parade.*

March /märch/ *n.* the third month of the year. *The weather begins to warm up in March.*

mark /märk/ *v.* to make a visible sign on or by. *Mark the wrong answers with an "X."*

mar•ket /mär′ kĭt/ *n.* a place where things can be bought and sold. *A supermarket is a large, modern market.* (**mar•ket•a•ble** *adj.*)

Mar•tin Lu•ther King Day *n.* United States commemoration of the birthday of Martin Luther King, Jr., observed on the third Monday in January. *There's no school on Martin Luther King Day, so we can think about a great leader.*

mas•ter /măs′ tər/ *v.* to become skilled in. *It takes time and practice to master a foreign language.*

may /mā/ *v.* (**might**) **a.** to be allowed to. *May I be excused from the table?* **b.** to be possible that. *The package may arrive today.*

May /mā/ *n.* the fifth month of the year. *Flowers bloom in May.*

may•be /mā′ bē/ *adv.* perhaps. *Maybe he hasn't left the train yet, and we can still find him.*

mean¹ /mēn/ *v.* (**means, meant, mean•ing**) **a.** to intend. *I didn't mean to hurt her feelings.* **b.** to signify; to carry the meaning of. *The sign "+" means "plus."*

mean² /mēn/ *adj.* unkind; wicked. *The boy was mean to the other children who walked in his yard.*

meant /mĕnt/ *v.* past tense of **mean**.

med•dle /mĕd′ l/ *v.* (**med•dles, med•dled, med•dling**) to interest oneself in what is not one's concern; to interfere without being asked. *It isn't courteous to meddle in other people's affairs.*

Me•mo•ri•al Day *n.* a United States holiday on May 30, officially observed on the last Monday in May, to remember those members of the armed forces killed in war. Also called Decoration Day. *We watched the parade on Memorial Day.*

-ment a Latin suffix that means "the result of an action or process," used to form nouns: *amusement.*

men•tion¹ /mĕn′ shən/ *v.* to talk about briefly; to say something about. *She mentioned the new teacher, but she didn't tell me his name.*

men•tion² /mĕn′ shən/ *n.* a brief statement. *There wasn't even a mention of the fire in the newspaper.*

men•u /mĕn′ yoo/ *n.* a list of dishes that may be ordered (in a restaurant) or served. *The menu listed several tasty appetizers.*

Mex•i•can¹ /mĕk′ sĭ kən/ *adj.* of or from Mexico. *A sombrero is a Mexican hat.*

Mex•i•can² /mĕk′ sĭ kən/ *n.* one born or living in Mexico. *Many Mexicans visit the United States each year.*

mice /mīs/ *n.* plural of **mouse**.

mid- an English prefix that means "middle": *midday.*

mid•day¹ /mĭd′ dā′/ *n.* the middle of the day; noon. *The parade began at midday.*

mid•day² /mĭd′ dā′/ *adj.* in the middle of the day: *the midday meal.*

mid•dle¹ /mĭd′ l/ *n.* the point or part located at the same distance from each side or end; the center. *Your nose is in the middle of your face.*

mid•dle² /mĭd′ l/ *adj.* occupying a central position. *His middle name is Michael.*

might /mīt/ *v.* past tense of **may**.

mild /mīld/ *adj.* **a.** not harsh; not severe; warm rather than cold. *We had a mild winter last year.* **b.** not sharp or biting to the taste. *We ordered mild sauce on our food.* (**mild•ness** *n.*)

mi•nor /mī′ nər/ *adj.* smaller; lesser; secondary. *Brian played a minor role, so he didn't have to learn many lines.*

mis- a Latin prefix that means "not, wrong, or less": *mislead.*

miss /mĭs/ *v.* (**mis•ses, missed, mis•sing**) fail to hit, reach, catch, or contact. *The dart will miss the target.*

➤ **Missed** sounds like **mist**.

mist /mĭst/ *n.* a fine spray of liquid, such as water or perfume. *The mist watered the vegetables at the grocery store.*

➤ **Mist** sounds like **missed**.

moist /moist/ *adj.* somewhat wet; damp. *The grass was still moist from the rain this morning.*

mois•ten /moi′ sən/ *v.* to make or become damp; to wet. *Moisten this cloth and use it to wipe the table.*

mo•ment /mō′ mənt/ *n.* **a.** an instant; a very brief period. *I saw him for a moment, but I lost sight of him in the crowd.* **b.** a specific point in time. *I called the moment I heard you were sick.*

Mon. Monday.

Mon•day /mŭn′ dē/ or /-dā′/ *n.* the second day of the week, coming after Sunday and before Tuesday. *Monday is the first school day in the week.* [Old English *monandæg,* the moon's day.]

month /mŭnth/ *n.* one of the twelve parts into which a year is divided. *We go to school for nine months of the year.*

month•ly[1] /mŭnth′ lē/ *adj.* happening once a month. *Did you pay the monthly bills?*

month•ly[2] /mŭnth′ lē/ *adv.* once each month. *This magazine is published monthly.*

morn•ing /môr′ nĭng/ *n.* the earliest part of the day, ending at noon. *We eat breakfast every morning.*

mot a Latin root that means "to move": *motion.*

mo•tel /mō tĕl′/ *n.* a hotel near a highway for people who are traveling by car. *We spent the night in a motel on our way to visit our cousins.*

moth•er /mŭth′ ər/ *n.* the female parent. *My mother likes to listen to me read.*

mother

mo•tion[1] /mō′ shən/ *n.* **a.** the act of moving; movement. *The motion of the train made us sleepy.* **b.** a suggestion made at a meeting. *The motion was passed by the club members.*

mo•tion[2] /mō′ shən/ *v.* to make a movement or a gesture. *The speaker motioned to us to sit down.*

mount /mount/ *v.* to climb onto; to get up on. *The rider mounted his horse and galloped away.*

mouse /mous/ *n.* (**mice** *pl.*) a small animal with white, gray, or brown fur, a long tail, and long, sharp front teeth. *The field mouse made a nest in the ground.*

mouth /mouth/ *n.* the opening in the head that contains the tongue and teeth and is used for taking in food and making sounds. *When you yawn, your mouth opens wide.*

move•ment /mōōv′ mənt/ *n.* action; a change in position or location. *The children watched the slow movement of the snail across the sidewalk.*

mov•ie /mōō′ vē/ *n.* (**mo•vies** *pl.*) the showing of motion pictures at a theater. *We saw Greg at the movies.*

mul•ti•pli•ca•tion /mŭl′ tə pli kā′ shən/ *n.* the adding of a number a certain number of times. *Knowing your times tables will help you solve problems in multiplication.*

mum•ble /mŭm′ bəl/ *v.* (**mum•bles, mum•bled, mum•bling**) to speak unclearly so that you are hard to understand. *If you mumble, no one will understand you.*

mu•sic /myōō′ zĭk/ *n.* **a.** the art of making and combining sounds using rhythm, melody, and harmony. *Music is one of the fine arts.* **b.** the sounds made and combined in this way. *We can hear many kinds of music on the radio.* **—idiom. music to your ears.** exactly what you want to hear.

mu•si•cian /myōō zĭsh′ ən/ *n.* a person who composes or performs music. *The players in the orchestra are fine musicians.*

nar•row /năr′ ō/ *adj.* **a.** not wide: *a narrow street.* **b.** close: *a narrow escape.*

na•tion /nā′ shən/ *n.* a group of people living together under one government, who usually have many of the same customs and speak the same language. *The United States, Japan, and Sweden are nations.* (**na•tion•al•i•ty** *n.*)

naugh•ty /nô′ tē/ *adj.* (**naugh•ti•er, naugh•ti•est**) behaving badly or mischievously. *The naughty students were punished for their behavior on the field trip.*

near[1] /nîr/ *adv.* not far away in time or distance. *The train drew near.*

near[2] /nîr/ *prep.* not far from. *The school is near my house, only a block away.*

near•by /nîr′ bī′/ *adj.* not far off. *They live in a nearby town.*

near•er /nîr′ ər/ *adj.* comparative form of **near;** being closer in time or distance than anyone or anything. *Your house is nearer the school than my house.*

near•est /nîr′ ĭst/ *adj.* superlative form of **near**; being closer in time or distance than everyone or everything. *The library that is nearest the school is three miles away.*

nee•dle /nēd′ l/ *n.* a thin, pointed steel tool used in sewing. *Can you thread a needle?*

nei•ther[1] /nē′ thər/ or /nī′-/ *pron.* not the one and not the other. *Neither of us was invited.*

nei•ther[2] /nē′ thər/ or /nī′-/ *conj.* also not. *If you're not going to the park, neither am I.*

nei•ther[3] /nē′ thər/ or /nī′-/ *adj.* not either. *Neither girl was tall enough for the part in the play.*

neph•ew /nĕf′ yōō/ *n.* a son of a person's sister, brother, sister-in-law, or brother-in-law. *My nephew calls me Aunt Tracie.*

-ness an English suffix that means "a state or quality," used to form nouns: *softness.*

nev•er /nĕv′ ər/ *adv.* not ever; not at any time. *Maria has never been late to school; she is always early.*

news /nōōz/ or /nyōōz/ *n.* recent happenings reported in newspapers and over television and radio. *We read the news in the paper.*

news•pa•per /nōōz′ pā pər/ or /nyōōz′-/ *n.* a printed paper that contains news, advertisements, cartoons, etc. *My grandfather likes to work the crossword puzzles in the newspaper.*

New York /nōō′ yôrk′/ or /nyōō′-/ *n.* a state in the eastern United States. *The state of New York has beautiful mountains and lakes.*

no•bod•y /nō′ bŏd′ ē/ or /nō′ bə dē/ *pron.* no one; no person. *Nobody is here at this time of day.*

nor /nôr/ *conj.* and not; not either. *There was neither milk nor fruit juice in the refrigerator.*

north /nôrth/ *n.* the direction to your right when you face the sunset. *Cold winds blow from the north.*

Nov. November.

No•vem•ber /nō vĕm′ bər/ *n.* the eleventh month of the year. *November has thirty days.*

o•bey /ō bā′/ *v.* **a.** to follow the orders of. *Children obey their parents.* **b.** to act in agreement with; to carry out. *Good citizens obey the law.*

Oct. October.

ă pat	ŏ pot	th **thin**
ā pay	ō toe	*th* **this**
âr care	ô paw, for	hw **which**
ä father	oi noise	zh vision
ĕ pet	ou out	ə about,
ē be	ōō took	item,
ĭ pit	ōō boot	pencil,
ī pie	ŭ cut	gallop,
îr pier	ûr urge	circus

Oc•to•ber /ŏk tō′ bər/ *n.* the tenth month of the year. *Many leaves change color in October.*

of•ten /ô′ fən/ or /ŏf′ ən/ *adv.* many times; frequently. *We often see our relatives during the holidays.*

o•ri•ole /ôr′ ē ōl′/ or /ōr′ ē ōl′/ *n.* a black and orange songbird. *The Baltimore oriole is Maryland's state bird.*

oth•er•wise /ŭth′ ər wīz′/ *adv.* in a different way or manner. *He thought he was right; she thought otherwise.*

ought /ôt/ *v.* should. *You ought to wear a coat on a cold day like this.*

-ous an English suffix that means "full of or having": *wondrous.*

out•doors[1] /out dôrz′/ or /-dōrz′/ *n.* the area outside a house or building; the open air. *Campers enjoy the outdoors.*

out•doors[2] /out dôrz′/ or /-dōrz′/ *adv.* outside a building; out in the open air. *We played outdoors on the first sunny day of spring.*

o•ver /ō′ vər/ *prep.* **a.** above. *The reading lamp is over the bed.* **b.** on top of. *Put the cover over the basket.* **c.** more than. *The flight took over three hours.*

own•er /ō′ nər/ *n.* one who owns or possesses something. *Who is the owner of this plaid jacket?*

ox /ŏks/ *n.* (**ox•en** *pl.*) an adult bull. *The ox pulled the cart.*

pack•age /**păk′** ĭj/ *n.* a wrapped box; a parcel. *How much will it cost to mail this package?*

page¹ /pāj/ *n.* one side of a sheet of paper in a book, magazine, newspaper, or letter. *Kurt knew from the first page that he would like the book.*

page² /pāj/ *v* (**pag•es, paged, pag•ing**) to summon a person in a crowd. *Will you please page my mother in the store?*

paint /pānt/ *v.* **a.** to cover a surface with paint. *They painted the fence.* **b.** to make a picture with paints. *Ms. Lindquist paints landscapes in her spare time.*

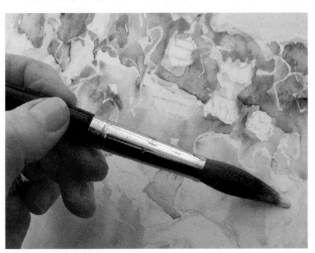

paint

paint•er /**pān′** tər/ *n.* **a.** a person who paints pictures; an artist. *Some painters make abstract designs.* **b.** a person whose job is painting buildings or furniture. *The painter stood on a ladder to paint the house.*

pa•per /**pā′** pər/ *n.* **a.** a material made in thin sheets of pulp, from wood or rags. *The pages of this book are made of paper.* **b.** a newspaper. *Have you seen the comics in today's paper?* **c.** a written article; a report. *The teacher asked us to write a paper about the moon.*

par•don /**pär′** dn/ *v.* to forgive or excuse. *Pardon me for disturbing you.*

par•ent /**păr′** ənt/ *n.* a father or a mother. *Either parent may write a note excusing an absence.*

part /pärt/ a Latin root that means "section or piece": *apart.*

part•ly /**pärt′** lē/ *adv.* in part; not completely. *My test is partly finished.*

pass¹ /păs/ *v.* **a.** to go by. *They pass the fire station on the way to school.* **b.** to hand over; to give; to send. *Please pass the salad.* **c.** to succeed in. *The entire fourth grade passed the test.*

pass² /păs/ *n.* **a.** a written note; a permit. *Did the teacher sign your pass?* **b.** a narrow road through mountains. *We saw snow at the top of the pass.*

passed /păst/ *v.* past tense of **pass**.

➤ **Passed** sounds like **past**.

pas•sen•ger /**păs′** ən jər/ *n.* a person traveling in, but not operating, a vehicle. *Each passenger is allowed one piece of carry-on luggage.*

past¹ /păst/ *n.* the time that has gone by. *In the distant past, dinosaurs lived on the earth.*

➤ **Past** sounds like **passed**.

past² /păst/ *adj.* gone by; previous. *In the past month we had three inches of rain.*

➤ **Past** sounds like **passed**.

pa•tient¹ /**pā′** shənt/ *adj.* able to put up with pain, trouble, delay, etc., without complaint. *The passenger was patient despite the traffic.*

pa•tient² /**pā′** shənt/ *n.* a person under the care of a doctor. *The doctor sees her patients in the morning.*

pave /pāv/ *v.* (**paves, paved, pav•ing**) to cover a road, street, etc., with a smooth, hard surface. *The dirt road will be paved next week.*

pave•ment /**pāv′** mənt/ *n.* the surface of a road or a street made by paving. *Some pavement is made with crushed rock, clay, and tar.*

pay•ment /**pā′** mənt/ *n.* an amount of money paid. *Most people who rent a house or an apartment make a monthly payment to the landlord.*

peace /pēs/ *n.* freedom from war. *The world's goal is to have peace.*

peace•ful /**pēs′** fəl/ *adj.* **a.** calm; quiet. *Early morning hours are peaceful.* **b.** not liking arguments or quarrels; liking peace. *Neutral nations are peaceful.*

peach /pēch/ *n.* (**peach•es** *pl.*) a sweet, juicy fruit with a large, rough stone in the center. *When ripe, a peach has a fuzzy, pinkish-yellow skin.*

pea•nut but•ter /**pē′** nŭt **bŭt′** ər/ *n.* a food made from roasted peanuts ground into a spreadable paste. *I like peanut butter on bananas.*

peb•ble /**pĕb′** əl/ *n.* a small stone. *Pebbles have been worn smooth by water running over them.*

peo•ple /**pē′** pəl/ *n.* human beings; persons; men, women, boys, and girls. *People of all ages attended the fair.*

per•fect /pûr′ fĭkt/ *adj.* **a.** having no flaws or errors; exactly right. *Charlene turned in a perfect paper in science.* **b.** excellent; unusually good. *Today is a perfect day for swimming.*

per•haps /pər hăps′/ *adv.* possibly, but not certainly; maybe. *Perhaps you should bring an umbrella, just in case it rains.*

per•son /pûr′ sən/ *n.* a human being; a man, woman, boy, or girl. *This elevator can hold six persons.*

pe•so /pā′ sō/ *n.* (**pe•sos** *pl.*) the currency used in some Latin American countries. *I found a peso on the ground in Mexico.*

pheas•ant /fĕz′ ənt/ *n.* (**pheas•ants** or **pheas•ant** *pl.*) a large, brightly colored bird with a long tail. *The ring-necked pheasant is South Dakota's state bird.*

pie /pī/ *n.* (**pies** *pl.*) baked goods made of fruit, meat, or pudding within a crust. *My mother made a pie for the holidays.*

piece /pēs/ *n.* a part; a segment. *Would you like a piece of my orange?*

pil•low /pĭl′ ō/ *n.* a support used for the head in resting or sleeping; a cushion. *Do you like to sleep on a feather pillow?*

pitch•er /pĭch′ ər/ *n.* a player in a baseball game who throws the ball to a person at bat. *The pitcher threw a curve ball for a strike.*

place•ment /plās′ mənt/ *n.* location; arrangement. *The placement of the flowers added the perfect touch to the dinner table.*

plaid¹ /plăd/ *n.* a pattern of checks or squares formed by stripes crossing at right angles. *Scottish clans have distinctive plaids, which they call tartans.* [Scottish Gaelic *plaide.*]

plaid² /plăd/ *adj.* having such a pattern: *a plaid scarf.*

play•er /plā′ ər/ *n.* **a.** a person who plays a game. *Beth is the shortest player on her soccer team.* **b.** a person who plays a musical instrument. *A guitar player is called a guitarist.*

play•ful /plā′ fəl/ *adj.* full of fun and enjoyment. *The baby was playful in his bath.*

pleas•ant /plĕz′ ənt/ *adj.* **a.** delightful; pleasing: *a pleasant vacation.* **b.** fair and warm: *a pleasant day.* **c.** agreeable; friendly: *pleasant teachers.*

pleas•ure /plĕzh′ ər/ *n.* **a.** joy; delight; satisfaction. *Her pleasure in meeting the famous guitarist showed on her face.* **b.** something that gives enjoyment or satisfaction. *Going to the zoo was a pleasure for the class.*

Pronunciation Key

ă	pat	ŏ	pot	th	**thin**
ā	pay	ō	toe	*th*	**th**is
âr	care	ô	paw, for	hw	**which**
ä	father	oi	n**oise**	zh	vision
ĕ	pet	ou	**out**	ə	about,
ē	be	ŏŏ	took		item,
ĭ	pit	ōō	boot		pencil,
ī	pie	ŭ	cut		gallop,
îr	pier	ûr	**urge**		circus

plow¹ /plou/ *n.* a tool used in farming for turning up soil. *Plows have sharp blades and are pulled by horses, oxen, or tractors.*

plow² /plou/ *v.* to work with a plow; to till. *Fields are plowed before crops are planted.*

poach /pōch/ *v.* (**poach•es, poached, poach•ing**) to cook in a simmering liquid. *I like to poach my eggs for breakfast.*

po•em /pō′ əm/ *n.* a verbal composition arranged so that it has rhythm and appeals to the imagination. *Not all poems rhyme.*

po•et /pō′ ĭt/ *n.* a person who writes poems. *Emily Dickinson was a famous American poet.*

po•ny /pō′ nē/ *n.* (**po•nies** *pl.*) a kind of horse that is small in size when fully grown. *Children ride a pony at an amusement park.*

pool /pōōl/ *n.* a small body of still water. *After it rained, there was a pool of water in our front yard.*

pop•corn /pŏp′ kôrn/ *n.* (**pop•corn** *pl.*) kernels of corn that burst open when heated. *Do you like butter on your popcorn?*

popcorn

port¹ /pôrt/ or /pōrt/ a Latin root that means "to carry": *portable.*

port² /pôrt/ or /pōrt/ *n.* **a.** a town with a harbor where ships may dock. *Boston and New York are Atlantic ports.* **b.** the left-hand side of a ship, boat, or airplane as one faces forward. *Ships show a red light toward port at night.*

pow•der /pou′ dər/ *n.* a substance made of fine grains. *It's easy to grind chalk into a powder.*

pow•er¹ /pou′ ər/ *n.* great strength, force, or control. *The police have power to enforce the law.*

pow•er² /pou′ ər/ *v.* to supply with power. *The boat is powered by an engine.*

pow•er•ful /pou′ ər fəl/ *adj.* having great power; strong. *The king was a powerful ruler.*

pow•er•less /pou′ ər lĭs/ *adj.* having no strength or power; helpless. *The farmers were powerless against the drought.*

pre- a prefix that means **a.** before: *preschool.* **b.** in advance: *prepay.*

pre•heat /prē hēt′/ *v.* to heat beforehand. *Please preheat the oven before you put the potatoes in to bake.*

pre•his•tor•ic /prē′ hĭ stôr′ ĭk/ or /-stŏr′-/ *adj.* having to do with the time before written history began. *Prehistoric paintings and tools have been found all over the world.*

pre•paid /prē pād′/ *v.* past tense of **prepay.**

pre•pay /prē pā′/ *v.* to pay beforehand. *The company will prepay the postage.*

pre•plan /prē′ plăn′/ *v.* (**pre•plans, pre•planned, pre•plan•ning**) to think or organize beforehand. *We will preplan the party before we send invitations.*

pre•re•cor•ded /prē rĭ kôrd′ əd/ *v.* recorded or taped in advance for later use. *We prerecorded this program to air over the holidays.*

pre•school /prē′ skool′/ *n.* a place of learning before elementary school. *Children aged three to five may attend preschool.*

Pres•i•dents′ Day *n.* a United States holiday on the third Monday in February to celebrate the birthdays of George Washington and Abraham Lincoln. *On Presidents' Day, we read about our country's leaders.*

pre•slice /prē slīs′/ *v.* (**pre•slic•es, pre•sliced, pre•slic•ing**) to cut beforehand. *Preslice the mushrooms before making a mushroom omelet.*

pre•soak /prē sōk′/ *v.* to soak beforehand. *Presoak the stained shirt before you wash it.*

pre•test /prē′ tĕst′/ *n.* a test given beforehand to determine readiness. *If you already know the spelling words, you'll do well on the pretest.*

pre•view /prē′ vyoo′/ *v.* to view or watch in advance. *We were invited to preview the art show.*

price /prīs/ *n.* the cost in money; the amount of money for which something is sold. *The price should be clearly labeled.*

prin•ci•ple /prĭn′ sə pəl/ *n.* a basic fact; a rule upon which other rules are based: *the principles of science.*

➤ **Principle** sounds like **principal.**

pro•fes•sor /prə fĕs′ ər/ *n.* a college teacher of the highest rank. *After Mr. Patel received his Ph.D., he became an assistant professor at the university.*

prompt /prŏmpt/ *adj.* (**prompt•er, prompt•est**) carried out or performed without delay. *We tipped the waiter well for his prompt service.*

pub•lic /pŭb′ lĭk/ *adj.* **a.** for the people; used by people. *Public parks are open to all.* **b.** of the people: *public opinion.*

pub•lish /pŭb′ lĭsh/ *v.* **a.** to prepare printed texts such as books or magazines for sale. *That company publishes a book we use in school.* **b.** to make known. *The newspaper published an account of the hearing.* [Latin *pūblicāre,* to make public.]

pub•lish•er /pŭb′ lĭ shər/ *n.* a person or company whose business is to prepare, print, and sell books, magazines, newspapers, etc. *You will find the publisher's name on the second page in this book.*

quail /kwāl/ *n.* (**quail** or **quails** *pl.*) a chicken-like bird with brown feathers and a short tail. *We saw some quail in the woods near our house.*

quaint /kwānt/ *adj.* (**quaint•er, quaint•est**) attractive in an old-fashioned way. *The quaint cottage seemed to be taken right out of a storybook.* (**quaint•ness** *n.*)

quake /kwāk/ *v.* (**quakes, quaked, quak•ing**) to vibrate or shake. *The ground quaked beneath us during the mild earthquake.*

quar•rel[1] /kwôr′ əl/ or /kwŏr′-/ *n.* an argument; a dispute. *The children had a quarrel about which program to watch.*

quar•rel[2] /kwôr′ əl/ or /kwŏr′-/ *v.* to fight; to disagree, using angry words. *They quarreled about whose turn it was to bat.*

quart /kwôrt/ *n.* a liquid measure equal to two pints; one-quarter of a gallon. *My mother sent me to the store for a quart of milk.*

quar•ter /kwôr′ tər/ *n.* a coin worth one fourth of a dollar, or twenty-five cents. *Two dimes and a nickel equal a quarter.*

quartz /kwôrts/ *n.* a mineral with hexagonal crystals. *Rose quartz is a pink-colored mineral used in jewelry.*

queen /kwēn/ *n.* **a.** a female ruler. *The queen issued a proclamation.* **b.** the wife of a king. *When she married the king, she became his queen.*

ques•tion[1] /kwĕs′ chən/ *n.* **a.** a sentence that asks something. *"What time is it?" is a question.* **b.** a problem. *The litter question will be discussed tonight.*

ques•tion[2] /kwĕs′ chən/ *v.* (**ques•tions, ques•tioned, ques•tion•ing**) to ask, doubt, or inquire. *I question your facts.*

quick /kwĭk/ *adj.* fast; swift. *The rabbit made a quick leap into the bushes.* (**quick•ness** *n.*)

quick•er /kwĭk′ ər/ *adj.* comparative form of **quick**; being faster or swifter than another. *A rabbit is quicker than a turtle.*

quick•est /kwĭk′ ĭst/ *adj.* superlative form of **quick**; being the fastest or swiftest of anyone or anything. *That pizza place has the quickest delivery of any pizza place in town.*

qui•et /kwī′ ĭt/ *adj.* **a.** silent; still; having little noise. *The hum of the airplane was the only sound in the quiet night.* **b.** peaceful; calm. *Alice spent a quiet afternoon reading.*

qui•et•er /kwī′ ĭt ər/ *adj.* comparative form of **quiet**; being more still or peaceful than another. *It is quieter out here at the lake than it is in the city.*

qui•et•est /kwī′ ĭt ĭst/ *adj.* superlative form of **quiet**; being the most still or peaceful of anyone or anything. *The library is the quietest place in this whole school.*

quill /kwĭl/ *n.* a large, stiff feather or its hollow stem. *Quills were once used to make pens.*

quilt /kwĭlt/ *n.* a bed cover made of layers of cloth and padding sewn together. *Grandma told me how she made the patchwork quilt.*

quilt

quit /kwĭt/ *v.* (**quits, quit** or **quit•ted, quit•ting**) **a.** to stop. *We'll quit raking leaves when it gets dark.* **b.** to leave; to give up. *Mr. Walters quit his job to start his own business.*

quite /kwīt/ *adv.* **a.** completely; entirely. *I haven't quite finished eating.* **b.** really; truly. *His drawings are quite good.*

quiv•er /kwĭv′ ər/ *v.* to shake or move with a slight trembling motion. *I can see how cold you are by the way you quiver!*

quiz /kwĭz/ *n.* (**quiz•zes** *pl.*) a brief test. *I missed two questions on the science quiz.*

quote[1] /kwōt/ *v.* (**quotes, quot•ed, quot•ing**) to repeat or refer to a passage from a story or poem. *Justin quoted a line from the poem in his essay.*

quote[2] /kwōt/ *n.* a quotation; a passage repeated from a story or a poem. *Quotes usually appear inside quotation marks.*

quo•tient /**kwō′** shənt/ *n.* the result obtained when one number is divided by another. *If you divide 16 by 2, the quotient is 8.*

rac•er /**rā′** sər/ *n.* one that races or takes part in a race. *The fastest racer came in first in the relay.*

ra•di•o /**rā′** dē ō/ *n.* **a.** a way of sending sounds from one place to another by electromagnetic waves. *Before radio was discovered, messages were sent over wires.* **b.** a device for receiving such sounds. *Rita heard the election results on her radio.*

rail /rāl/ *n.* **a.** a bar of wood or metal. *She sat on the top rail of the fence.* **b.** railroad. *Send this package by rail.*

rain•bow /**rān′** bō′/ *n.* a curved band of colored light in the sky, caused by the rays of the sun passing through drops of rain, mist, or spray. *We saw a rainbow where the waves broke against the rocks.*

rainbow

range /rānj/ *v.* (**rang•es, ranged, rang•ing**) **a.** to extend or vary within certain limits. *The stories in this book range from sad to funny.* **b.** to travel over; to wander through. *Giraffes range the plains of Africa.*

rare /râr/ *adj.* not often found or seen. *My uncle saves rare postage stamps.*

rath•er /**ră***th***′** ər/ *adv.* **a.** somewhat. *The baby is rather tired after the long ride.* **b.** more readily; more gladly. *I would rather stay inside today.*

rat•tle /**răt′** l/ *v.* (**rat•tles, rat•tled, rat•tling**) **a.** to make a number of short, sharp sounds. *The windows rattle when the wind blows.* **b.** to move with short, sharp sounds. *The old car rattled over the bumpy road.* —*idiom.* **rattle a cage.** to annoy.

ra•zor /**rā′** zər/ *n.* a tool for cutting or shaving, often used for hair. *My dad uses a razor to shave every morning.*

re- a Latin prefix that means: **a.** "again": *rebuild.* **b.** "back": *recall.*

reach /rēch/ *v.* **a.** to stretch out one's hand or arm. *Joel reached for the book on the top shelf.* **b.** to extend to. *The old road reaches the river and stops.*

read /rēd/ *v.* (**reads, read, read•ing**) to decode the meaning of (written or printed characters, words, or sentences). *I can't read your writing.*

read•er /**rē′** dər/ *n.* a person who reads. *The teacher chose Kathy to be the reader of our lunchtime story this week.*

read•y /**rĕd′** ē/ *adj.* (**read•i•er, read•i•est; read•i•ly** *adv.*) **a.** prepared. *We are ready for school.* **b.** willing. *My older brother is always ready to help me with my homework.*

rear[1] /rîr/ *n.* the back part. *We stood in the rear of the room.* —*idiom.* **bring up the rear.** to be the last in line.

rear[2] /rîr/ *adj.* at or of the back. *Use the rear entrance.*

rear[3] /rîr/ *v.* to rise on the hind legs. *The horse reared suddenly and the rider fell off.*

rear[4] /rîr/ *v.* (**rears, reared, rear•ing**) to care for (children or a child) during the early stages of life. *They promised to rear their adopted children as their own.*

rea•son[1] /**rē′** zən/ *n.* **a.** a cause or explanation. *Your parents will write the reason for your absence.* **b.** logic; the power to think. *Use reason to solve the problem.*

rea•son[2] /**rē′** zən/ *v.* to think in a sensible way; to use logic. *See if you can reason out the meaning of the word.*

re•build /rē bĭld′/ *v.* (**re•builds, re•built, re•build•ing**) to build again. *They are planning to rebuild the old school.*

re•check /rē chĕk′/ *v.* to check again. *After he finished the test, Pedro went back and rechecked his answers.*

re•claim /rĭ klām′/ or /rē-/ v. **a.** to restore to a usable condition. *We can reclaim land used for mining and set up a nature preserve.* **b.** to claim back; to ask for the return of. *They reclaimed their furniture from storage.* (**rec•la•ma•tion** *n.*)

re•cord[1] /rĭ kôrd′/ v. **a.** to keep an account of. *The story of our country's beginning is recorded in history.* **b.** to put sounds on a magnetic tape, phonograph record, or compact disc.

re•cord[2] /rĕk′ ərd/ n. **a.** an account of facts or events. *The secretary keeps the club's records.* **b.** the best performance. *Who holds the record for the race?* **c.** a thin disc used on a phonograph to produce sound.

re•cov•er /rĭ kŭv′ ər/ v. **a.** to get back. *The police recovered the stolen goods.* **b.** to regain health. *Tracy recovered quickly after her illness.*

red•der /rĕd′ ər/ adj. (**red, red•dest**) having more red than something else. *Her hair is redder than his.*

red•dest /rĕd′ ĭst/ adj. having the most red of anyone or anything else. *That cardinal is the reddest bird I have ever seen.*

re•fill /rē fĭl′/ v. to fill again; to replenish. *Please refill the soap dispenser because it is empty.*

re•form /rĭ fôrm′/ v. to make better by correcting or removing faults. *We discussed how to reform the old rules.*

re•frain[1] /rĭ frān′/ v. (**re•frains, re•frained, re•frain•ing**) to hold oneself back from doing something. *I try to refrain from gossiping.*

re•frain[2] /rĭ frān′/ n. a phrase, verse, or group of verses repeated throughout a song or poem. *The song's refrain is stuck in my head.*

re•fresh /rĭ frĕsh′/ v. to make fresh again; to revive; to renew. *The cool lemonade refreshed us after our hike.*

re•gain /rē gān′/ v. to get back again. *He will regain consciousness after the medicine has worn off.*

re•group /rē groop′/ v. to arrange differently; to put into a new grouping. *You must sometimes regroup numbers before you can subtract.*

re•heat /rē hēt′/ v. to heat again. *Dad reheated some leftovers for dinner.*

rein•deer /rān′ dîr′/ n. (**rein•deer** or **rein•deers** pl.) an animal with antlers that resembles a caribou.

re•lay[1] /rē′ lā/ or /rĭ lā′/ v. (**re•layed, re•lay•ing, re•lays**) to take and pass along to another person or place. *Will you relay a message to Joan when you see her?*

Pronunciation Key

ă	pat	ŏ	pot	th	thin
ā	pay	ō	toe	*th*	this
âr	care	ô	paw, for	hw	which
ä	father	oi	noise	zh	vision
ĕ	pet	ou	out	ə	about,
ē	be	o͝o	took		item,
ĭ	pit	o͞o	boot		pencil,
ī	pie	ŭ	cut		gallop,
îr	pier	ûr	urge		circus

re•lay[2] /rē′ lā/ n. **a.** a relay race. *Our team finished second in the relay race.* **b.** a division of a relay race. *Kara is training for the 200-mile distance team relay.*

relay

re•ly /rĭ lī′/ v. (**re•lies, re•lied, re•ly•ing**) to depend on. *Many who are visually impaired rely on guide dogs to help them travel safely.*

re•main /rĭ mān′/ v. **a.** to continue without change; to stay. *The nurse reported that the patient's condition remained good.* **b.** to be left over. *After the picnic only a few sandwiches remained.*

re•name /rē nām′/ v. (**re•names, re•named, re•nam•ing**) to call by a different name; to give a new name to. *We can rename one ten as ten ones.*

re•or•der /rē ôr′ dər/ v. to order again. *The product was damaged, so I need to reorder it.*

re•peat /rĭ pēt′/ v. **a.** to say again. *Will you repeat the question, please?* **b.** to say from memory. *Tomorrow each of you will be asked to repeat this poem.*

re•play /rē′ plā′/ *n.* something shown again on television, especially an exciting part of a sporting event. *After watching the replay, the referee changed his call.*

re•ply¹ /rĭ plī′/ *n.* (**re•plies** *pl.*) an answer. *I did not hear his reply because he spoke so softly.*

re•ply² /rĭ plī′/ *v.* (**re•plies, re•plied, re•ply•ing**) to give an answer; to respond. *She replied to my letter immediately.*

re•port¹ /rĭ pôrt′/ or /-pōrt′/ *n.* a detailed written or spoken account. *The newspaper report of the election listed the winners.*

re•port² /rĭ pôrt′/ or /-pōrt′/ *v.* to give an account or statement of. *The president of the company reported that sales had increased.*

re•port•er /rĭ pôr′ tər/ or /-pōrt′-/ *n.* a person who gathers news for radio, television, or newspapers. *A reporter interviewed the candidates.*

re•read /rē rēd′/ *v.* (**re•reads, re•read, re•read•ing**) to read again. *I often reread my favorite books.*

rest•ful /rĕst′ fəl/ *adj.* offering rest, peace, or quiet. *My aunt finds sewing restful after a busy day.*

rest•ful•ness /rĕst′ fəl nĭs/ *n.* the condition of having peace and quiet. *The restfulness was much needed after such a busy week!*

rest•less /rĕst′ lĭs/ *adj.* impatient; unable to be still. *The small children grew restless after the long delay.*

re•turn /rĭ tûrn′/ *v.* **a.** to come or go back. *We will return after the game is over.* **b.** to bring, send, or give back. *Return the book when you have finished reading it.*

re•view /rĭ vyōō′/ *v.* to study again; to go over. *She reviewed the chapter before she took the test.*

re•write /rē rīt′/ *v.* (**re•writes, re•wrote, re•writ•ten, re•writ•ing**) to write again. *The teacher asked us to rewrite our book reports, after correcting the spelling and punctuation.*

ridge /rĭj/ *n.* **a.** a narrow, raised line or strip; a crest. *Corduroy is a type of cloth that has ridges.* **b.** a long, narrow hill or mountain. *The sun sank behind the ridge.*

right /rīt/ *adj.* **a.** just; good. *Obeying the law is the right thing to do.* **b.** correct; true; accurate. *Abby's answers were all right.* (**right•ness** *n.*)

rig•id /rĭj′ ĭd/ *adj.* very stiff; not able to be bent. *A cast holds a broken arm in a rigid position so it can heal.*

rise¹ /rīz/ *v.* (**ris•es, rose, ris•en, ris•ing**) **a.** to get up. *He rose from his chair to greet us.* **b.** to move upward; to ascend. *We saw the balloon rise over the heads of the crowd.*

rise² /rīz/ *n.* an increase in height or amount. *The store announced a rise in prices.*

role /rōl/ *n.* a part or a character in a play. *Who will play the role of Peter Pan?*

  ➤ **Role** sounds like **roll**.

roll /rōl/ *v.* **a.** to move by turning over and over. *The ball rolled down the hill.* **b.** to wrap something around itself. *She rolled the yarn into a ball and put it in a drawer.*

  ➤ **Roll** sounds like **role**.

rough /rŭf/ *adj.* **a.** not smooth or even. *The car bounced and rattled over the rough road.* **b.** harsh; violent; not gentle. *The apples were bruised by rough handling.*

round /round/ *adj.* **a.** shaped like a ball. *The earth is round.* **b.** shaped like a circle. *Our swimming pool is square, but theirs is round.* (**round•ness** *n.*)

roy•al /roi′ əl/ *adj.* having to do with kings and queens. *The king and queen live in the royal palace.*

rub•ber /rŭb′ ər/ *n.* elastic material used in products such as tires, containers, and rubberbands. *We have rubber tires on the car.*

rule /rōōl/ *n.* **a.** a law; a regulation. *Always obey the school safety rules.* **b.** an instruction; a direction. *The rules describe how to play the game.* —*idiom.* **rule the roost.** be in charge.

rum•mage /rŭm′ ĭj/ *v.* (**rum•mag•es, rum•maged, rum•mag•ing**) to search for something by moving things around. *The hidden camera caught the thief trying to rummage around the office.*

run•ner /rŭn′ ər/ *n.* one who runs. *The runners were very tired after the race.*

runner

Rus•sia /rŭsh′ ə/ *n.* a large country in eastern Europe and northern Asia. *Russia was the largest republic in the former U.S.S.R.*

Rus•sian¹ /rŭsh′ ən/ *adj.* of or from Russia. *Borscht is a Russian soup.*

Rus•sian² /rŭsh′ ən/ *n.* **a.** one born or living in Russia. *Russians must dress warmly in winter.* **b.** the language of Russia. *Russian uses a different alphabet from English.*

Pronunciation Key

ă	pat	ŏ	pot	th	thin
ā	pay	ō	toe	*th*	this
âr	care	ô	paw, for	hw	which
ä	father	oi	noise	zh	vision
ĕ	pet	ou	out	ə	about,
ē	be	ŏŏ	took		item,
ĭ	pit	ōō	boot		pencil,
ī	pie	ŭ	cut		gallop,
îr	pier	ûr	urge		circus

sad•der /săd′ ər/ *adj.* (**sad, sad•dest**) more unhappy than someone else. *I am sadder about losing the game than I thought I would be.*

sad•ness /săd′ nĭs/ *n.* sorrow; grief. *Tears can be an expression of sadness.*

safe /sāf/ *adj.* free from risk or harm. *The sidewalk is a safe place to walk.*

saf•er /sāf′ ər/ *adj.* (**safe, saf•est**) more protected from harm than something or someone else. *Wearing a seatbelt makes driving a car safer.*

saf•est /sāf′ ĭst/ *adj.* (**safe, saf•er**) most protected from harm. *Walking may be the safest mode of traveling.*

said /sĕd/ *v.* past tense and past participle of **say.** *I said I would not be in school today.*

sam•ple¹ /săm′ pəl/ *n.* a part that shows what the rest is like. *The store gave away free samples of the new soap.*

sam•ple² /săm′ pəl/ *v.* (**sam•ples, sam•pled, sam•pling**) to test; to try. *We sampled the cookies we had baked for the party.*

Sat. Saturday.

Sat•ur•day /săt′ ər dē/ or /-dā′/ *n.* the seventh day of the week, coming after Friday. *We have no school on Saturday.* [Old English *Sæternesdæg*, translated from Latin *dies Saturni*, Saturn's day.]

say /sā/ *v.* (**says, said, say•ing**) to utter out loud; pronounce. *Could you please say that more slowly?*

scale¹ /skāl/ *n.* a device or machine for weighing things. *According to the scale in the doctor's office, she weighed seventy pounds.* [Old Norse *skāl.*]

scale² /skāl/ *v.* (**scaled, scal•ing, scales**) to climb up or over. *The climbers used ropes to scale the cliff.*

scare /skâr/ *v.* (**scares, scared, scar•ing**) to frighten. *The sudden loud noise scared me.*

scowl /skoul/ *n.* a facial expression of displeasure; a frown. *He made a scowl when he spilled his milk.*

sea•son /sē′ zən/ *n.* one of the four parts into which a year is divided. *Spring is my favorite season.*

seat belt /sēt′ bĕlt′/ *n.* a safety strap designed to hold a person securely in a seat. *The flight attendant asked the passengers to fasten their seat belts.*

self /sĕlf/ *n.* (**selves** *pl.*) individual. *Bess is finally acting like her old self again.*

sell•er /sĕl′ ər/ *n.* a person who sells; a vendor. *The flower seller had a stand on the street corner.*

➤ **Seller** sounds like **cellar.**

sense•less /sĕns′ lĭs/ *adj.* lacking sense; foolish or stupid. *It is senseless not to use sunscreen when going to the beach.*

Sept. September.

Sep•tem•ber /sĕp tĕm′ bər/ *n.* the ninth month of the year. *Many schools start in September.*

serve /sûrv/ *v.* **a.** to prepare and offer food. *We were served a delicious dinner.* **b.** to help others by performing a task. *Sarah will serve as club treasurer.*

set•tle /sĕt′ l/ *v.* **a.** to agree; to decide. *The class settled on Saturday as the day of the picnic.* **b.** to establish residence. *Their family settled in California years ago.*

shad•ow /shăd′ ō/ *n.* a dark shape made on a surface by something that blocks the light. *The afternoon sun casts a long shadow of the tree.* [Old English *sceadu*, shade, shadow.]

share¹ /shâr/ *n.* a part; a portion. *Todd always does his share of work.*

283

share² /shâr/ *v.* (**shares, shared, shar•ing**) to use together. *The brothers share the same room.*

sharp•er /shär′ pər/ *adj.* (**sharp, sharp•est**) having a thinner edge or finer point suitable for cutting or piercing. *Some species of cactus have sharper spines than others.*

sheep /shēp/ *n.* (**sheep** *pl.*) a hoofed animal with a thick, woolly coat. *Farmers raise sheep both for meat and for wool.*

shell /shĕl/ *n.* the hard outer covering of certain animals. *Snails, turtles, and clams have shells.*

shel•ter¹ /shĕl′ tər/ *n.* something that covers, protects, or shields. *The old barn served as a shelter from the storm.*

shel•ter² /shĕl′ tər/ *v.* to protect; to give shelter to. *Our house shelters us from cold weather.* [Old English *scield,* "shield."]

ship•ment /shĭp′ mənt/ *n.* goods sent or delivered to a certain place. *The store received a shipment of clothing from the manufacturer.*

short•en /shôr′ tn/ *v.* (**short** *adj.*) to make short or shorter. *The sleeves are too long so I will shorten them.*

shoul•der /shōl′ dər/ *n.* **a.** the part of the body between the neck and an arm. *The gym teacher said, "Shoulders straight!"* **b.** the edge of a road. *The truck driver pulled onto the shoulder.*

show /shō/ *v.* (**shows, showed, shown or showed, show•ing**) to point out; to cause to be seen. *Show me the picture you liked.*

show•er /shou′ ər/ *n.* **a.** a short fall of rain. *During the afternoon there were three showers.* **b.** a bath in which water comes down in a spray. *I take a shower every morning.*

shown /shōn/ *v.* a form of **show**.

shy /shī/ *adj.* **a.** reserved; quiet. *After Josh made friends at his new school, he was no longer shy.* **b.** easily frightened. *A deer is shy.*

sick•ness /sĭk′ nĭs/ *n.* (**sick•ness•es** *pl.*) **a.** illness; poor health. *Good nutrition helps prevent sickness.* **b.** a certain disease. *Chicken pox is usually a mild sickness.*

si•lent /sī′ lənt/ *adj.* **a.** quiet; still; with no sound or noise. *The morning was silent until the birds began to sing.* **b.** not said out loud. *The "e" in "rake" is silent.*

sil•ver /sĭl′ vər/ *n.* a whitish precious metal. *Silver is used in making coins such as dimes and quarters.*

sim•ple /sĭm′ pəl/ *adj.* **a.** easy to understand. *The simple questions did not take long to answer.* **b.** plain; bare; with nothing fancy added. *She chose a simple red dress.*

sing•er /sĭng′ ər/ *n.* one who sings. *A choir is a group of singers.*

sin•gle /sĭng′ gəl/ *adj.* one alone; only one. *A single orange was left in the box.*

sis•ter /sĭs′ tər/ *n.* a girl or woman having the same parents as another person. *The two sisters were planning a surprise party for their parents' anniversary.*

size /sīz/ *n.* the physical measurements of an object. *Which size paintbrush do you need?*

skat•er /skā′ tər/ *n.* a person who skates. *The skaters checked the ice before skating on the pond.*

skill /skĭl/ *n.* the ability to do something well as a result of practice. *His skill in playing the violin may someday make him famous.*

skill•ful /skĭl′ fəl/ *adj.* displaying much skill; expert. *The skillful mason laid the brick quickly and perfectly.*

skirt /skûrt/ *v.* (**skirts, skirt•ed, skirt•ing**) pass around or avoid. *He will skirt the issue because he is uncomfortable talking about it.*

sleep•less /slēp′ lĭs/ *adj.* not able to sleep; being without sleep. *After drinking a lot of caffeine, I was quite sleepless last night.*

slight /slīt/ *adj.* not big; small; slender. *Although it looks sunny, there's a slight chance it will rain later today.*

slim•mer /slĭm′ ər/ *adj.* thinner or more slender than something or someone else. *Joe chose the slimmer book to read on vacation.*

slim•mest /slĭm′ ĭst/ *adj.* thinnest or most slender of anyone or anything. *That giraffe has the slimmest neck in the entire herd.*

smart /smärt/ *adj.* intelligent; clever; quick in mind. *A smart dog can learn many tricks.*

smell¹ /smĕl/ *v.* to get the odor or scent of through the nose. *We could smell dinner cooking as we came in.*

smell² /smĕl/ *n.* an odor; a scent. *The smell of orange blossoms filled the air.*

smooth•ness /smōō*th*′ nĭs/ *n.* the condition of having no rough parts. *I like the smoothness of leather couches.*

snare /snâr/ *v.* (**snares, snared, snar•ing**) to trap or to catch. *The ranger was hoping to snare a bear.*

snug•gle /snŭg′ əl/ v. (**snug•gles, snug•gled, snug•gling**) to lie or press together; to cuddle. *The puppies snuggled close to their mother to keep warm.*

soap /sōp/ n. a substance used for washing. *Use plenty of soap when you wash your hands.*

soar /sôr/ or /sōr/ v. to rise or fly high; to glide. *Eagles soar gracefully in the sky.*

➤ **Soar** sounds like **sore**.

soar

soft•en /sô′ fən/ or /sŏf′ ən/ v. to make or become soft. *Ice cream softens in the heat.* (**soft•ly** adv.)

soft•ness /sôft′ nĭs/ or /sŏft′-/ n. the state or condition of being soft. *The softness of the wool blanket made it pleasant to use.*

some•one /sŭm′ wŭn′/ or /sŭm′ wən/ pron. somebody; some person. *Someone ought to fix that front door.*

some•thing /sŭm′ thĭng/ pron. a certain thing that is not specifically named. *Give the dog something to eat.*

some•times /sŭm′ tīmz/ adv. once in a while; now and then. *The sun sometimes shines when it is raining.*

son /sŭn/ n. a male child. *The mother took her son to a baseball game.*

sore /sôr/ or /sōr/ adj. painful; tender when touched. *His foot was sore after he stubbed his toe.*

➤ **Sore** sounds like **soar**.

sort /sôrt/ v. to separate things into like groups. *The child can sort the blocks into two piles by color.*

south /south/ n. the direction to the left when a person faces the sunset. *A warm wind blew from the south.*

Span•ish¹ /spăn′ ĭsh/ adj. of or from Spain. *The flamenco is a Spanish dance.*

Span•ish² /spăn′ ĭsh/ n. the language of Spain, Mexico, Central America, and most of South America. *Spanish is taught in many schools.*

spare /spâr/ adj. extra. *Every automobile should have a spare tire.*

spark /spärk/ n. **a.** a tiny particle of fire. *As the wood burned, it gave off bright sparks.* **b.** a brief, bright flash of light. *We saw the sparks of fireflies in the night.*

spar•kle /spär′ kəl/ v. (**spar•kles, spar•kled, spar•kling**) to glitter or shine; to flash. *Most diamonds will sparkle in the sun.*

speak /spēk/ v. (**speaks, spoke, spo•ken, speak•ing**) to talk; to say words. *Speak clearly so that we can understand you!*

speak•er /spē′ kər/ n. **a.** a person who speaks or delivers public speeches. *The speaker at tonight's meeting will discuss the election.* **b.** a device that transmits sound. *These speakers will help everyone hear the music.*

speech /spēch/ n. (**speech•es** pl.) a talk given in public. *The President made a speech on television.*

speed¹ /spēd/ n. **a.** swiftness; quickness. *An antelope has great speed.* **b.** the rate of movement. *The airplane flies at a speed of six hundred miles an hour.*

speed² /spēd/ v. (**speeds, sped** or **speed•ed, speed•ing**) to go fast. *We watched the train speed past.*

spill¹ /spĭl/ v. to run out; to flow over. *The juice spilled on the tablecloth.*

spill² /spĭl/ n. an act of spilling: *an oil spill.*

spin•ach /**spĭn′** ĭch/ *n.* a leafy green vegetable. *Spinach provides iron, which a healthy body needs.*

spoil /spoil/ *v.* **a.** to ruin; to damage; to destroy. *The stain will spoil your shirt if you don't wash it out quickly.* **b.** to become rotten or not fit for use. *The meat spoiled when it was left in the hot sun.*

spoke /spōk/ *v.* past tense of **speak**.

sport /spôrt/ or /spōrt/ *n.* any game involving exercise; recreation. *Swimming is a common summer sport.*

spout[1] /spout/ *v.* to shoot out in a forceful stream or in spurts. *Whales spout water from their blowholes in order to breathe.*

spout[2] /spout/ *n.* a pipe or narrow opening through which liquid is discharged in a stream. *The water won't come out because the pump's spout is rusted.*

spread /sprĕd/ *v.* (**spreads, spread, spread•ing**) **a.** to open out; to unfold. *Spread out the map on the table.* **b.** to stretch out. *The bird spread its wings and flew away.*

spring /sprĭng/ *n.* the season of the year that begins about March 21 and ends around June 21. *The weather begins to get warm in the spring.*

square[1] /skwâr/ *n.* a rectangle with four equal sides. *A checkerboard is made up of squares.*

square[2] /skwâr/ *adj.* having four equal sides. *This room is square.*

squash /skwŏsh/ *n.* a fruit with a hard rind and edible flesh. *Zucchini is a type of squash.* [Narragansett *askútasquash.*]

squeal[1] /skwēl/ *n.* a sharp, high-pitched cry. *The squeals of the pigs got louder as they saw the farmer bringing their food.*

squeal[2] /skwēl/ *v.* to make a sharp, high-pitched cry. *The baby squealed with delight.*

squeeze /skwēz/ *v.* (**squeez•es, squeezed, squeez•ing**) to press together hard; to compress. *Squeeze the sponge so that all the water comes out.*

squid /skwĭd/ *n.* (**squids** or **squid** *pl.*) a marine animal that has ten arms, a long tapered body, and a fin on each side. *The giant squid can grow as long as 100 feet.*

squint /skwĭnt/ *v.* (**squint•ed, squint•ing**) to look at with partly opened eyes. *The sun was so bright we had to squint to see.*

squirm /skwûrm/ *v.* (**squirm•ed, squirm•ing**) to turn and twist the body. *We laughed to see the puppy squirm in the child's arms.*

squir•rel /**skwûr′** əl/ *n.* a small rodent with a long bushy tail. *Squirrels eat nuts and live in trees.*

squirrel

squirt /skwûrt/ *v.* to come forth in a sudden, rapid stream from a narrow opening. *Be careful; the water may squirt out of the hose unexpectedly.*

sta•di•um /**stā′** dē əm/ *n.* (**sta•di•ums** or **sta•di•a** *pl.*) a large, usually unroofed building with tiers of seats for spectators at sports events. *This football stadium will seat more than 100,000 people.*

stake /stāk/ *n.* a stick or post with a pointed end that can be pounded into the ground. *The tent will stand straight when we tie it to these stakes.*

➤ **Stake** sounds like **steak**.

stare /stâr/ *v.* (**stares, stared, star•ing**) to look at with a steady gaze. *Mei Li stared at the painting, fascinated by the bright colors.*

sta•tion /**stā′** shən/ *n.* the place from which a service is provided or operations are directed. *The local radio station will broadcast the game.*

sta•tion•ar•y /**stā′** shə nĕr′ ē/ *adj.* not moving. *I exercise on a stationary bike.*

steak /stāk/ *n.* a slice of meat or fish for cooking. *For dinner he ordered a steak, a baked potato, a salad, and a roll with butter.*

➤ **Steak** sounds like **stake**.

steal /stēl/ *v.* (**steals, stole, sto•len, steal•ing**) **a.** to take without permission. *He locked his bike so nobody would steal it.* **b.** to move quietly and secretly. *We decided to steal away before the play was over.*

➤ **Steal** sounds like **steel**.

steam /stēm/ *n.* the vapor into which water is changed by heating. *We could see steam rising from the iron.*

steel /stēl/ *n.* a strong metal made from iron by mixing it with carbon. *Steel is used for making strong tools.*

➤ **Steel** sounds like **steal.**

steer[1] /stîr/ *v.* to cause to move in the correct direction. *Use the handlebars to steer the bike.* —*idiom.* **steer clear.** to avoid.

steer[2] /stîr/ *n.* a male of domestic cattle that is raised especially for beef. *They herded the steers into the corral.*

still•ness /stĭl′ nĭs/ *n.* quiet; silence. *After the city noise, the stillness of the country was a relief.*

stor•y /stôr′ ē/ or /stōr′ ē/ *n.* (**stor•ies** *pl.*) a tale or account of an adventure or happening. *Mr. Lee told us a story about his grandfather.*

straight•en /strāt′ n/ *v.* **a.** to make or become straight. *After miles of curving, the road began to straighten.* **b.** to put in order. *Straighten your room before dinner.*

strange /strānj/ *adj.* unusual; odd. *We were startled by the strange noise.*

street /strēt/ *n.* a road in a city or town. *This street is always crowded during rush hour.*

stroll[1] /strōl/ *v.* to walk slowly and easily. *We strolled through the park.*

stroll[2] /strōl/ *n.* a slow walk for pleasure. *Our stroll in the neighborhood was pleasant.*

stroll

stu•dent /stŏŏd′ nt/ or /styŏŏd′-/ *n.* a person who studies or goes to school. *There are three hundred students in our school.*

stum•ble /stŭm′ bəl/ *v.* to trip and almost fall. *Carlos stumbled over his sister's foot.*

style /stīl/ *n.* **a.** a way of doing or making something. *Some authors have a simple style of writing.* **b.** fashion. *This year's style in dresses is different from last year's.*

sub•head /sŭb′ hĕd′/ *n.* a less important heading or title. *Rosa's outline had three subheads under each of the two main headings.*

suc•tion /sŭk′ shən/ *n.* a drawing in by removing part of the air. *The suction of the vacuum was not very strong.*

suit•case /sŏŏt′ kās′/ *n.* a usually rectangular bag used to hold clothes when a person travels. *I had to sit on my suitcase to close it after it was packed.*

sum•mer /sŭm′ ər/ *n.* the warmest season of the year. *Summer comes between spring and fall.*

Sun. Sunday.

Sun•day /sŭn′ dē/ or /-dā′/ *n.* the first day of the week. *Sunday comes before Monday.* [Old English *sunnerdæg,* translated from Latin *dies solis,* day of the sun.]

sunk•en /sŭng′ kən/ *adj.* to be beneath the surface. *They found old coins underwater in the sunken ship.*

sun•ni•er /sŭn′ ē ər/ *adj.* more exposed to or more abounding in sunshine. *We placed the plant in the sunnier room.*

sup•ply /sə plī′/ *v.* (**sup•plies, sup•plied, sup•ply•ing**) to provide; to furnish; to give. *Who will supply the lemonade for the picnic?* (**sup•pli•er** *n.*)

sur•prise[1] /sər prīz′/ *v.* (**sur•pris•es, sur•prised, sur•pris•ing**) to cause to feel wonder or delight; to astonish. *They surprised us by singing the song they had written.*

sur•prise² /sər prīz'/ *n.* something unexpected. *The flowers from Aunt Laura were a nice surprise.*

sweat•er /swĕt' ər/ *n.* a knitted garment worn on the upper part of the body. *Aunt Ellie is knitting me a new sweater.*

sweater

sweat•shirt /swĕt' shûrt'/ *n.* a heavy cotton pullover with long sleeves, often worn for exercise. *Grandpa wears a sweatshirt when he goes jogging.*

sweet•en /swĕt' n/ *v.* (**sweet**) **a.** to make sweeter by adding sugar, honey, or some other sweetener. *She added honey to sweeten the tea.* **b.** to make more pleasant. *He tried to sweeten her mood by telling a joke.*

swift /swĭft/ *adj.* **a.** very fast: *a swift runner.* **b.** prompt: *a swift answer.*

syl•la•ble /sĭl' ə bəl/ *n.* a word or a part of a word that is pronounced as a unit. *We divide words into syllables to know where to hyphenate them at the end of a line.*

ta•ble /tā' bəl/ *n.* a piece of furniture that has legs and a smooth, flat top. *We eat supper at the kitchen table.*

ta•ble•cloth /tā' bəl klôth'/ or /-klŏth'/ *n.* a cloth used for covering a table. *Tony brushed the crumbs off the tablecloth.*

tan•gle /tăng' gəl/ *v.* (**tan•gles, tan•gled, tan•gling**) to intertwine or twist in a confused mass. *If you don't comb your hair, it will tangle.*

tar•di•ness /tär' dē nĭs/ *n.* slowness; lateness. *Steve's forgetfulness contributes to his tardiness.*

tar•dy /tär' dē/ *adj.* (**tar•di•er, tar•di•est**) late or delayed. *Our teacher requires us to be on time, not tardy.* (**tar•dies** *n., pl.*)

taught /tôt/ *v.* past tense of **teach**.

teach /tēch/ *v.* (**teach•es, taught, teach•ing**) to help to learn; to instruct. *Will you teach me how to play this game?*

teach•er /tē' chər/ *n.* a person who teaches. *Who is your piano teacher?*

tear¹ /târ/ *v.* (**tears, tore, torn, tear•ing**) to pull apart or into pieces. *Be careful not to tear the letter as you open the envelope.*

tear² /tîr/ *n.* a drop of liquid from the eye. *She stopped crying and wiped the tears from her face.* (**tear•ful** *adj.*, **tear•ful•ly** *adv.*)

teeth /tēth/ *n. pl.* more than one tooth. *Did you brush your teeth this morning?*

tem•ple /tĕm' pəl/ *n.* a building for religious worship. *The ancient Greeks built many temples.*

term /tûrm/ *n.* a period of time. *The winter school term seems long because there aren't many holidays.*

terse /tûrs/ *adj.* (**ters•er, ters•est**) short and brusque. *Her terse tone suggested she was upset about something.* (**terse•ly** *adv.*)

test /tĕst/ *n.* an examination or trial, often consisting of a series of questions or problems. *There were twenty problems on the arithmetic test.*

Tex•as /tĕk' səs/ *n.* a state in the south central United States. *Texas is the second-largest state in the United States.*

thank•ful /thăngk' fəl/ *adj.* feeling or showing gratitude; grateful. *She was thankful when I returned her lost purse.*

thank•less /thăngk' lĭs/ *adj.* not showing appreciation; ungrateful. *Be sure to write Uncle Jeff a thank-you note for his gift so you won't seem like a thankless person.*

Thanks•giv•ing Day /thăngks gĭv' ĭng dā'/ *n.* the fourth Thursday in November observed as a legal holiday in the United States celebrating the friendship between the Pilgrims and the Native Americans. *On Thanksgiving Day, my family comes to our house for dinner.*

their /thâr/ *adj.* of, belonging to, or relating to them. *Is that your cat or their cat?*

➤ **Their** sounds like **there**.

there /*th*âr/ *adv.* **a.** in or at that place. *Put the flowers over there.* **b.** to that place; into that place. *I went there last week.*

➤ **There** sounds like **their.**

they're they are.

thick•en /thĭk′ ən/ *v.* to make heavier or thicker. *You can use flour to thicken gravy.*

thick•ness /thĭk′ nĭs/ *n.* the condition of being heavy or thick. *The thickness of the paint made it difficult to apply.*

thin /thĭn/ *adj.* slender; not thick. *A sheet of paper is thin.*

think /thĭngk/ *v.* (**thinks, thought, think•ing**) to consider, ponder, or reflect in the mind. *I think I would like to go to college.*

thin•ner /thĭn′ ər/ *adj.* comparative form of **thin**; being more slender than another. *Thread for sewing is thinner than string for kites.*

thin•nest /thĭn′ əst/ *adj.* superlative form of **thin**; being the most slender of anyone or anything. *This pen makes the thinnest line of all my pens.*

third base /thûrd bās/ *n.* the base that must be touched third by a base runner in baseball. *The runner slid into third base.*

thirst /thûrst/ *n.* a desire for something to drink caused by a dry feeling in the mouth or throat. *The horses satisfied their thirst by drinking from a stream.* (**thirst•y** *adj.,* **thirst•i•ly** *adv.*)

thor•ough /thûr′ ō/ *adj.* **a.** complete. *She did a thorough job.* **b.** careful and exact. *The police were thorough in examining the evidence.*

though[1] /thō/ *adv.* however. *You must admit, though, that she was partly right.*

though[2] /thō/ *conj.* in spite of the fact that; although. *Though it was getting late, we kept playing for a while longer.*

thought[1] /thôt/ *v.* past tense of **think.**

thought[2] /thôt/ *n.* **a.** the act or process of thinking. *She spent many hours in thought about the problem.* **b.** an idea, opinion, or belief. *Do you have any thoughts about how to improve our school?*

thought•ful /thôt′ fəl/ *adj.* **a.** engaged in thought; serious; meditative: *a thoughtful mood.* **b.** having consideration for others. *She is thoughtful of her friends and never hurts their feelings.*

thou•sand /thou′ zənd/ *n.* the next number after 999; 10 × 100; 1,000. *The figure for one thousand has four numerals.*

Pronunciation Key

ă	pat	ŏ	pot	th	thin
ā	pay	ō	toe	*th*	this
âr	care	ô	paw, for	hw	which
ä	father	oi	noise	zh	vision
ĕ	pet	ou	out	ə	about,
ē	be	ŏŏ	took		item,
ĭ	pit	ōō	boot		pencil,
ī	pie	ŭ	cut		gallop,
îr	pier	ûr	urge		circus

threat /thrĕt/ *n.* a sign of trouble, impending doom, or danger. *The threat of rain changed our plans for going swimming.*

threw /thrōō/ *v.* (**throws, threw, thrown, throw•ing**) tossed or cast through the air. *The pitcher threw the ball to first base.*

thun•der[1] /thŭn′ dər/ *n.* the loud noise caused by the violent expansion of air heated by lightning. *Thunder often comes before rain.* (**thun•der•ous** *adj.*)

thun•der[2] /thŭn′ dər/ *v.* to make this noise. *When it began to thunder, we headed for home.*

Thurs. Thursday.

Thurs•day /thûrz′ dē/ or /-dā/ *n.* the fifth day of the week, coming between Wednesday and Friday. *Our spring vacation begins on Thursday.* [Old English *dunresdæg,* Thor's day.]

tick•et /tĭk′ ĭt/ *n.* a document that gives the owner the right to be admitted or to be served. *I forgot my movie ticket at home!*

tick•le[1] /tĭk′ əl/ *n.* the act of tickling. *The tickle of the feather made me sneeze.*

tick•le[2] /tĭk′ əl/ *v.* (**tick•les, tick•led, tick•ling**) **a.** to touch lightly to produce a shivering feeling and laughter. *She tickled me until I laughed.* **b.** to have this feeling. *His nose tickles when he has to sneeze.* —*idiom.* **tickled pink.** to make happy.

tight /tīt/ *adj.* **a.** not loose; firm. *The knot was so tight that we couldn't untie it.* **b.** fitting very closely. *My old shoes are too tight.*

tight•en /tīt′ n/ *v.* to make or become tighter. *Mother tightened her seat belt before driving away.*

ti•ny /tī′ nē/ *adj.* (**ti•ni•er, ti•ni•est**) very small; wee. *An ant is a tiny animal.* (**ti•ni•ness** *n.*)

tire¹ /tīr/ *v.* (**tired, tir•ing, tires**) to make weary or exhausted. *Exercising for a long time tires me.*

tire² /tīr/ *n.* an outer rim of rubber, often filled with air, that is fitted around the rim of a wheel. *I pumped air into my bicycle tire.* [Middle English *tyre,* covering for a wheel, from *tyr,* attire.]

ti•tle /tīt′ l/ *n.* the name of a book, movie, painting, etc. *When I had finished reading the story, I couldn't remember its title.*

to•geth•er /tə gĕ*th*′ ər/ *adv.* with each other; in one group. *We all walked to the game together.*

touch /tŭch/ *v.* to feel with the hand or other part of the body. *The builder touched the cement to see if it was still soft.*

tough /tŭf/ *adj.* strong; not easily torn or broken. *The rug is made of very tough materials.*

tour•ist /toor′ ĭst/ *n.* a person traveling for pleasure. *The tourists all took pictures of the castle.*

to•ward /tôrd/, /tōrd/, or /tə wôrd′/ *prep.* in the direction of. *We ran toward the shelter to get out of the rain.*

tow•er /tou′ ər/ *n.* a tall, narrow structure. *The bell tower stands next to the church.*

trac•tor /trăk′ tər/ *n.* a large machine on wheels, used for pulling trucks or farm equipment. *The farmer drove the tractor through the field.*

tractor

trail•er /trā′ lər/ *n.* a large vehicle pulled or hauled by a car, truck, or tractor. *We used a trailer attached to our car to move our furniture.*

train•er /trā′ nər/ *n.* a person that trains; a coach. *The team's trainer suggested everyone get a full night's rest before the big game.*

tra•peze /tră pēz′/ or /trə pēz′/ *n.* a short, horizontal bar suspended by ropes, used by acrobats. *The crowd gasped as the acrobat leapt from one trapeze to the next.*

trea•son /trē′ zən/ *n.* the act of betraying one's home country by aiding the enemy. *The jury found the spies guilty of treason.*

treat•ment /trēt′ mənt/ *n.* **a.** a way of handling. *Baby animals receive special treatment at the zoo.* **b.** anything used to treat something. *The doctor said that ice was the best treatment for my sprain.*

trem•ble /trĕm′ bəl/ *v.* (**trem•bles, trem•bled, trem•bling**) to shake or quiver. *I was so nervous that my hands trembled.*

tri•an•gle /trī′ ăng′ gəl/ *n.* a closed figure in which three straight lines form three angles. *There are 180 degrees in a triangle.*

trick /trĭk/ *n.* **a.** something done to deceive. *The phone call was just a trick to get me out of the room while they planned the surprise party.* **b.** an act that requires a special skill. *Seth taught his dog the trick of rolling over.*

trou•ble /trŭb′ əl/ *n.* **a.** something that causes worry or distress; difficulty. *The trouble with our car is that the motor won't run.* **b.** a bother; an extra effort. *It was no trouble to help her clean her room.*

true /troo/ *adj.* right; accurate; not false. *It is true that ostriches cannot fly.*

trust /trŭst/ *v.* **a.** to believe in; to depend or rely on. *We trust the doctor to do what is best for us.* **b.** to expect; to assume. *I trust you have finished your homework.*

truth /trooth/ *n.* **a.** that which agrees with the facts. *The truth is that we were wrong.* **b.** honesty. *Her apology had a feeling of truth.* —**idiom. grain of truth.** partly true.

tube /toob/ or /tyoob/ *n.* a long, hollow cylinder used to carry or hold liquids and gases. *A drinking straw is a tube.*

Tues. Tuesday.

Tues•day /tooz′ dē/ or /-dā′/ or /tyooz′-/ *n.* the third day of the week, coming after Monday. *Elections are usually held on a Tuesday.* [Old English *Tiwesdæg,* Tiu's day.]

tu•lip /tōō′ lĭp/ or /tyōō′-/ *n.* a plant of the lily family that grows from a bulb and blooms in the spring. *Tulips have large cup-shaped flowers.*

tulip

tu•na /tōō′ nə/ or /tyōō′ nə/ *n.* (**tu•na** or **tu•nas** *pl.*) a large fish. *The yellowfin tuna is a popular food.*

tur•key /tûr′ kē/ *n.* (**tur•keys** *pl.*) a large North American bird covered with thick feathers. *A turkey can weigh more than thirty pounds.* —*idiom.* **talk turkey.** to speak frankly.

um•pire /ŭm′ pīr′/ *n.* a person who rules on the play of a game. *In baseball, the umpire calls the balls and strikes.*

un- a Latin prefix that means "not" or "the opposite of": *unafraid.*

un•a•ble /ŭn ā′ bəl/ *adj.* not able to do something. *I promised to keep a secret, so I am unable to tell you where we are going.*

un•cer•tain /ŭn sûr′ tn/ *adj.* not known beyond a doubt. *We were uncertain what time the train was supposed to arrive.*

un•cle /ŭng′ kəl/ *n.* **a.** the brother of one's father or mother. *I have two uncles on my mother's side.* **b.** the husband of one's aunt. *We visited our aunt and uncle last spring.*

un•cov•er /ŭn kŭv′ ər/ *v.* **a.** to remove the cover from. *Steam rose from the hot dish as Dad uncovered it.* **b.** to reveal or expose. *The truth was uncovered during the trial.*

un•der•line /ŭn′ dər līn′/ *v.* (**un•der•lines, un•der•lined, un•der•lin•ing**) to draw a line under. *Underline the part of the sentence that contains an error.*

Pronunciation Key

ă	pat	ŏ	pot	th	**thin**
ā	pay	ō	toe	*th*	**this**
âr	care	ô	paw, for	hw	**wh**ich
ä	father	oi	n**oi**se	zh	vi**si**on
ĕ	pet	ou	**ou**t	ə	**a**bout,
ē	be	ōō	t**oo**k		it**e**m,
ĭ	pit	ōō	b**oo**t		penc**i**l,
ī	pie	ŭ	cut		gall**o**p,
îr	pier	ûr	**ur**ge		circ**u**s

un•e•qual /ŭn ē′ kwəl/ *adj.* **a.** not the same; not equal: *unequal amounts.* **b.** poorly matched; unfair. *The race between the tortoise and the hare was an unequal contest.*

un•fair /ŭn fâr′/ *adj.* not fair; not honest or just. *Cheating is unfair.* (**un•fair•ness** *n.*)

un•friend•ly /ŭn frĕnd′ lē/ *adj.* (**un•friend•li•er, un•friend•li•est**) not friendly; hostile; mean. *The unfriendly boy sat by himself at the party.* (**un•friend•li•ness** *n.*)

un•hap•py /ŭn hăp′ ē/ *adj.* (**un•hap•pi•er, un•hap•pi•est; un•hap•pi•ly** *adv.*) not happy; sad; full of sorrow. *When Maria was unhappy, we tried to cheer her up.* (**un•hap•pi•ness** *n.*)

un•kind /ŭn kīnd′/ *adj.* not nice or friendly; mean. *It hurts my feelings when you say unkind things to me.* (**un•kind•ness** *n.*)

un•known /ŭn nōn′/ *adj.* not known; strange; unfamiliar. *A stranger is an unknown person.*

un•lock /ŭn lŏk′/ *v.* to undo a lock by turning a key. *Mr. Hughes unlocked the door and let us in.*

un•luck•y /ŭn lŭk′ ē/ *adj.* (**un•luck•i•er, un•luck•i•est; un•luck•i•ly** *adv.*) not lucky; disappointing. *It was unlucky that we missed the bus.*

un•pack /ŭn păk′/ *v.* to remove the contents of a suitcase or a package. *After we moved, it took a week to unpack all the boxes.*

un•safe /ŭn sāf′/ *adj.* not safe; dangerous. *Running into a crowded hallway is unsafe.*

un•tie /ŭn tī′/ *v.* (**un•ties, un•tied, un•ty•ing**) to loosen something that has been tied. *She untied the ribbon and opened the gift.*

up•stairs¹ /ŭp′ stârz′/ *adv.* up the stairs; to a higher floor. *I went upstairs to bed.*

up•stairs² /ŭp′ stârz′/ *adj.* on a higher floor. *Did you clean the upstairs hall?*

up-to-date /ŭp′ tə dāt′/ *adj.* including any recent changes; current; modern. *This edition of the dictionary is the most up-to-date version.*

use /yo͞oz/ *v.* (**us•es, used, us•ing**) to put into service. *Use the cloth to dust the shelf.*

used¹ /yo͞ozd/ *v.* past tense of **use**.

used² /yo͞ozd/ *adj.* not new; owned by another person in the past. *A used bike costs less than a new one.*

use•ful /yo͞os′ fəl/ *adj.* of use; helpful. *She gave me some useful advice about studying for the test.*

use•less /yo͞os′ lĭs/ *adj.* of no use; serving no purpose. *My sled is useless in the summer.*

vain /vān/ *adj.* **a.** too proud of oneself. *After Elaine won the prize she became vain about her accomplishment.* **b.** not successful; useless. *I soon gave up my vain efforts to attract his attention.*

➤ **Vain** sounds like **vane** and **vein**.

vane /vān/ *n.* a device to show which way the wind is blowing. *The weather vane turns as the wind changes direction.*

➤ **Vane** sounds like **vain** and **vein**.

vein /vān/ *n.* one of the many branching tubes through which blood is carried to the heart from all parts of the body. *Can you see the veins in your arms?*

➤ **Vein** sounds like **vain** and **vane**.

view /vyo͞o/ *n.* **a.** what is seen; scene. *The view from the window by the beach is breathtaking.* **b.** opinion; idea. *His view was that we should change our plans.* —*idiom.* **bird's eye view.** to see clearly from above.

vil•lage /vĭl′ ĭj/ *n.* a number of houses and buildings in an area that is smaller than a town. *Everyone knows everyone else in our village.*

vin•e•gar /vĭn′ ĭ gər/ *n.* a sour liquid produced from fermented liquids and used as a condiment or preservative. *Aunt Brenda likes to put oil and vinegar on her salad.*

vi•sion /vĭʒ′ zhən/ *n.* **a.** something that is or has been seen. *Jan was a vision of beauty in her costume.* **b.** the sense of sight. *He has perfect vision in both eyes.*

vow•el /vou′ əl/ *n.* **a.** a sound made with the voice when the breath is allowed to pass out of the mouth freely. *The sound of "o" in "go" is a vowel.* **b.** any of the letters that stand for such a sound. *The most common vowels are a, e, i, o, and u.*

waist /wāst/ *n.* the narrow part of the body between the ribs and the hips. *Belts are worn around the waist.*

➤ **Waist** sounds like **waste**.

Wash•ing•ton /wŏsh′ ĭng tən/ or /wôsh′-/ *n.* a state in the northwestern United States. *Washington is known for its delicious apples.*

waste /wāst/ *v.* (**wastes, wast•ed, wast•ing**) to use up carelessly or foolishly. *He wasted his money on toys he didn't need.*

➤ **Waste** sounds like **waist**.

waste•ful /wāst′ fəl/ *adj.* tending to waste; using or spending too much. *Taking more food than you can eat is wasteful.*

watch /wŏch/ *n.* (**watch•es** *pl.*) a small clock worn on the wrist or carried in a pocket. *I checked my watch to be sure I had the correct time.*

wa•ter¹ /wô′ tər/ or /wŏt′ ər/ *n.* the clear liquid that falls as rain. *Water becomes ice when it freezes.*

wa•ter² /wô′ tər/ or /wŏt′ ər/ *v.* to put water on. *Did you water the flowers today?*

weak•en /wē′ kən/ *v.* to make weak; to become weak. *His legs weakened as he climbed up the mountain.*

weak•ness /wēk′ nĭs/ *n.* (**weak•ness•es** *pl.*) **a.** lack of strength or power. *An illness can cause weakness.* **b.** a weak point; a fault. *Poor fielding is the baseball team's only weakness.*

wealth /wĕlth/ *n.* an abundance of valuable material possessions or money. *I wish you much wealth and fortune.* (**wealth•y,** *adj.,* **wealth•i•er,** *comp.,* **wealth•i•est,** *sup.*)

Wed. Wednesday.

Wednes•day /wĕnz′ dē/ or /-dā′/ *n.* the fourth day of the week. *Wednesday is the day after Tuesday.* [Old English *Wodnesdæg,* Woden's day.]

week /wēk/ *n.* a period of seven days, especially from Sunday to Saturday. *This is the third week of the month.*

week•end /wĕk′ ĕnd′/ *n.* Saturday and Sunday, as a time for rest, play, visiting, etc. *We are going bowling this weekend.*

weight•less /wāt′ lĭs/ *adj.* not experiencing the effects of gravity. *We are weightless in space.*

west¹ /wĕst/ *n.* the direction in which the sun sets. *East and west are opposite directions.*

west² /wĕst/ *adj.* **a.** in the west; of the west; toward the west. *Cindy lives in the west end.* **b.** from the west. *A west wind was blowing.*

west³ /wĕst/ *adv.* toward the west. *We walked west.*

when•ev•er /hwĕn ĕv′ ər/ *conj.* at any time that. *I'm ready whenever you are.*

wheth•er /hwĕ*th*′ ər/ *conj.* if. *He didn't know whether he should laugh or cry.*

whis•tle¹ /hwĭs′ əl/ or /wĭs′ əl/ *v.* (**whis•tles, whis•tled, whis•tling**) to utter a shrill sound by blowing or drawing air through the puckered lips. *Pa likes to whistle while he works.*

whis•tle² /hwĭs′ əl/ or /wĭs′ əl/ *n.* a small wind instrument in which sound is produced by the forcible passage of breath through a slit in a short tube. *The coach blew his whistle to end practice.*

who /hoō/ *pron.* what or which person or persons: *Who wants dinner?* **whom** *pron.* objective case, **whose** *pronoun adj.* possessive form.

whose /hoōz/ *pron.* of whom; of which. *Whose jacket did you borrow?*

wide /wīd′/ *adj.* (**wid•er, wid•est**) covering or having more space from side to side than something else. *Because I broke my foot, I need wide shoes.* (**wi•den** *v.*)

wid•est /wīd′ ĭst/ *adj.* (**wide, wid•er**) covering or having the most space from side to side than anything else. *They placed the large painting on the widest wall.*

wife /wīf/ *n.* (**wives** *pl.*) the woman a man is married to. *He brought flowers to his wife on her birthday.*

wild /wīld/ *adj.* not tamed; not cultivated; living or growing in a natural condition. *Wild plants grew along the side of the road.*

win•ter¹ /wĭn′ tər/ *n.* the coldest season of the year. *Winter comes between autumn and spring.*

win•ter² /wĭn′ tər/ *adj.* of or for the winter. *Ice skating is a winter sport.*

wise /wīz/ *adj.* (**wi•ser, wis•est**) **a.** having good sense; showing good judgment. *She made a wise decision.* **b.** having much knowledge or information. *Scientists and professors are wise.*

ă	pat	ŏ	pot	th	**thin**
ā	pay	ō	toe	*th*	**th**is
âr	care	ô	paw, for	hw	**wh**ich
ä	father	oi	noise	zh	vision
ĕ	pet	ou	**ou**t	ə	about,
ē	be	oͦo	took		item,
ĭ	pit	oōo	boot		pencil,
ī	pie	ŭ	cut		gallop,
îr	pier	ûr	**ur**ge		circus

wis•er /wīz′ ər/ *adj.* more sensible than before. *He was wiser about the hiking trail because he had hiked it before.*

wives /wīvz/ *n.* plural of **wife**.

wolf /woͦolf/ *n.* (**wolves** *pl.*) a wild animal of the dog family, slightly larger than a German shepherd. *Arctic wolves eat mice and travel in packs.*

wolf

wom•an /woͦom′ ən/ *n.* (**wom•en** *pl.*) a grown female person. *Your mother is a woman.*

wom•en /wĭm′ ĭn/ *n.* (**wom•an** *sing.*) grown females. *These women are my aunts.*

won•der /wŭn′ dər/ *v.* to be curious to know. *I wonder how the story will end.* (**won•drous** *adj.*)

won•der•ment /wŭn′ dər mənt/ *n.* the condition of surprise or amazement. *The baby played with the new toy in wonderment.*

wood•en /wŏŏd′ n/ *adj.* made or consisting of wood. *We need to repaint our wooden shed.*

wool•en /wŏŏl′ ən/ *adj.* made or consisting of wool. *This woolen sweater makes me itch.*

work•er /wûr′ kər/ *n.* one who works. *Our server in the restaurant was a good worker.*

wrap /răp/ *v.* (**wraps, wrapped, wrap•ping**) **a.** to enclose in something by winding or folding. *Wrap the baby in warm blankets.* **b.** to cover with paper. *Did you wrap the gift for your mother?*

wrap

wreath /rēth/ *n.* (**wreaths** *pl.*) a ring made of flowers, leaves, or small branches. *This wreath is made out of pine branches.*

wretch•ed /rĕch′ ĭd/ *adj.* in a terrible, miserable state. *The wretched conditions after the flood caused many to come help.*

wrig•gle /rĭg′ əl/ *v.* (**wrig•gles, wrig•gled, wrig•gling**) to move the body or a bodily part back and forth like a worm; to squirm. *Our hamster likes to wriggle when you hold him.*

wring /rĭng/ *v.* (**wrings, wrung, wring•ing**) to twist and squeeze. *Wring out that wet cloth before you wipe the table.*

wrin•kle¹ /rĭng′ kəl/ *n.* a small crease or fold. *Rosa ironed the wrinkles out of her skirt.*

wrin•kle² /rĭng′ kəl/ *v.* to crease or crumple. *Your forehead wrinkles when you frown.*

write /rīt/ *v.* (**writes, wrote, writ•ten, writ•ing**) **a.** to form letters or words with a pen, pencil, or other instrument. *Most people learn to write in school.* **b.** to be the author of. *He will write a story for the school newspaper.*

➤ **Write** sounds like **right**.

writ•ten /rĭt′ n/ *v.* a form of **write**.

wrong /rông/ or /rŏng/ *adj.* **a.** not right; bad; wicked. *Telling lies is wrong.* **b.** not correct; not true. *Your answer was wrong.* **c.** out of order. *Do you know what's wrong with the phone?*

wrote /rōt/ *v.* past tense of **write**.

-y a Greek adjective suffix that means "somewhat like": *juicy.*

year /yîr/ *n.* a period of 365 days or 12 months. *The calendar year begins on January 1.*

year•book /yîr′ bŏŏk′/ *n.* a school publication that is usually compiled by students in a graduating class and that serves as a record of the year's activities. *My picture is in the yearbook seven times.*

yen /yĕn/ *n.* the currency used in Japan. *My grandparents gave me twenty yen for my birthday.*

young /yŭng/ *adj.* not old or fully grown. *A fawn is a young deer.*

youth /yōōth/ *n.* **a.** a young person, especially a young man. *Who is the tall youth with the red hair?* **b.** the quality or the time period of being young. *Youth is followed by adulthood.*

zip code /zĭp′ kōd/ *n.* a system that uses a set of numbers to identify each postal delivery area in the United States. *I live in Fort Worth, Texas, and my zip code is 76112.*

zip•per /zĭp′ ər/ *n.* a fastening device with two rows of tiny teeth that can be closed together by a sliding tab. *My boots close with a zipper.*

Using the Thesaurus

The **Writing Thesaurus** provides synonyms—words that mean the same or nearly the same—and antonyms—words that mean the opposite—for your spelling words. Use this sample to identify the various parts of each thesaurus entry.

- **Entry words** are listed in alphabetical order and are printed in boldface type.
- The abbreviation for the **part of speech** of each entry word follows the boldface entry word.
- The **definition** of the entry word matches the definition of the word in your **Spelling Dictionary**. A **sample sentence** shows the correct use of the word in context.

- Each **synonym** for the entry word is listed under the entry word. Again, a sample sentence shows the correct use of the synonym in context.
- Where appropriate, **antonyms** for the entry word are listed at the end of the entry.

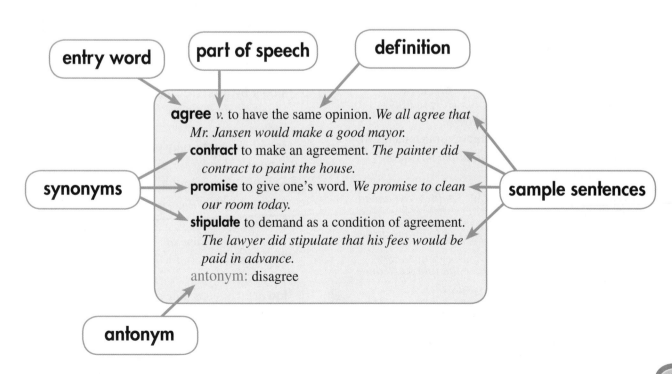

entry word · part of speech · definition

agree *v.* to have the same opinion. *We all agree that Mr. Jansen would make a good mayor.*
contract to make an agreement. *The painter did contract to paint the house.*
promise to give one's word. *We promise to clean our room today.*
stipulate to demand as a condition of agreement. *The lawyer did stipulate that his fees would be paid in advance.*
antonym: disagree

synonyms · sample sentences · antonym

able *adj.* having power, skill, or talent. *With practice you will be able to play the piano.*
  competent able; qualified. *The meal was prepared by a very competent chef.*
  skillful having skill. *The skillful player won the tennis game.*
  talented gifted; having natural ability. *The talented musician played the piano for us.*
  antonym: unable

agree *v.* to have the same opinion. *We all agree that Mr. Jansen would make a good mayor.*
  contract to make an agreement. *The painter did contract to paint the house.*
  promise to give one's word. *We promise to clean our room today.*
  stipulate to demand as a condition of agreement. *The lawyer did stipulate that her fees would be paid in advance.*
  antonym: disagree

agreement *n.* an arrangement or understanding between two persons or groups. *The students came to an agreement about the best day for the litter cleanup.*
  arrangement settlement; agreement. *The new arrangement satisfied everyone.*
  contract an agreement. *The contract had specific terms for the car loan.*
  settlement an arrangement; agreement. *The president worked for a quick settlement on wages for post office employees.*
  understanding an agreement or arrangement. *We have an understanding about the terms for buying the house.*

ahead *adv.* in advance; in front. *Dad walked ahead to look for a campsite.*
  before in front; ahead. *He walked before us to see that the path was clear.*
  forward in front; ahead. *Once the line started to move, we all stepped forward.*
  antonym: behind

aim *v.* to point at; direct toward. *Aim the arrow at the center of the target.*
  beam to send out; direct. *The machine will beam the light at the sign.*
  direct to point or aim. *He will direct the traffic away from the parade route.*
  level to keep even. *The police officer will level his rifle at the target.*
  point to aim; direct. *Ask John to point at the deer standing behind the bush.*
  train to point; aim. *She will train the spotlight on the actor.*

alarm *n.* a signal warning that danger is near. *The alarm went off moments after the fire started.*
  beacon light or fire used to warn. *The beacon was placed on the shoreline.*
  bell anything that makes a ringing sound. *The bell rang to warn the ships in the fog.*
  signal a sign of warning or notice. *A red light was the signal to indicate danger.*
  siren a loud whistle. *The fire siren warned us that a fire truck was coming.*

alive *adj.* living; not dead. *People sometimes forget that trees are alive.*
  existing living; having life. *The existing animals were saved from starvation.*
  living being alive; having life. *The artificial plants looked like living ones.*
  antonym: dead

alone *adv.* without anyone else. *The box was too heavy for one person to lift alone.*
  singly by itself; separately. *Let us review each person singly to see how well his or her job is done.*
  solely alone; the only one or ones. *I am solely responsible for the picnic plans.*

also *adv.* too; in addition; likewise. *Geraniums grow well not only in flowerpots but also in gardens.*
  besides in addition; also. *Many people besides the parents came to the play.*
  likewise also; too. *I will be there on time, and she will likewise.*
  too also; besides. *The cats and dogs are hungry, too.*

amount *n.* the total or sum. *We raised the amount of money needed for the books.*

  figure price; amount. *The figure for the car was less because of the rebates.*

  number amount; total. *A number of people were invited to the party.*

  sum amount; total. *We paid a large sum for the new house.*

  total amount; sum. *A total of 100 tickets were sold for the community play.*

answer *n.* a reply. *I must send my answer to her letter quickly.*

  acknowledgment something done to let one know that a service or gift was received. *An acknowledgment was sent to thank us for the gift.*

  reply response; answer. *Your reply was very easy to understand.*

  response an answer. *The response she gave was very prompt.*

apart *adv.* to pieces; in separate pieces. *The puzzle fell apart when it slipped off the table.*

  independently on one's own. *The class members selected projects independently.*

  separately individually; one at a time. *We worked separately on the project.*

  antonym: together

apartment *n.* a group of rooms to live in, generally in a building housing more than one family. *They live in an apartment on the second floor.*

  flat apartment or set of rooms. *We lived in a flat above the store.*

  room a part of a building with walls of its own. *The hotel rented us a room for the night.*

  suite set of rooms connected to each other. *The hotel suite had five rooms.*

army *n.* a large group of people who are organized and trained to serve as soldiers. *The United States Army fought in Europe during World War II.*

  armed forces the army, navy, and air force of a country. *The armed forces took part in the Fourth of July parade.*

  soldiers men or women in the army. *The soldiers were trained in Louisiana.*

  troops soldiers. *The troops helped to rescue people after the earthquake.*

babysitter *n.* one who takes care of young children. *Juan's mother called a babysitter to stay with him for the afternoon.*

  nanny a person who takes care of children. *The nanny took the children to the park.*

  nursemaid a girl or woman hired to care for children. *The nursemaid knew how to prepare the baby's food.*

badge *n.* something worn to show that a person is a member of a group or an organization. *Each firefighter wore a badge.*

  emblem a badge or sign. *The police officer had an emblem on her uniform.*

  name tag a badge worn that gives a name. *Everyone at the meeting wore a name tag to help people learn names.*

baggage *n.* suitcases; luggage. *Airline passengers may pick up their baggage inside the terminal.*

  luggage baggage. *The passengers checked their luggage at the ticket counter.*

  suitcase a flat, rectangular-shaped bag for traveling. *We packed our clothes in the suitcase.*

battle *n.* a fight between armies, navies, etc., during a war. *That battle was the turning point of the war.*

  combat a fight or struggle. *The argument was settled without any combat.*

  conflict a fight or struggle. *The conflict over employee wages lasted for years.*

  encounter a meeting of enemies; battle; fight. *The peaceful encounter between the two groups led to a settlement.*

  war a fight or conflict. *The war between the two groups lasted only a few days.*

because *conj.* for the reason that. *I study because I want to learn.*

  as because. *As she knew how to act better than anyone else, she became the star of the show.*

  for because. *We can't stay outside, for it is raining.*

  since because. *Since you want a new toy, you should save your money.*

begin *v.* to start. *We will begin our school day with an arithmetic lesson.*
>   **commence** to begin; start. *The play will commence when the curtain opens.*
>   **open** to start or set up. *They will open a new store in the shopping center.*
>   **start** to begin. *We will start reading at the beginning of the chapter.*
>   **undertake** to try; attempt. *We will undertake the new assignment as soon as we get to work this morning.*
>   antonyms: end, finish

believe *v.* to accept something as true or real. *Do you believe that cats have nine lives?*
>   **assume** to suppose; to believe something to be true or real. *We could assume that the bus driver knew the correct route.*
>   **suppose** to believe, think, or imagine. *I suppose we could try to fix the toy.*
>   **think** to believe; to have an opinion. *I think it will rain today.*
>   **trust** to have faith; believe. *I trust you know how to solve the math problem.*

beside *prep.* at the side of; near to. *The carton was left beside the trash cans.*
>   **abreast** side by side. *In the parade the Boy Scouts marched four abreast.*
>   **alongside** by the side of; side by side. *The trees were alongside the building.*

between *prep.* in the space that separates two things. *There were four people between me and the door.*
>   **in the midst** in the middle of. *The toys were put in the midst of the children.*

bitter *adj.* tasting sharp and unpleasant. *Do you think black walnuts have a bitter taste?*
>   **sharp** strongly affecting the senses. *The lemon drops had a very sharp taste.*
>   **sour** having a sharp, bitter taste. *The sour lemon juice was used in the tea.*

boast *v.* to brag; to talk too much about oneself and about what one can do. *Judy likes to boast about how fast she can run.*
>   **bluster** to talk in a noisy manner. *The man tried to complain and bluster at the clerk.*

>   **brag** to boast; praise oneself. *Tom always seems to brag about his bicycle.*
>   **crow** to show one's pride; boast. *We listened to the winners crow about how well they ran.*

bold *adj.* not afraid to face danger; brave and daring. *The bold gymnast attempted a difficult vault.*
>   **brave** showing courage; without fear. *The brave firefighter saved the people in the burning house.*
>   **courageous** brave; fearless. *The courageous child saved the animals from the cold winter storm.*
>   **fearless** without fear. *The fearless woman raced to catch the falling child.*
>   antonyms: cowardly, afraid, weak

break *v.* to come apart; separate into pieces. *The dish will break if it falls on the floor.*
>   **crack** to break without separating into parts. *The dish might crack when it lands on the floor.*
>   **shatter** to break into pieces. *The glass will shatter when it hits the floor.*
>   **snap** to break suddenly. *The rope did snap when we pulled on it.*
>   **split** to separate into pieces. *The seam split as he pulled on his jacket.*

brief *adj.* short; quick; direct. *Our meeting was brief.*
>   **concise** short; brief. *He gave a concise report to the group.*
>   **little** not long in time; short. *Please wait a little while before you go.*
>   **short** not long. *It took only a few minutes to read the short story.*
>   **succinct** brief; short. *The succinct comments really told the whole story.*
>   **terse** brief; to the point. *A one-word answer is a terse reply.*

brighten *v.* to lighten; make or become bright. *The lamp will brighten the living room.*
>   **illuminate** to light up; make bright. *The lights will illuminate the sky.*
>   **lighten** to make brighter; to add light to. *The new paint does lighten the room.*
>   antonym: darken

bubble *n.* a thin, round film of liquid that forms a ball around a pocket of gas or air. *The slightest touch can pop a bubble.*

  bead any small, round object like a bubble. *A bead of water formed on the newly waxed car.*

  blob a small drop. *A blob of jelly fell on the floor.*

build *v.* to make; put together. *Doug wants to build a model house out of toothpicks.*

  construct to build; fit together. *The builders will construct a new office tower.*

  erect to put up; build. *The landscaping crew can erect a new flag pole.*

  make to build; put together. *We will make a tree house in the backyard.*

  put up to build. *We followed the directions when we put up the tent.*

burst *v.* to break open suddenly. *The balloon will burst if it touches the light bulb.*

  blow up to explode. *The balloon will blow up when Horace jumps on it.*

  explode to burst with a loud noise. *The fireworks explode high in the sky.*

  rupture to break; burst. *Where did the water main rupture?*

buy *v.* to purchase. *Sally had to buy a new pair of shoes before winter.*

  purchase to buy. *He can purchase the jewelry at the shop by our house.*

  shop to go to stores to look at or buy things. *We plan to shop for a new coat.*

  antonyms: sell, market

calm *adj.* quiet; peaceful; motionless. *There wasn't even a breeze on that calm evening.*

  composed quiet; calm. *The composed officer came forward to receive the award.*

  cool calm; not excited. *The people kept cool and walked to the nearest exit.*

  serene calm; peaceful. *A serene smile could be seen on her face.*

  tranquil peaceful; quiet; calm. *The tranquil night air was very relaxing.*

  antonyms: nervous, anxious

careful *adj.* cautious; full of care. *Be careful when you cross the busy street.*

  cautious very careful. *The cautious player watched the ball at all times.*

  considered carefully thought out. *His considered opinion was respected by everyone.*

  diligent careful; steady. *He is a diligent worker.*

  antonym: careless

careless *adj.* reckless; not cautious. *You can't afford to be careless with matches.*

  negligent careless. *No one liked the negligent way Pat drove.*

  thoughtless without thought. *Her thoughtless behavior made me angry.*

  antonym: careful

cart *n.* a two-wheeled vehicle pulled by a horse or another animal. *The pony pulled a cart in the parade.*

  buggy a small carriage pulled by a horse. *We rode in a buggy around the park.*

  wagon a four-wheeled vehicle. *The wagon was pulled by a horse.*

case *n.* a large box; container. *Our music teacher carries her violin in a case.*

  bin a box or container. *The grain was stored in a large bin.*

  box container with four sides, a bottom, and a lid. *We packed the dishes in a box.*

  carton a box made of cardboard. *The books were packed in a carton.*

  container a box, can, etc. used to hold things. *She put the paper clips in a small container.*

certain *adj.* confident; sure; convinced. *She was certain you would win.*

  decided definite; clear. *There is a decided difference between the two books on hamsters.*

  definite clear; exact. *I want a definite answer to my question.*

  sure certain; positive. *I am sure that is the right way to go.*

  antonym: uncertain

charge *n.* an amount asked or made as payment. *There is no charge for this service.*

  amount the total or sum. *We raised the amount of money needed to buy the books for our new library.*

  cost the price paid. *The cost of the shirt was more than I was willing to pay.*

  price the amount charged for something. *The price of cars goes up every year.*

charm *v.* to delight; please. *The child's smile did charm the audience.*

  delight to please greatly. *The pony rides will delight the children.*

  enchant to delight. *The magician can enchant the audience with his tricks.*

  fascinate to attract; enchant. *The music will fascinate all of us.*

chart *v.* to make a map or a diagram of. *My job is to chart our class's spelling progress.*

  diagram to put a sketch on paper. *The builder will diagram the house plan for us.*

  map to plan; arrange. *We will map out our work.*

  outline to sketch; make a plan. *She tried to outline the entire trip for us.*

  plot to plan secretly. *The pirate will plot a way to get the treasure.*

cheer *v.* to shout words of approval; to encourage by yelling. *We all cheer for our star player as he comes on the field.*

  encourage to give courage. *The coach tried to encourage the players to do their best.*

  shout to say loudly. *We shout encouragement to the runners.*

  yell to shout loudly. *The fans yell cheers to the home team.*

cheerful *adj.* happy; joyful. *Kari gave a cheerful smile.*

  good-humored cheerful; pleasant. *The good-humored clown entertained everyone.*

  joyful full of joy. *The first and last days of school are always joyful.*

  rosy bright; cheerful. *The good news meant there would be a rosy future.*

  sunny happy, cheerful; bright. *May had a sunny personality that cheered everyone around her.*

  antonyms: cheerless, sad, gloomy

chief *n.* a leader; a head of a tribe or group. *The chief leads the tribal council.*

  captain head of a group; chief; leader. *John is the captain of the football team.*

  head leader; chief person. *The head of the school was Mr. Smith.*

  leader person who leads. *Jan was the leader of the debate team.*

  officer person who holds an office in a club or organization. *The president is the top officer of the business.*

choice *n.* a decision; selection. *For dinner we will go to the restaurant of your choice.*

  decision a choice. *I have made a decision about the theme for the food, costumes, and invitations for the big Fourth of July party.*

  option choice; a choosing. *We have the option of taking a car, a bus, or a train to get to work.*

  selection choice; act of selecting. *The store had a good selection of clothes for children.*

clear *adj.* having no clouds; bright. *The sun shone in the clear sky.*

  bright very light or clear. *The bright day convinced us it would be a good day for a picnic.*

  light clear; bright. *The lamp makes the room as light as day.*

  sunny having much sunlight. *We wanted a sunny day for the parade.*

climb *v.* to go up, often using both hands and feet; to move on a steep slope. *The club members climb mountains all over the state.*

  mount to go up. *We tried to mount the stairs as fast as we could.*

  scale to climb. *We used ropes and hooks to scale the mountainside.*

clothes *n.* garments; articles of dress; clothing. *Some people order all of their clothes through a catalog.*

  apparel clothing; dress. *This store sells very expensive women's apparel.*

  dress clothing. *We studied about the dress of people from years ago.*

  garments articles of clothing. *The queen's garments were made of velvet.*

clue *n.* a piece of information that helps solve a problem or mystery. *In this game we use a word clue to solve the puzzle.*

hint a sign; a suggestion. *The hint he gave us did not help us find the treasure.*

suggestion something suggested. *They gave us a suggestion to help us solve the problem.*

coast *n.* the seashore; land along the sea or ocean. *There are many beaches along the coast of the Pacific Ocean.*

seacoast coast; land by the sea. *Maine has a beautiful seacoast.*

shore land along the sea, ocean, lake, etc. *We walked along the shore until we reached the path.*

shoreline place where water and shore meet. *The rising water changed the shoreline.*

compare *v.* to examine things for similarities or differences. *If you compare prices, you can save money when you shop.*

contrast to compare to show differences. *A list was made to contrast city living with country living.*

liken to compare. *The art collector did liken my painting to one hanging in the museum.*

match to fit together; be alike. *The curtains almost match the colors in the couch.*

cottage *n.* a small house. *We spent our vacation in a cottage on the beach.*

bungalow a small, one-floor house. *The family lived in a bungalow.*

cabin a small house, roughly built. *The mountain cabin was made of logs.*

crowd *v.* to push or squeeze together in a small space. *Many people tried to crowd into the small room.*

cram to put too many into a space. *Twenty people tried to cram into the small waiting room.*

jam to squeeze things or people together. *The riders tried to jam onto the train.*

swarm to crowd. *Hundreds of fans might swarm onto the field after the game.*

cute *adj.* delightfully attractive or appealing. *The child looked cute in her rabbit costume.*

attractive pretty; pleasing. *The attractive lady wore a black suit.*

charming attractive; very pleasing. *The children had charming roles in the play.*

pretty pleasing; attractive. *The pretty pictures decorated the walls.*

antonym: ugly

dampen *v.* to make moist or wet. *Dampen the cloth before you begin cleaning.*

moisten to make or become moist. *We will moisten the towel with water and clean up the mess.*

wet to make or become moist. *He can wet the soap to get lather.*

danger *n.* peril; chance of injury or harm. *Learning safety rules can help you avoid danger.*

hazard chance or harm. *The railroad crossing has been a serious safety hazard.*

peril chance of danger or harm. *The storm put the city in peril.*

darkness *n.* the state or quality of being without light or brightness. *The darkness of the sky warned of a coming storm.*

blackout a lack of light in a city or place due to loss of power. *The blackout lasted for two hours.*

dusk the time just before dark. *We got home at dusk.*

gloom darkness. *The gloom spread over the city as the sun set.*

deal *v.* to handle in a certain way; cope. *It is important to know how to deal with emergencies.*

cope to handle. *We will cope with the problem when it arises.*

handle to deal with. *The director will handle all of the problems.*

dew *n.* water droplets that form at night on cool surfaces. *In the morning you may see dew on the leaves.*

mist fine drops of water in the air. *We can see the mist out in the yard.*

moisture small drops of water in the air. *The moisture in the air made the car wet.*

vapor moisture in the air. *The water vapor in the air made the windows steam up.*

dodge *v.* to try to avoid; stay away from. *The batter stepped back from the plate to dodge the wild pitch.*

    duck to move suddenly to keep from being hit. *She had to duck quickly to avoid the ball.*

    lurch to lean or stagger. *The man began to lurch forward when he lost his balance.*

    sidestep to step aside. *The pitcher had to sidestep to avoid being hit by the line drive.*

drag *v.* to pull slowly along the ground; haul. *They drag the sled to the top of the hill and then slide down.*

    pull to move; drag. *We can pull the wagon up the hill.*

    tow to pull. *The truck will tow the car to the garage.*

    tug to pull hard. *He must tug on the rope to lead the horse to the barn.*

eager *adj.* excitedly or impatiently wanting or expecting something. *We were eager for school to begin that day.*

    avid very eager. *The avid fans cheered their team to victory.*

    enthusiastic eager; interested. *The class was very enthusiastic about the field trip.*

    zealous enthusiastic; eager. *The zealous efforts of the players made us feel we could win.*

easy *adj.* not hard or difficult. *The quiz was easy for me.*

    effortless easy; using little effort. *Because the work was so easy, it was an effortless job.*

    elementary basic; simple. *The computer instructor showed us the elementary steps for using the computer.*

    simple not hard; easy. *The simple problems were the best part of the test we had today.*

    antonyms: hard, difficult

echo *v.* to send back a sound. *Our shouts can echo throughout the canyon.*

    reverberate to echo back. *Our voices reverberate off the walls of the cave.*

    vibrate to resound; echo. *The clanging of the bells would vibrate in our ears.*

edge *n.* border; side. *The cup fell off the edge of the table.*

    border side or edge of something. *We crossed the state border at noon.*

    boundary a border or limit. *The river is the western boundary of our county.*

    brim edge or border. *The cup was filled to the brim.*

enjoy *v.* to get pleasure from. *Did you enjoy the movie last night?*

    delight to please greatly. *The clowns will delight the children.*

    like to wish for; enjoy. *The children like the new game a lot.*

enough *adj.* as much or as many as needed. *The backpackers had enough food and water for three days.*

    adequate enough; sufficient. *The food supply was adequate for a family of four.*

    ample as much as is needed; enough. *My ample allowance easily covers lunches and supplies.*

    sufficient as much as is needed. *We took sufficient food for the long trip.*

everyday *adj.* ordinary; all right for the usual day or event. *You should wear your everyday clothes to play outside.*

    common usual; ordinary. *Having a lot of rain is common in this area.*

    familiar common; well-known. *Coloring is a familiar activity for young children.*

    ordinary everyday; common. *Today is a very ordinary day.*

example *n.* a sample; model; something that may be imitated. *If you don't understand how to do the problems, look at the example.*

    case a special condition; example. *The doctor treated a bad case of measles.*

    model something to be copied or imitated. *Use the pattern as the model for your drawing.*

    sample something to show what the rest are like. *The sample gave us a taste of various French foods.*

eye *v.* to look at or watch. *We wanted to eye the visitors to see if we knew any of them.*

   observe to see; notice. *We tried to observe the workers to discover ways to improve production.*

   peer at to look closely. *She likes to peer at the people in the cars on the street below.*

   view to look at; see. *We can view the craters on the moon with our new telescope.*

   watch to look at; observe. *The class will watch the movie about space travel.*

fame *n.* the state of being well-known; respect; recognition. *George Washington was a man of great fame.*

   dignity position of honor; rank; title. *The dignity of the office of President is upheld through traditions.*

   majesty nobility. *The majesty of the queen impressed all the guests.*

   nobility people of noble title. *The nobility ruled the country until the revolution.*

fasten *v.* to join; attach. *We can fasten this lamp to the wall over my desk.*

   attach to fasten; fix in place. *Attach the rope to the front of the sled.*

   bind to hold together. *We can bind sticks together as a bundle.*

   join to put together. *Let's join hands and walk in a circle.*

   tie to fasten; bind. *I will tie the packages together with string.*

fear *n.* a feeling of fright or alarm. *A dog shows fear by putting its tail between its legs.*

   fright fear; alarm. *The screeching brakes gave us a fright.*

   panic fear in many people. *The earthquake caused a panic in our city.*

   scare fright. *The loud noises sent a scare through all of us.*

   terror great fear; fright. *The sound of thunder caused terror in the child.*

few *adj.* not many. *There are few copies of this rare book available.*

   scant not enough. *The scant supplies worried the captain of the ship.*

   scarce hard to get. *Some coins have become very scarce.*

   sparse meager; scant. *The lack of food put everyone on a very sparse diet.*

   antonym: many

firm *adj.* hard; solid. *They left the muddy road and walked on firm ground.*

   solid hard; firm. *The solid ground turned to mud because of the rain.*

   stable firm; steady. *The steel construction made the building very stable.*

   steady firm; solid. *He used a steady hand to guide the animal to safety.*

   antonym: soft

flavor *n.* a particular taste. *Lemonade can have a sweet or tart flavor.*

   tang a strong flavor. *The chili powder gave the stew a zesty tang.*

   taste the special flavor of food. *The meat left a strange taste in my mouth.*

flood *n.* water that flows over normally dry land. *The low bridge was underwater for an hour after the flash flood.*

   deluge a great flood. *The deluge washed the bridge away.*

   downpour a very heavy rain. *The downpour caused flooding in the streets.*

flour *n.* a fine powder of ground grain, usually wheat. *Flour is used in breads.*

   bran the covering of grains of wheat, rye, etc. *The cereal contained bran.*

   meal anything ground to a powder. *The corn meal was ground to a fine powder.*

flower *n.* the blossom of a plant. *Tulips are flowers that bloom in the spring.*

> **bloom** a blossom; flower. *There was one perfect rose bloom in the vase.*
>
> **blossom** the flower of a seed plant. *The peach blossom smells beautiful.*
>
> **bud** a partly opened flower. *The bud will soon open into a lovely flower.*
>
> **floret** a small flower. *The floret was purple and pink.*

fold *v.* to close or bend parts of something together in order to fit it into a smaller space. *When we take down the flag, we fold it into the shape of a triangle.*

> **bend** to curve; to be crooked. *Bend the paper around the edges of the box.*
>
> **crease** to make a fold. *She will crease the paper as she wraps the package.*
>
> **crinkle** to wrinkle. *The paper will crinkle when it is crushed.*

forth *adv.* forward; onward. *From that day forth they were good friends.*

> **ahead** in the front; forward. *We will go ahead with the project.*
>
> **forward** toward the front. *Come forward and get your prize.*
>
> **onward** toward the front. *We will move onward to see the monument.*

friend *n.* a person one knows and likes. *Erin is my good friend.*

> **acquaintance** a person one knows but not as a close friend. *Almost every day I made a new acquaintance.*
>
> **classmate** member of the same class. *Our new classmate studied with us for the test.*
>
> **companion** a comrade; friend. *Jane and her companion worked and played together.*
>
> **comrade** a close friend; companion. *The police officer and her comrade directed traffic.*
>
> **mate** companion; friend. *My mate and I will try to go to a movie.*
>
> antonym: enemy

funny *adj.* causing laughter or amusement. *The joke was funny.*

> **amusing** entertaining; funny. *The author wrote many amusing stories.*
>
> **humorous** amusing; funny. *I like the humorous stories he tells.*
>
> **witty** showing wit; clever and amusing. *The witty speaker made the audience laugh.*

gather *v.* to bring or come together. *When clouds gather, it often means rain.*

> **accumulate** to gather little by little. *Dust can accumulate under the sofa.*
>
> **assemble** to gather or bring together. *The students will assemble outside the museum.*
>
> **collect** to gather together. *The students want to collect aluminum cans for recycling.*

gentle *adj.* light; soft. *The gentle breeze rustled the leaves.*

> **easy** smooth and pleasant. *His quiet, easy way made everyone around him feel relaxed.*
>
> **mild** not harsh; not severe. *She had a very mild manner.*
>
> **soft** quiet; gentle; mild. *She has a soft voice.*
>
> antonym: harsh

gigantic *adj.* extremely large. *Elephants and whales are gigantic.*

> **huge** very big; extremely large. *The huge truck was loaded with steel rails.*
>
> **stupendous** immense; extremely large. *The stupendous mountains were a beautiful sight to see.*

glow *v.* to give off light; to shine. *Fireflies glow in the dark.*

> **gleam** to give off light. *The little lamp will gleam in the darkness.*
>
> **glitter** to shine with sparkling light. *The beads on the costumes seemed to glitter.*
>
> **shine** to send out light; glow. *Please shine your flashlight over here.*
>
> **twinkle** to shine and glitter. *Stars twinkle in the night sky.*

glue *n.* a sticky liquid that hardens to hold things together. *Broken toys can be mended with glue.*
cement something that hardens to hold things together. *Rubber cement is used to hold the pictures in the album.*
paste mixture used to hold things together. *We used white paste to make the paper chains.*

goal *n.* a purpose; aim. *Mark's goal is to play the double bass in a symphony orchestra.*
aim a purpose; goal. *The aim of the exercise is to build up leg muscles.*
objective a goal; aim. *We each wrote an objective for our science project.*
purpose an aim; plan. *The purpose of the game is to find all the numbers.*
target a goal; objective. *Our target was to walk a mile in eight minutes.*

group *n.* a gathering or arrangement of people or objects. *There is a large group of people in the hotel lobby.*
branch a part; division; local office. *That branch of the company is located in Sweden.*
division one part of a whole; group; section. *This division of the company handles the manufacturing of our product.*
section part of a city, region, etc. *The city offices are in this section of town.*

happy *adj.* feeling or showing pleasure; joyful. *The happy man whistled as he worked.*
cheerful happy; joyful. *Kari gave us a cheerful smile.*
contented pleased; satisfied. *The contented cat lay by the fire and purred.*
delighted very glad; very pleased. *I am delighted that you came to visit.*
ecstatic very happy; joyful. *The winner had an ecstatic look on her face.*
glad happy; pleased. *We are glad that you won the prize.*
antonym: sad

harden *v.* to make or become hard. *The ground does harden during the cold weather.*
temper to bring to a proper condition of hardness. *A special process of heating and cooling will temper the steel.*
toughen to make or become tough. *The hard work will toughen our hands and our bodies.*

haul *v.* to pull with force; drag. *We tried to haul the rowboat out of the water.*
lug to drag or pull along. *We must lug the boxes down the stairs.*
pull to move; drag. *We can pull the wagon up the hill.*
tug to pull hard. *He must tug on the rope to lead the horse to the barn.*

heavy *adj.* hard to move because of its weight; not light. *We will need two people to lift this heavy trunk.*
hefty weighty; heavy. *The hefty man easily picked up the big boxes.*
husky big and strong. *The job required a husky person to lift the crates.*
ponderous very heavy. *An elephant is a ponderous animal.*
weighty heavy. *The hasty decisions caused weighty problems for the city.*
antonym: light

hedge *n.* a thick row of bushes planted as a fence or boundary. *A hedge should be trimmed evenly.*
fence a wall put around a yard or field. *The bushes made a fence around the yard.*
wall a structure built around an area. *The plants made a wall of flowers around the patio.*

helpless *adj.* not able to help oneself or others. *We felt helpless to stop the school's litter problem.*
incapable lacking ability. *He is incapable of performing that complicated task.*
incompetent lacking power or ability. *She is incompetent when it comes to flying a helicopter.*
powerless without power; helpless. *The powerless leader was finally removed from office.*
useless of no use. *The old motor is useless.*
antonym: capable

hero *n.* a person admired for bravery or fine qualities. *Abraham Lincoln is a national hero.*
  adventurer person who seeks adventure. *The adventurer set out to explore the jungle.*
  star a person with exceptional qualities. *The little child was the star of the show.*

high *adj.* tall; far above the ground. *Eagles build nests on high cliffs.*
  alpine like high mountains. *The alpine trees rise high into the sky.*
  tall having great height. *The tall building could be seen for miles.*
  towering very high. *They climbed up the towering mountain.*
  antonym: low

highway *n.* a main road. *A highway is usually numbered to simplify maps and road signs.*
  boulevard a broad street. *The boulevard was named after a president.*
  interstate a highway that connects two or more states. *Hundreds of cars, trucks, and buses use the interstate.*
  road a way for cars, trucks, etc. to travel. *The road went from town to the farm in the country.*
  thoroughfare a main road; highway. *Route 66 was a main thoroughfare in years past.*

hire *v.* to employ; pay a person for working. *Because business is good, the store can hire three more clerks.*
  employ to hire or give work to. *The company does employ many people.*
  engage to hire. *We must engage a crew to rake the leaves and mow the lawn.*
  antonym: fire

holiday *n.* a day on which a special event is celebrated. *The family went to Grandmother's house for the holiday.*
  fiesta a holiday or festival. *The community planned a summer fiesta.*
  vacation a time with no school, work, or other duties. *The summer vacation gave us time to swim and play.*

honest *adj.* tending not to lie, cheat, or steal; able to be trusted. *An honest person always tells the truth.*

  conscientious taking care to do what is right. *The children were conscientious workers in school.*
  honorable showing a sense of what is right. *The honorable man was elected to the city council.*
  sincere real; honest. *His sincere efforts showed how much he cared about his work.*
  trustworthy reliable; dependable. *The bank employees were trustworthy.*
  truthful telling the truth. *The witness gave a truthful account of the accident.*
  upstanding honorable. *The upstanding judge was respected by the townspeople.*
  antonym: dishonest

hopeless *adj.* having very little chance of working out right. *After darkness fell, they decided the search for the ball was hopeless.*
  desperate not caring; without hope. *After the tornado, they made a desperate search for the mailbox.*
  despondent having lost hope; discouraged. *The helpers were despondent over the conditions left by the storm.*
  discouraged lacking in courage. *The discouraged partners tried to sell the business.*
  dismayed greatly troubled. *She was dismayed that she failed to get to school on time.*
  antonym: hopeful

hotel *n.* a place that provides guests with lodging, meals, and other services. *Our grandparents stayed in a hotel near the beach.*
  inn a place where travelers can get food and rooms. *The inn was built near a major highway.*
  lodge a place to live in. *The ski lodge was located in Aspen, Colorado.*
  resort a place people go to vacation. *The resort by the ocean had water sports and many other things to do.*

however *conj.* nevertheless. *I've never tasted eggplant before; however, it looks delicious.*
  nevertheless however; nonetheless. *We knew what to do; nevertheless, we waited.*
  yet nevertheless; however. *The game was well played, yet it would have been better if we had won.*

huge *adj.* very large. *A skyscraper is a huge building.*

enormous extremely large. *The enormous hippopotamus wandered down to the river.*

immense very large; huge. *The immense shopping center was the largest in the United States.*

tremendous very large; enormous. *The tremendous whale slowly swam in front of the ship.*

antonyms: tiny, little, small

idea *n.* a thought; a plan. *Bringing plants to decorate the room was Kristin's idea.*

impression idea; notion. *My impression of him changed when I saw how hard he worked.*

inspiration brilliant idea. *My inspiration for the design came from the patterns in the wallpaper.*

notion idea or understanding. *I don't think he has any notion of what I said.*

thought idea; what one thinks. *My thought on the topic was written in my report.*

view an idea; picture. *The outline will give you a general view of the story.*

illness *n.* poor health; a disease. *Craig went home from school because of illness.*

ailment sickness; illness. *The ailment caused her to be very tired.*

malady a disease or deep-seated illness. *Cancer is a very serious malady.*

sickness an illness. *The fever was caused by the sickness.*

invite *v.* to ask a person to go somewhere or do something. *My mother will invite my friend to lunch.*

ask to invite. *We must ask everyone to come to the school party.*

request to ask. *She did request that we go to hear the speech on safety.*

island *n.* a piece of land with water all around it. *People must take a boat or an airplane to get to an island.*

cay a low island; reef. *The cay was to the north of our hotel.*

isle a small island. *Only the lighthouse was left on the isle.*

joyful *adj.* full of joy. *The first and last days of school are always joyful.*

enjoyable giving joy. *We had a very enjoyable day at the zoo.*

pleasurable pleasant; enjoyable. *The trip was a pleasurable time for all of us.*

judge *n.* one who presides over a court of law by hearing cases and making decisions. *A judge must be completely fair.*

justice of the peace a local official who handles small cases and other minor duties. *The justice of the peace performed the wedding ceremony.*

magistrate a judge in a court. *The court magistrate asked the jury to give its verdict.*

jumble *v.* to mix up. *We had to jumble the letters of the word for the puzzle.*

muddle to make a mess of. *He did muddle his speech because he lost his notes.*

snarl to tangle. *As it ran around the room, the cat managed to snarl the yarn.*

tangle to twist together. *The rope might tangle around the post.*

jungle *n.* wild land near the equator with thickly grown tropical plants. *Parrots and monkeys live in a jungle.*

bush wild, unsettled land. *The explorers roamed the bush of Australia.*

chaparral an area of thick shrubs and small trees. *Animals live in the chaparral of the southwestern United States.*

kettle *n.* a pot used for heating liquids. *Put the kettle on the stove.*

> **boiler** large container. *The water was heated in the boiler.*
>
> **caldron** a large kettle. *We made soup in the old, black caldron.*

kind *adj.* friendly; thoughtful of others. *Everyone likes kind people.*

> **friendly** like a friend. *The friendly salesperson helped us with our problem.*
>
> **goodhearted** caring; generous. *The goodhearted neighbor helped everyone.*
>
> **gracious** kindly; pleasant. *The gracious hostess tried to make sure that her guests had a good time.*
>
> **hospitable** kind and friendly. *The town was hospitable to newcomers.*
>
> **thoughtful** considerate; kind. *The mayor was always thoughtful of our wishes.*
>
> antonyms: cruel, mean

knock *v.* to strike with the fist or with a hard object. *I did knock on the door but no one answered.*

> **hit** to strike; knock. *The stick hit the ground with great force.*
>
> **punch** to hit with the fist. *He continued to punch the bag until it ripped.*
>
> **slap** to strike with an open hand. *She thought she had to slap the horse to make it move.*

lady *n.* a polite term for a woman. *We knew by her manners that she was a real lady.*

> **female** woman; girl. *Is the new student a female or a male?*
>
> **woman** a grown female person. *Do you know the woman in the blue gown?*

laugh *v.* to make sounds with the voice that show amusement. *Everyone seemed to laugh at the funny movie.*

> **giggle** to give high-pitched laughs. *The little children tried not to giggle at the cartoons.*
>
> **snicker** to make a sly or silly laugh. *The teens liked to snicker at the old movie.*

lead *v.* to direct or show the way. *She will lead the hikers home.*

> **direct** to tell or show the way. *Please direct me to the registration desk.*
>
> **guide** to direct; lead. *The ranger did guide the tourists through the forest preserve.*
>
> **show** to guide; direct. *I will show you the way to the museum.*

leader *n.* one who leads. *The Scout troop needs a new leader.*

> **captain** head of a group; chief; leader. *John is the captain of the football team.*
>
> **chief** a leader; a head of a tribe or group. *The chief of the tribe wore a headdress of feathers and beads.*
>
> **director** person who manages or directs. *The director told the actors where to stand.*
>
> **guide** person who leads or directs. *The guide showed us the way to the campsite.*
>
> **manager** a person who manages. *Have you met the new store manager?*
>
> **master** one who has power over others. *The master of the house made the rules.*

learner *n.* one who learns; student. *A good learner listens carefully.*

> **pupil** a person who is learning. *He is the new pupil in the dance class.*
>
> **scholar** a person in school; a learner. *The scholar studies her lessons every day.*
>
> **student** a person who studies. *Which student is doing the spelling assignment?*
>
> **trainee** a person who is being trained. *She is a trainee at the hospital.*

least *adj.* smallest in size or amount. *Which game costs the least money?*

> **lowest** not tall; not high. *This is the lowest score on the test.*
>
> **slightest** smallest of its kind. *The slightest one is four feet tall.*
>
> **smallest** littler than others. *This is the smallest doll I have ever seen.*
>
> antonym: most

lighten *v.* to make brighter; to add light to. *The new paint does lighten the room.*

brighten to lighten; make or become brighter. *The lamp will brighten the living room.*

illuminate to light up; make bright. *The lights seem to illuminate the sky.*

antonym: darken

listen *v.* to pay attention; try to hear. *The audience did listen closely to the speaker.*

eavesdrop to listen secretly. *You can eavesdrop by putting your ear against the wall.*

hear to listen; to take in sounds. *We could hear everything that she said.*

heed to give attention to. *We must heed the advice we were given.*

lose *v.* to be unable to find; misplace. *Put the key in your pocket so you won't lose it.*

mislay to put away and forget where. *Where did you mislay your science book?*

misplace to put in the wrong place. *I always seem to misplace my gloves.*

antonym: find

major *adj.* larger; greater; primary. *We spent the major part of the day at the beach.*

greater better; larger. *The greater part of the afternoon was devoted to studying.*

larger bigger; greater. *The larger section of the office was used for the accounting division.*

superior better; greater. *This clothing is of superior quality.*

mark *v.* to make a visible sign on or by. *Mark the wrong answers with an "X."*

initial to mark or sign with initials. *Each member of the family needed to initial the document.*

inscribe to mark with letters, words, etc. *The jeweler will inscribe her initials on the bracelet.*

stamp to mark with some tool. *She needed to stamp the date on each letter.*

market *n.* a place where things can be bought and sold. *A supermarket is a large, modern market.*

emporium a large store selling many kinds of things. *At the emporium you can buy clothes, shoes, and things for the home.*

shop a place where things are sold. *The dress shop had an assortment of clothes to sell.*

store a place where things are kept for sale. *The store was located near my house.*

master *v.* to become skilled in. *It takes time and practice to master a foreign language.*

conquer to overcome; to get the better of. *If we want to conquer a difficult task, first divide it into small parts.*

learn to gain skill or knowledge. *We will learn about Africa in Social Studies.*

middle *n.* the point or part located at the same distance from each side or end; center. *Your nose is in the middle of your face.*

center the middle point. *The table is in the center of the room.*

midst the center. *The child is in the midst of the group.*

moment *n.* an instant; a very brief period. *I saw him for a moment but lost sight of him in the crowd.*

instant a moment in time. *The horse stopped for an instant and then raced away.*

second instant; moment. *He paused for a second before turning the key.*

mount *v.* to climb onto; to get up on. *The rider wants to mount his horse and gallop away.*

ascend to go up. *The group can ascend the steps to the platform.*

climb to go up; ascend. *We tried to climb to the top of the tower.*

vault to leap or jump. *She could vault over the hedge.*

movement *n.* action; change in position or location. *The children watched the slow movement of the snail across the sidewalk.*

action movement; way of moving. *She enjoys the action of a hockey game.*

gesture movement of the body to give an idea. *Waving her hand was a gesture to say she did not want to be disturbed.*

mumble *v.* to speak unclearly so that you are hard to understand. *If you mumble, no one will understand you.*

> **murmur** to say softly. *We told her not to murmur her thanks, so everyone can hear her.*
> **mutter** to speak unclearly. *He always seems to mutter when he gets tired.*
> **whisper** to speak softly. *I like to whisper secrets to my closest friend.*

near *adv.* not far away in time or distance. *The train drew near.*

> **alongside** by the side of. *The big car pulled up and parked alongside our car.*
> **closely** near; next to. *The books are stacked closely together.*
> antonym: far

nearby *adj.* not far off. *They live in a nearby town.*

> **adjacent** near or close. *The new store will be on the adjacent lot.*
> **adjoining** next to; bordering. *The adjoining lakes were connected by a stream.*
> **close** near; together. *The buildings are very close to each other.*

newspaper *n.* a printed paper that contains news, advertisements, cartoons, etc. *My grandfather likes to work the crossword puzzles in the newspaper.*

> **daily** a newspaper printed every day. *The article appeared in the daily.*
> **paper** a newspaper. *Have you seen the comics in today's paper?*

obey *v.* to follow the orders of. *Children are taught to obey their parents.*

> **comply** to follow a request. *I will comply with the captain's orders.*

conform to follow a law or rule. *She didn't like to conform to the rules of the tennis club.*

> **observe** to keep; follow. *We always try to observe the rules about being quiet in the library.*
> antonym: disobey

often *adv.* many times; frequently. *We often see our relatives during the holidays.*

> **frequently** often; repeatedly. *We frequently shop at the grocery store in our neighborhood.*
> **recurrently** repeatedly. *He had to cough recurrently.*
> **repeatedly** more than once. *She repeatedly asked for news of her lost puppy.*

owner *n.* one who owns or possesses something. *Who is the owner of this plaid jacket?*

> **landlord** person who owns a building. *We paid the rent to the landlord.*
> **partner** one of a group who owns a company. *Each partner invested a lot of money in the new business.*
> **proprietor** owner. *The proprietor of the store was very helpful to every customer.*

package *n.* a wrapped box; parcel. *How much will it cost to mail this package?*

> **bundle** things tied or wrapped together; package. *The bundle of gifts contained many games and toys.*
> **parcel** a package. *The driver delivered the parcel this morning.*

paper *n.* a written article; a report. *The teacher asked us to write a paper about the moon.*

> **article** a written report; composition. *The article contained factual information about air pollution.*
> **document** written information; report. *The lawyer found the document she wanted to use in court.*
> **report** a written account of something. *The report was prepared by a committee.*

pass *v.* to hand over; give; send. *Please pass the salad.*

   deliver to hand over; give out. *The postal carrier will deliver the mail in the morning.*

   hand to pass; give. *Please hand me the jar of jam.*

   transfer to move from one place to another; to hand over. *We had to transfer the order to the New York office.*

past *adj.* gone by; previous. *This past month we had three inches of rain.*

   earlier previous; coming before. *The earlier report said the president would arrive on Tuesday.*

   previous coming before; earlier. *The previous lesson showed us how to multiply.*

   prior earlier; coming before. *The job did not require prior experience.*

payment *n.* an amount of money paid. *Most people who rent a house or apartment make a monthly payment to the landlord.*

   compensation an amount paid. *We were given compensation for our work.*

   installment part of a payment. *The loan was to be paid back in twelve monthly installments.*

   settlement payment. *The court settlement helped her pay the legal fees.*

perfect *adj.* having no flaws or errors; exactly right. *Charlene turned in a perfect paper in science.*

   flawless perfect; without flaw. *The flawless diamond was very valuable.*

   ideal perfect; having no flaws. *This is an ideal day to go to the beach.*

   impeccable perfect; faultless. *The group had impeccable manners.*

piece *n.* a part; a segment. *Would you like a piece of my orange?*

   fragment a piece broken off. *We found a fragment of the broken dish near the sink.*

   part a piece; less than the whole. *The best part of the dinner was the dessert.*

   portion a part; share. *One portion of the work was already completed.*

   segment piece or part of a whole. *She picked the shortest segment of the straw.*

placement *n.* location; arrangement. *The placement of the flowers added the perfect touch to the dinner table.*

   arrangement items in proper order. *The arrangement of pictures told the story of the Little Red Hen.*

   location place; position. *The store's location was ideal because it was on a corner of a busy street.*

playful *adj.* full of fun and enjoyment. *The baby was playful in his bath.*

   frisky lively; playful. *The frisky puppy ran all around the yard.*

   frivolous silly; full of fun. *Her frivolous behavior made us laugh.*

   mischievous teasing; full of fun. *The mischievous kitten unraveled the yarn.*

port *n.* a town with a harbor where ships may dock. *Boston is an Atlantic port.*

   dock platform built over water. *The ship unloaded at the dock.*

   harbor a place to dock ships and boats. *The steamship docked at the harbor.*

   wharf a dock; platform built out from shore. *The huge ship was tied at the wharf.*

powder *n.* a substance made of fine grains. *It's easy to grind chalk into a powder.*

   dust fine, dry earth. *The dust settled all over the road.*

   grit fine bits of sand or gravel. *The boat was covered with grit.*

   sand tiny bits of stone in large amounts, found in the deserts and on shores along oceans, lakes, and rivers. *This beach has smooth sand.*

power *n.* great strength, force, or control. *The police have power to enforce the law.*

   control power to direct. *The police have control over the traffic.*

   force power; strength. *The force of the wind blew the door open.*

   strength power; force. *He had the strength of a giant.*

powerful *adj.* having great power; strong. *The king was a powerful leader.*

  able having power, skill, or talent. *He is an able warrior.*

  forceful having much force or strength. *The forceful leader told everyone what to do.*

  mighty showing strength. *The mighty ruler rode off to battle.*

  strong having much force or power. *The strong woman lifted weights every day.*

  antonym: powerless

powerless *adj.* having no strength or power; helpless. *The farmers were powerless against the drought.*

  helpless not able to help oneself. *The helpless child needed his parents.*

  sickly not strong. *A sickly person should not go hiking in the mountains.*

  unable not able. *I would like to help you, but I am unable.*

  antonym: powerful

preschool *n.* a place of learning before elementary school. *Children aged three to five may attend preschool.*

  daycare center a place where young children are cared for while parents work. *Our community has a new daycare center.*

  nursery school a place for children under the age of five. *The nursery school helps the young children learn about numbers and letters.*

quake *v.* to vibrate or shake. *The ground did quake beneath us during the mild earthquake.*

  quaver tremble; shake. *The old house seemed to quaver as the strong winds blew.*

  shake to move quickly. *Please shake the dirt off your boots.*

  tremble to shake from fear, cold, etc. *We started to tremble when we heard the storm was near.*

  vibrate to move rapidly. *The strings of the violin vibrate as he plays.*

quarrel *v.* to fight; to disagree, using angry words. *They always quarrel about whose turn it is to bat.*

  argue to give reasons for and against an issue. *The students argued about the playground rules.*

  bicker to quarrel. *The children started to bicker over whose turn was next.*

  brawl to quarrel in a loud manner. *Two players started to brawl during the hockey game.*

  wrangle to argue or quarrel. *The group seemed to wrangle over every topic that was brought up at the meeting.*

queen *n.* a female ruler. *The queen issued a proclamation.*

  czarina a Russian empress. *The czarina wore beautiful clothes.*

  empress a woman who rules an empire. *The empress was admired by everyone.*

question *n.* a problem. *The litter question will be discussed tonight.*

  issue a problem; a point or topic. *The tax issue was always hotly debated.*

  problem a difficult question. *The new economic problem troubled the country.*

  topic subject that people write or talk about. *The topic of my report is health.*

  antonym: answer

quick *adj.* fast; swift. *The rabbit made a quick leap into the bushes.*

  fast moving with speed; quick. *The fast runner took the lead and won the race.*

  rapid fast; quick. *They keep up a rapid pace on the assembly line.*

  speedy fast; rapid; quick. *The speedy messenger delivered the package on time.*

  swift very fast; rapid. *He gave a swift response to every test question.*

  antonym: slow

quit *v.* to stop. *We'll quit raking leaves when it gets dark.*

  cease to stop; put to an end. *The noise will cease when the speaker begins.*

  stop to halt; to keep from doing something. *We couldn't stop them from winning.*

quiz *n.* a brief test. *I missed only two questions on the science quiz.*

  checkup an examination; inspection. *I saw my doctor for a checkup yesterday.*

  examination a test; set of questions. *We were given an examination by our teacher.*

  test an examination, often consisting of a series of questions or problems. *There were twenty items on the test.*

quote *v.* to repeat or refer to a passage from a story or poem. *Justin wanted to quote a line from the poem in his essay.*

  recite to say from memory. *We had to choose a poem to recite in class.*

  repeat to say again. *Please repeat what you said about using the dictionary.*

range *v.* to extend or vary within certain limits. *The stories in this book range from sad to funny.*

  encompass to include; contain. *The article will encompass a lot of information.*

  span to extend. *The new bridge will span the rocky canyon.*

  vary to change; be different. *The colors may vary in shades from light to dark.*

rare *adj.* not often found or seen. *My uncle saves rare postage stamps.*

  scarce rare; hard to get. *Some jungle animals have become very scarce.*

  uncommon rare; unusual. *Hummingbirds are uncommon in this state.*

  unusual not common; rare. *This unusual flower grows only in the desert.*

rattle *v.* to make a number of short, sharp sounds. *The windows rattle when the wind blows.*

  bang to make a loud noise. *The wind caused the shutters to bang against the house.*

  clang to make a loud, harsh sound. *The bells began to clang as the wind blew.*

  clatter to make a loud noise. *The dishes clatter as we stack them in the kitchen sink.*

reader *n.* a person who reads. *The teacher chose Kathy to be the reader of our lunchtime story this week.*

  bookworm a person who loves to read. *Karl is a bookworm; he reads all the time.*

  browser a person who looks through materials. *Robert is only a browser; he seldom reads a whole book.*

ready *adj.* prepared. *We are ready for school.*

  available able to be used. *She is available to start work tomorrow.*

  prepared ready. *The prepared lessons were put on tape.*

reason *n.* a cause or explanation. *Your parents will write the reason for your absence.*

  cause reason for action. *What was the cause of the accident?*

  explanation something that explains. *He didn't give an explanation for his absence.*

  motive reason; thought or feeling. *My motive for the trip was to hike farther than any of my friends had.*

  purpose reason for which something is done. *The major purpose of the lesson was to learn how to divide.*

rebuild *v.* to build again. *They are planning to rebuild the old school.*

  reconstruct to construct again. *The townspeople wanted to reconstruct the library after the fire.*

  restore to put back; establish again. *My uncle likes to restore old furniture.*

record *n.* an account of facts or events. *The secretary keeps the record of the club's activities.*

  diary a personal record of daily events. *Her diary told about the events of her life.*

  memo a short written statement. *The memo announced a special company picnic.*

remain *v.* to continue without change; stay. *The nurse reported that the patient's condition did remain good.*

  continued to stay; remain. *The weather will continue to be sunny and nice.*

  linger to stay on. *He could linger for hours in the library.*

  loiter to linger. *We liked to loiter along the way and to look in the store windows.*

  stay to continue; remain. *She decided to stay near the child until he fell asleep.*

report *v.* to give an account or statement. *The president of the company did report that sales had increased.*

  disclose to tell; to make known. *I will never disclose my friend's secret.*

  reveal to make known. *I will reveal my findings to the press next week.*

  tell to say; put in words. *The travel agent will tell us about France and Italy.*

restful *adj.* offering rest, peace, or quiet. *My aunt finds sewing restful after a busy day.*

  calm quiet; peaceful; motionless. *There wasn't even a breeze on that calm evening.*

  cozy warm; comfortable. *The cozy cottage was difficult to leave.*

  peaceful calm; quiet. *Early morning hours are peaceful.*

  quiet stillness; peace. *The quiet library was a good place to study.*

  snug warm; comfortable. *I felt snug in a warm coat.*

  tranquil peaceful; quiet; calm. *The tranquil night air was very relaxing.*

  antonym: restless

restless *adj.* impatient; unable to be still. *The small children grew restless after the long delay.*

  agitated restless; impatient. *The agitated crowd began to yell at the speaker.*

  impatient not patient; restless. *We became impatient while waiting in line.*

  nervous upset; excited. *A nervous person tends to fidget a lot.*

  uneasy restless; disturbed. *The tornado warnings gave us an uneasy feeling.*

  antonym: restful

return *v.* to come or go back. *We will return after the game is over.*

  reappear to appear again. *After the clouds pass, the stars will reappear in the night sky.*

  recur to occur again. *The problem will recur if we don't make any changes.*

review *v.* to study again; go over. *She did review the chapter before she took the test.*

  critique to review critically. *He had to critique the play and analyze the plot.*

  examine to look closely at. *I will examine all of the information before I decide what to do.*

  study to try to learn. *I will study my spelling words tonight.*

  survey to examine; look over. *She will survey the situation before she decides what to do.*

rigid *adj.* very stiff; unbending. *A cast holds a broken arm in a rigid position so it can heal.*

  firm solid; hard. *The sailors were glad to set foot on firm ground.*

  hard not soft; firm. *We couldn't pound the stakes into the hard ground.*

  stiff rigid; not able to bend. *The stiff paper could not be bent around the package.*

  tense stiff; stretched tight. *The tent was held up by the tense ropes.*

rise *n.* an increase in height or amount. *The store announced a rise in prices.*

  boost an increase in price, amount, etc. *The boost in prices made food cost more this year.*

  growth an increase; amount grown. *This year's growth has made the company very successful.*

  raise an increase in amount. *The workers were given a yearly raise in pay.*

  swell an increase in amount. *The swell of shoppers made the store owners happy.*

role *n.* a part or character in a play. *Who will play the role of Peter Pan?*

  character a person or animal in a book, play, etc. *The main character was a big monster from outer space.*

  impersonation a representation. *The woman gave an impersonation of a movie star.*

  part a role; character in a play. *The students will try out for each part in the school play.*

roll *v.* to move by turning over and over. *The ball started to roll down the hill.*

  revolve to move in a circle. *The planets revolve around the sun.*

  rotate to turn about a center. *Earth does rotate on its axis.*

  turn to rotate; move around. *The wheels will turn as the horse pulls the wagon.*

  whirl to spin; turn round and round. *The dancers whirl around the stage.*

rough *adj.* not smooth or even. *The car bounced and rattled over the rough road.*

  bumpy full of bumps. *We took a bumpy ride in an old wagon.*

  rocky bumpy; full of rocks. *The car made lots of noise as it bounced over the rocky mountain road.*

  uneven not level or flat. *The uneven ground made it hard to walk.*

royal *adj.* having to do with kings and queens. *The king and queen live in a royal palace.*

  regal belonging to royalty. *The regal party was held in the palace of the king.*

  sovereign having the power of a ruler. *The queen was the sovereign leader of the British Commonwealth.*

rule *n.* a law; regulation. *Always obey each and every school safety rule.*

  fundamental a basic principle. *You can't learn a sport one fundamental at a time.*

  law a rule or regulation made by a state, country, etc. *Each law was made by the state government.*

  principle a basic law or assumption. *It is a scientific principle that what goes up must come down.*

  regulation rule; law. *This regulation controls flights to all airports.*

sadness *n.* sorrow; grief. *Tears can be an expression of sadness.*

  grief sadness; sorrow. *His grief made him a very quiet person.*

  melancholy sadness; low spirits. *Her melancholy was caused by several painful events.*

  sorrow grief; sadness. *Her sorrow was caused by the loss of her pet.*

  unhappiness sorrow; sadness. *His illness caused his family much unhappiness.*
  antonym: happiness

safe *adj.* free from risk or harm. *This sidewalk is a safe place to walk.*

  armored protected with armor. *An armored car is a safe way to transport money.*

  protected guarded; safe. *He led a very protected life.*

  secure safe. *They built a secure fence all around the farm.*

sample *n.* a part that shows what the rest are like. *The store gave away a free sample of the new soap.*

  example one thing that shows what others are like. *He used Dallas as an example of a Texas city.*

  specimen one of a group used to show what others are like. *Janet collected a new rock specimen from her world travels.*

scale *v.* to climb up or over. *The climbers used ropes to scale the cliff.*

  climb to go up; ascend. *We tried to climb to the top of the tower.*

  mount to climb onto; to get up on. *The rider wanted to mount his horse and gallop away.*

  vault to leap or jump. *She could vault over the hedge.*

scare *v.* to frighten. *The sudden loud noise did scare me.*

  alarm to frighten; fill with fear. *The loud whistle and siren seemed to alarm everyone.*

  frighten to scare; fill with fright. *The thunder did frighten us.*

  startle to frighten suddenly. *He made a loud noise to startle the birds out of the tree.*

season *v.* to improve the taste. *The chef will season the soup with herbs.*

  flavor to season. *The spices flavor the pot of stew.*

  salt to sprinkle with salt. *He always seems to salt his food more than anyone else does.*

  spice to season; add spice. *She decided to spice the pie with nutmeg and cloves.*

seller *n.* a person who sells; a vendor. *The flower seller had a stand on the street corner.*
  merchant a person who buys and sells. *The merchant in the shopping center is having a special sale.*
  vendor a seller; peddler. *The vendor services the candy machines once a week.*

serve *v.* to help others by performing a task. *Sarah will serve as club treasurer.*
  administer to be helpful; contribute. *Their job is to administer to the elderly.*
  help to do what is needed. *I can help you fix up the old house.*
  perform to do. *She did perform many duties as an officer of the company.*

settle *v.* to establish residence. *Their family did settle in California years ago.*
  locate to establish in a place. *She will locate her business near San Francisco.*
  place to put. *We will place the sign near the busy intersection.*
  reside to occupy a home or place. *The decision to reside at this address was made years ago.*

share *n.* a part; a portion. *Todd always does his share of work.*
  allotment a part; share. *The largest allotment was for food and housing.*
  part a share. *We wanted only the part of the reward that belonged to us.*
  portion a share; part. *A portion of time at the end of the day is set aside for storytime and cleanup.*

shipment *n.* the goods sent or delivered to a certain place. *The store received a clothing shipment from the manufacturer.*
  cargo the freight carried on a ship or another vehicle. *The barge carried a cargo of lumber to the mill.*
  freight goods carried by plane, truck, ship, or train. *The dockworker sent the freight by truck.*
  load something that is carried. *The load was too heavy for the small car.*

shower *n.* a short fall of rain. *During the afternoon there was a thunder shower.*
  cloudburst a sudden rain; violent rainstorm. *We were caught in the cloudburst and got very wet.*

downpour a very heavy rain. *The downpour started while we were at a picnic.*
  rain water falling from the clouds in drops. *The rain came down all morning.*
  torrent an outpouring. *A torrent of rain caused the river to flood the whole valley.*

shy *adj.* reserved; quiet. *After Josh made friends at his new school, he was no longer shy.*
  bashful reserved; shy; easily embarrassed. *As a bashful child, she did not like to be with groups of people.*
  quiet peaceful; calm. *Alice spent a quiet afternoon reading.*
  reserved quiet; keeping to oneself. *The reserved child seldom spoke to anyone in his class at school.*
  unsociable reserved; bashful. *Ann was an unsociable child and often kept away from other people.*

simple *adj.* easy to understand. *The simple questions did not take long to answer.*
  easy not hard to do. *The science experiment was easy.*
  effortless requiring little effort. *Typing is an effortless task for him.*
  elementary simple; easy to learn first. *When learning a new sport, begin with the elementary principles.*

singer *n.* one who sings. *The singer joined a choir.*
  artist one skilled in the performance of an art. *The opera singer was a talented artist.*
  crooner a person who sings in a soft, sentimental style. *Crooners were popular in the forties.*
  songster a singer. *The songster sang everyone's favorite songs.*
  vocalist a singer. *The vocalist had an excellent soprano voice.*

single *adj.* one alone; only one. *A single orange was left in the box.*
  lone alone; single. *A lone cloud floated in the blue sky.*
  one a single unit. *One apple fell from the tree.*
  only single; sole. *Rose was the only child to win two races.*
  sole single; only one. *The pilot was the sole survivor of the plane crash.*

patterns, (cont.)
  spelling patterns
    consonants
      complex consonants (see complex consonants)
      double consonants, 15, 18, 53, 80, 112, 128–133, 144, 156, 158, 159
      patterns with (see consonants)
      silent consonants, 42, 102–107, 120, 122, 135, 138, 176, 182, 188, 189, 194, 195, 214
      more letters than sounds, 96–101, 120, 121
      sorting by, 85 (see also sorting words)
      vowels (see also vowels)
        /ô/, 70–75, 82
        schwa + r, 140–145, 158, 160
    structural patterns
      compound words, 180, 195, 222–227, 234, 236
      plurals (see plurals)
      possessives, 50, 210–215, 234, 235
      prefixes (see prefixes)
      suffixes (see suffixes)
personal pronouns, 164, 165
persuasive essay, writing, 131, 165
persuasive writing
  advertisement, 213, 231
  letter, 117
  letter to the editor, 225, 241
  newspaper ad, 35, 67
  persuasive essay, 131, 165
  poster, 41
phonics skills. See also dictionary skills; sounds
  digraphs, 36, 52
  rhyme, 18, 24, 30, 34, 36, 37, 45, 55, 56, 91, 92, 100, 109, 118, 122, 129, 132, 138, 142, 144, 195, 236

phonics skills, (cont.)
  syllables (see syllables)
  word building, 59, 121, 122, 132, 144, 159, 167, 188
  word structure, 27, 39, 56, 59, 97, 129, 167, 191
plot. See writing skills
plurals
  irregular, 56, 166–171, 196, 197, 211
  possessive nouns, 50, 210, 211, 214, 215
  proper nouns and, 232
  regular, 15, 30, 56, 62, 77, 112, 166–171, 211, 214, 223
poetry
  completing, 192
  proofreading, 55
  writing, 55
possessive nouns, 50, 210–215, 234, 235
possessive pronouns, 164, 165
postcard, writing, 155
poster, writing, 41
prefixes, 226
  base word and, 68, 172–177, 196, 197
  dis-, 36, 68
  mid-, 30
  mis-, 36
  pre-, 172–177, 196, 197
  re-, 30, 42, 172–177, 196, 197
  un-, 62, 112, 172–177, 196, 197
present perfect tense, 112
present tense, 42, 112
prewriting, 17, 23, 29, 35, 41, 51, 55, 61, 67, 73, 79, 89, 93, 99, 105, 111, 117, 127, 131, 143, 149, 155, 169, 175, 181, 193, 203, 207, 213, 219, 225, 231, 241
problem solving, 105, 187
pronouns, 164, 165, 202

proofreading
  advertisements, 213, 231
  book reviews, 99
  descriptions, 143, 181
  descriptive essays, 61, 89
  diary entries, 29, 207
  e-mail messages, 111, 127
  instructions, 149
  letters, 23, 105, 117, 137, 187, 203, 219, 225, 241
  lists, 175
  marks for, 17, 23, 29, 35, 41, 55, 61, 67, 73, 79, 93, 99, 105, 111, 117, 131, 137, 143, 149, 155, 169, 175, 181, 187, 193, 207, 213, 219, 225, 231
  newspaper ads, 35, 67
  persuasive essays, 131, 165
  poetry, 55
  postcards, 155
  posters, 41
  realistic stories, 17, 51
  stories, 73, 169
  thank-you notes, 93
  travel report, 79
proper nouns, 51, 88, 89, 127, 165, 203, 232, 241
publishing, 17, 23, 29, 35, 41, 51, 55, 61, 67, 73, 79, 89, 93, 99, 105, 111, 117, 127, 131, 143, 149, 155, 169, 175, 181, 193, 203, 207, 213, 219, 225, 231, 241
punctuation. See specific kinds of punctuation

quotation marks, use, 51, 89, 127, 165, 203, 241

Credits

Photography: Cover image © George C. Anderson Photography; p. 3 top © Chet Baron/MCA+; p. 3 bottom © PhotoDisc; p. 4 © Jupiter Images/Getty Images; p. 5 © iStockphoto.com/kcline; p. 6 © iStockphoto.com/fujean; p. 7 top © istockphoto/narvikk; p. 7 bottom © istockphoto/lovemovement; p. 8 © iStockphoto.com/Melissa Carroll; p. 9 © Jack Hollingsworth/Getty Images, Inc.; p. 10 top © George C. Anderson; p. 10 bottom © 2001–2009 Smart Technologies ULC. All rights reserved; pp. 11–13 © George C. Anderson; p. 15 © Image Source/Corbis; p. 16 © Chet Baron/MCA+; p. 19 © iStockphoto.cpm/Donna Heatfield; p. 21 © Jupiter Images/Getty Images; p. 22 © iStockphoto.com/Peter Marshall; p. 25 © Carl Iwasaki/Time & Life Pictures/Getty Images; p. 27 © Blend Images/Alamy; p. 28 © iStockphoto.com; p. 31 © AP Images; p. 33 © iStockphoto.com/Melissa Carroll; p. 34 © iStockphoto.com/John Pauls; p. 37 © PCN Chrome/Alamy; p. 39 © iStockphoto.com/Luminis; p. 40 © Creatas/Jupiter Images; p. 43 © Jack Hollingsworth/Getty Images, Inc.; p. 45 © iStockphoto.com/Cheryl Paquin; p. 46 © Jupiter Images/Getty Images; p. 50 © iStockphoto/Giorgio Fochesato; p. 53 © iStockphoto.com; p. 54 © iStockphoto.com/Francisco Romero; p. 57 © Radius Images/Alamy; p. 59 © Visions of America, LLC/Alamy; p. 60 © Geoff du Feu/Alamy; p. 63 © MBI/Alamy; p. 65 © iStockphoto.com/Kevin Eaves; p. 66 © iStockphoto.com/Lifephoto; p. 69 © Moodboard/Corbis; p. 71 © iStockphoto.com/Atlaspix; p. 72 © Jupiter Images/Getty Images; p. 75 © iStockphoto.comm/Francisco Romero; p. 77 © iStockphoto.com/D. Huss; p. 78 © iStockphoto.com/Chepko Danil; p. 81 © Andrew B. Graham/The Bridgeman Art Library/Getty Images; p. 83 © iStockphoto.com/Paul Hill; p. 84 © iStockphoto.com/Paul Yates; p. 88 © iStockphoto.com/Angie Stadler; p. 91 © iStockphoto/digitalskillet; p. 92 © iStockphoto.com/Christine Kublanski; p. 95 © Bettmann/CORBIS; p. 97 © iStockphoto.com/Arvind Balaraman; p. 98 © Jeff Greenberg/Alamy; p. 101 © Picture Partners/Alamy; p. 103 © iStockphoto.com/Eric Gevaert; p. 104 © Ted Foxx/Alamy; p. 107 © iStockphoto.com/Michael Lynch; p. 109 © iStockphoto.com/Zsolt Biczó; p. 110 © Jupiter Images/Getty Images; p. 113 © D. Hurst/Alamy; p. 115 © Lucinda Hutson; p. 116 © Jupiter Images/Getty Images; p. 119 © iStockphoto.com/blackred; p. 121 © iStockphoto.com/Floortje; p. 122 © iStockphoto.com/Pablo Demetrio Scapinachis; p. 126 © iStockphoto.com/Linda Armstrong; p. 129 © iStockphoto.com/John Prescott; p. 130 © James Forte/Photolibrary; p. 133 © John Mitchell/Alamy; p. 135 © iStockphoto.com/lisafx; p. 136 © iStockphoto.com/Karen Town; p. 139 © Jose Luis Pelaez, Inc./Corbis; p. 141 © iStockphoto.com/Clint Spencer; p. 142 © imagebroker/Alamy; p. 145 © Image Source/Getty Images; p. 147 © iStockphoto.com/Colleen Butler; p. 148 © PhotoDisc;

p. 151 © Zaner-Bloser; p. 153 © iStockphoto.com/Joe Cicak; p. 154 © iStockphoto.com/Martil57900; p. 157 © Bettmann/Corbis; p. 159 © First Light/Alamy; p. 160 © Jupiter Images/Getty Images; p. 164 © iStockphoto.com/kcline; p. 167 © istockphoto/narvikk; p. 168 © Betty LaRue/Alamy; p. 171 © istockphoto/lovemovement; p. 173 © istockphoto/kate_sept2004; p. 174 © istockphoto/iofoto; p. 177 © Stockbyte/Getty Images; p. 179 © istockphoto/Glenn Frank; p. 180 © Ariel Skelley/Blend Images/Corbis; p. 183 © Stockbyte/Getty Images; p. 185 © istockphoto/asiseeit; p. 186 © istockphoto/jamiestokes; p. 189 © Corbis/Bettman; p. 191 © Ron Sherman/Getty Images; p. 192 © Jupiter Images/Getty Images; p. 195 © Jupiter Images/Getty Images; p. 197 © iStockphoto.com/fujean; p. 198 © Ariel Skelley/CORBIS; p. 202 © ColorBlind Images; p. 205 © iStockphoto.com; p. 206 © iStockphoto.com/Kyle McMahon; p. 209 © iStockphoto.com/Lisa F. Young; p. 211 © Jupiter Images/Getty Images; p. 212 © Jupiter Images/Getty Images; p. 215 © SuperStock; p. 217 © Jupiter Images p. 218 © Image Source/Getty Images; p. 221 © PhotoAlto/Sigrid Olsson/Getty Images; p. 223 © iStockphoto.com/Andrew Rich; p. 224 © Corbis/PhotoLibrary; p. 227 © Sandy Jones/Getty Images; p. 229 © Jupiter Images/Getty Images; p. 230 © Jupiter Images/Getty Images; p. 233 © iStockphoto.com/Rich Legg; p. 235 © Jupiter Images/Getty Images; p. 236 © istockphoto/Jasna Hrovatin; p. 240 © Peter Arnold, Inc./Alamy; p. 250 © iStockphoto.com/Geoffrey Holman; p. 252 © Ariel Skelley/Blend Images/Corbis; p. 54 © iStockphoto.com/Floortje; p. 256 © iStockphoto.com/D. Huss; p. 258 © Lucinda Hutson; p. 260 © William Manning/Alamy; p. 263 © iStockphoto.com/kcline; p. 264 © iStockphoto.com/Murat Koc; p. 266 © Rolf Nussbaumer/Alamy; p. 269 © iStockphoto.com/Pablo Demetrio Scapinachis; p. 271 © iStockphoto.com/Eric Gevaert; p. 272 © iStockphoto.com/Wellford Tiller; p. 274 © Image Source/Corbis; p. 276 © iStockphoto.com/Chris At; p. 277 © istockphoto/lovemovement; p. 279 © D. Hurst/Alamy; p. 280 © iStockphoto.com/Daniel Grill; p. 281 © image100/Alamy; p. 282 © Image Source/Corbis; p. 285 © Creatas/Jupiter Images; p. 286 © iStockphoto.com/Andrew Dean; p. 287 © iStockphoto.com/Justin Horrocks; p. 288 © iStockphoto.com/Arvind Balaraman; p. 290 © Jupiter Images/Getty Images; p. 291 © Geoff du Feu/Alamy; p. 293 © Creatas/Jupiter Images; p. 294 © iStockphoto.com/monkeybusinessimages.

Illustrations: Alessia Girasole: 24, 30, 36, 42, 56, 62, 68, 74, 80, 94, 100, 106, 112, 118, 132, 138, 144, 150, 156, 170, 176, 182, 188, 194, 208, 214, 220, 226, 232